Gorbachev's Challenge

BY MARSHALL I. GOLDMAN

Gorbachev's Challenge

Economic Reform in the Age of High Technology

MARSHALL I. GOLDMAN

W · W · NORTON & COMPANY
New York · London

Copyright © 1987 by W. W. Norton & Company, Inc.

Published simultaneously in Canada by Penguin Books Canada Ltd.,
2801 John Street, Markham, Ontario L3R 1B4.
Printed in the United States of America.

The text of this book is composed in Times Roman, with display type set in Benguiat
Medium. Composition and manufacturing by The Haddon Craftsmen Inc.
Book design by Jacques Chazaud.

First Edition

Library of Congress Cataloging-in-Publication Data

Goldman, Marshall I.
  Gorbachev's challenge.

  Includes bibliographical references and index.
  1. Soviet Union—Economic policy—1981- .
2. Soviet Union—Economic conditions—1976- .
3. Technology transfer—Soviet Union. i. Title.
HC336.25.G6365   1987   338.947   86-33187

ISBN 0-393-02454-7

W. W. Norton & Company, Inc., 500 Fifth Avenue, New York, N. Y. 10110
W. W. Norton & Company Ltd., 37 Great Russell Street, London WC1B 3NU

1 2 3 4 5 6 7 8 9 0

To

JESSICA

the first of a new generation

"The Czar himself is powerless against the bureaucratic body; he can send any one of them to Siberia, but he cannot govern without them, or against their will. On every decree of his they have a tacit veto, by merely refraining from carrying it into effect."

—JOHN STUART MILL, 1859

Contents

Contents

List of Tables

List of Illustrations

Preface

Studying the Soviet Union from afar is not always easy. Nor, given the emotional attitudes in the United States toward the Soviet Union and those in the Soviet Union toward the United States, is it easy to analyze the Soviet economy unemotionally and objectively, as one would analyze, say, the Canadian economy. Soviet economists have traditionally attacked studies by American Sovietologists as being biased. Admittedly, we often tend to focus on the pathological side. In part that is because the Soviets restrict information available to outside observers, and one therefore, very often has to rely on the Soviets' analyses of their own problems. We sometimes focus too much on those problems.

It turns out, however, that the Soviets do have some very real problems. In my earlier books, I looked at some of those difficulties. This has not always endeared me to Soviet officials and probably helps explain why I had difficulty in the past in obtaining visas to visit the Soviet Union. I was denied entrance in 1979 and 1980. I was in 1983 invited to the Soviet Union as a houseguest of Ambassador Arthur Hartman, the American representative in Moscow. When the Soviets finally did issue me a visa, I was kept at the airport for an hour after the lights had been turned off; and after I was allowed to proceed to town, lectures I had been scheduled to deliver were canceled. Many of my former friends were told they should not meet with me. This was also undoubtedly a consequence of my refusal to promise not to meet with dissidents.

Much to my surprise, when I reapplied to go to the Soviet Union in 1986, as a lecturer for the U.S. Information Agency, not only was I able to obtain a visa in a record eleven days but Soviet economists and officials received me as if there had been no problem previously. In fact, many Soviet scholars sought me out, and I was invited for discussions at institutes I had never heard of before. When I remarked about the change in attitude, one Soviet official said that much of my problem had been due to the fact that I had been too critical of the Soviet Union during Brezhnev's time. That criticism was no longer offensive: as he put it, "We now know more about Brezhnev than you did, and you were not hard enough."

There also seems to have occurred a marked change in the Soviet Union since Mikhail S. Gorbachev assumed control. His call for openness *(glasnost)* and his determination to push through with economic reform have opened up areas of debate that were closed earlier. Part of that debate involves examining the evaluations of others, including Sovietologists in the United States. At a briefing in April 1986, a Soviet official told a visiting American group, "[the] new era of Gorbachev's openness means that we now not only invite our critics, such as Marshall Goldman, but we read what he has to say." Similarly, a visiting American correspondent from the *Chicago Tribune* was told by an official of the Institute of the U.S.A. and Canada that in his search for ideas about the reform, Gorbachev has adopted "the Russian Research Center line."

After years of having been attacked for our comments about the Soviet Union, I now find it gratifying that some of our views are apparently receiving serious attention in Moscow itself. This book is an effort to examine the challenges that face Gorbachev. In addition to all the old problems, he now must also deal with the need to master what we have come to call new high technology. This complicates his task in a way that did not bother his predecessors. It may be presumptuous, but this study is meant as a guidebook for him and thus ends with a series of suggestions about the steps that he might profitably pursue. As one Soviet official put it, people in the Soviet Union are very often inhibited in what they say, for political reasons; and when they do take a candid look, they tend to be too much taken with the trees to see the forest. I hope this provides some of that forest.

Any study like this owes much to many people and institutions. First, I would like to thank Wellesley College for providing me with sabbatical help and being so tolerant of my wanderings. The Russian Research Center has also been very helpful in providing me with materials for study and a research climate available at few other places in this world. The staff has been patient and long-suffering, to say the least. In particular, Catherine Reed has put up with deadlines and subtle requests for immediate performance that do little for longevity or peace of mind.

I should also like to express my thanks to the Soviet colleagues who have provided me with guidance over the years regarding what is happening in the Soviet Union, to the Western and Japanese businessmen who took the time to share their experiences with me, to the U.S. Information Agency for providing me with opportunities to visit the Soviet Union, and to Ambassador and Mrs. Arthur Hartman for being so hospitable when I do visit.

Finally, I want to thank Barney Schwalberg for his critical review of an early draft of the manuscript and to my editor, Don Lamm, who treated the manuscript as if it were his own. I must also express my appreciation to the members of my family, who have put up with a schedule that has not always been the most conducive to good family relations. My son, Seth, helped me with some of the editing, and, as usual, Merle, my wife, went over the manuscript in an effort to spare me needless embarrassment. Despite her best efforts, and this represented the most energetic editing work ever, there certainly will be such criticism. But thanks to Merle, there will be less.

Gorbachev's Challenge

1

The Challenge

Mikhail S. Gorbachev is not the kind of person who elicits deep feelings of sympathy. He looks and acts like a man who can handle and has handled himself with cunning, skill, and heavy-handedness. One cannot become the general secretary of the Communist party of the Soviet Union without having had to resort to a little ruthlessness now and then. As Andrei Gromyko was reported to have said about Gorbachev, "This man has a nice smile, but he has iron teeth."[1] But reforming the Soviet economy, the first priority he has set for himself, may prove to be too much of a challenge, even for the gifted Gorbachev. Successful reform withstood the best efforts of his predecessors.

At first glance, it would seem that Gorbachev should have no trouble doing anything he wants in the Soviet Union with the economy or anything else. Consider how effective he has been in dealing with the Soviet problem of alcoholism. Knowing full well that he would meet resistance, he nonetheless decided to crack down, even though that meant attacking social mores that are centuries old. Although Yuri Andropov, Gorbachev's mentor, first began the anti-alcohol campaign in 1982, Gorbachev is the one who has put teeth into it. To make it more difficult to buy vodka and other alcoholic products, he ordered that such beverages could no longer be sold before 2:00 P.M. Simultaneously, he reduced the number of sales outlets, so that in Moscow, for example, almost 50 percent of the stores that used to sell alcoholic products no longer do.[2] As a further disincentive, he has gradually raised prices. Prices were increased 20 to 25 percent on August 1, 1986. As a consequence of such measures, retail sales of alcoholic beverages in the first half of 1986 were one-third less than they had been in the preceding year.[3] At the same time, sales of nonalcoholic beverages have increased by almost 30 percent.[4] This means that unless workers exercise considerable forethought, they will be sober until at least two in the afternoon. According to Gorbachev, this is the primary reason that the accident rate fell 20 percent in six months. Because there are fewer men drunk in the evening, there also seems to be less wife beating; as a consequence, in the second half of 1985, the number of divorces fell by 19 percent.[5] In some regions of the country, enforcement is less effective than elsewhere. Yet, that Gorbachev has had any success in changing something as deeply rooted as Russian drinking habits is a measure of how ambitious and determined he is.

Gorbachev's efforts have won something less than unanimous enthusiasm, but many Soviets do support them. That is evident in the countless jokes that have sprung up. They reflect the frustration of those who must now stand in block-long lines in order to buy vodka, as well as the relief of those who are grateful that they must no longer drink themselves into a daily stupor. Here are two examples:

After two hours in line, one drunk says to the other, "Enough of this. I'm going down to the Kremlin and punch Gorbachev." Two hours later, he returns. His friend, who is still in line, asks, "Well, what happened?" "Nothing, the line was too long!"

The next day the two drunks are in line again. After three hours, one complains to the other, "The whole problem is that Gorbachev is a teetotaler." His friend replies, "Count your blessings. Imagine what would have happened if he were celibate?"

Such bittersweet humor suggests a grudging respect for Gorbachev's power. This sense of power makes Gorbachev's quest for economic reform all the more fascinating. If he cannot succeed, who can? After all, in many respects he is probably the strongest, most effective political manipulator the Soviet Union has had since the Bolshevik Revolution. Because this includes Lenin and Stalin, that is a strong statement to make. Obviously, it does not mean that Gorbachev can wave his hand and send opponents off to prison or death, as did Stalin, or that he commands the deity-like worship of a Lenin. Nor does it mean that Gorbachev can ignore the Politburo or its members. In some ways, he is no more than the chairman of the board. But that he knows how to wield power is evident from the way he assumed control of the Politburo. No one, not even Lenin or Stalin, was able to establish himself as the sole head of the Soviet Union in less than three months, as did Gorbachev. When he purged Grigorii Romanov from the Politburo, in June 1985, and kicked Andrei Gromyko upstairs to be president of the Supreme Soviet, Gorbachev effectively removed his major rivals. After he added several new supporters to the Politburo a few months later, he had assured himself of a solid base of support. (See Table 10.) He may not have removed all vestiges of the Brezhnev era (Gromyko, Dinmukhamed Kunayev, and Vladimir Shcherbitsky remained as members, even after the February 1986 party congress; Kunayev, however, was removed in December 1986), but no other leader has been able to assume complete control of both the party and the government in less than a year. It took Stalin several years to rid himself of his rivals. In the same way, Nikita Khrushchev had to share power with Nikolai Bulganin for a few years, just as Leonid Brezhnev found it desirable or necessary to share state duties with Alexei Kosygin for an extended period. Even though Nikolai Ryzhkov is officially the prime minister, no one doubts that he is in fact very much subordinate to Gorbachev.

All of this indicates that few if any Soviet leaders in the last few decades were as well positioned as Gorbachev to attempt to reform the Soviet economy. But why is there a need for such

a reform? After all, the Soviet Union's gross national product
(GNP) is second only to that of the United States. The Soviet
Union produces almost twice as much steel as the United States
does. It is the world's largest pumper of petroleum and natural
gas and produces more machine tools than any other country.
Even more impressive, it was the first to send unmanned and
manned satellites into space, and it has an armed military force
with conventional as well as rocket and other space weaponry
that is equal or superior to what we have in the United States.
Moreover, the Soviets have had some impressive achievements
on the social front as well. They have eliminated most overt
forms of unemployment and inflation, boosted literacy rates to
a reported 100 percent, and instituted a safety net to prevent
homelessness and some of the other extreme forms of poverty
that occur in the West.

But the Soviet economy is a paradox. Despite evident
strength, the Soviet economy is widely regarded, even by Soviet
leaders, to be seriously flawed. For example, 20 percent of the
Soviet urban population continues to live in communal apart-
ments, with only one room for each family and a toilet and
kitchen that must be shared with the other families in the same
apartment.[6] Careful estimates of per capita GNP indicate that,
as of 1984, Soviet citizens, with a per capita income of $7,120,
lag behind fellow communists in East Germany, with $9,800,
and in Czechoslovakia, with $8,250.[7] Soviet per capita income
lagged slightly behind that of Hungary, which was $7,200. The
Soviets are also embarrassed by the fact that, despite their
safety net, life expectancy was until recently falling while infant
mortality was rising, just the opposite of what should be happening.

The Soviets have also been embarrassed by a series of disasters that reflect badly on both Soviet technology and management practices. The near meltdown at the Chernobyl nuclear
energy station in late April 1986 was particularly distressing
because some of the radioactivity spread outside Soviet borders.
That was bad enough. But, as we shall see, while the Soviet
authorities, including Gorbachev, were immediately informed

about the problem, no indication that anything was amiss was provided to the outside world until nearly three full days after the explosion. Circumstantial evidence seemed to suggest that if they could have, Soviet authorities would have kept the whole affair a secret, much in the manner they had kept similar disasters secret in years past. Having been severely criticized for the way they handled the Chernobyl disaster, Soviet officials decided they should be more open in the future.

Unfortunately for them, this policy coincided with a string of misfortunes, including the collision and subsequent sinking of the passenger ship *Admiral Nakhimov,* on August 31, 1986, with the loss of more than one hundred lives. Shortly thereafter, on October 3, came the acknowledgment that a Soviet submarine carrying ballistic missiles had caught fire and sunk off the coast of Bermuda. Equally embarrassing, the government announced in December that students in Alma-Ata, the capital of Kazakhstan, had rioted in protest of the replacement of Kunayev, a Kazakh, by Gennadi Kolbin, a Russian. None of this did much for the image of the Soviet Union in the world or among the Soviet people.

Nor did it help that daily living conditions were often unsatisfactory. For example, Soviet consumers have had to live with major, recurring shortages of basic and not especially sophisticated consumer goods. The Soviet press berates Soviet planners for failing to provide adequate supplies of such essential products as matches, shoes, fruits, potatoes, other vegetables, and, on occasion, bread.[8] Even Moscow suffers from shortages.[9] For that matter, meat (even sausage) has been in perennial short supply for almost a decade. It was necessary to introduce rationing in many Soviet cities in the early 1980s.[10] A great many Soviet goods intended for consumers and for industry are continually criticized for their poor quality.[11] In one instance, Gorbachev complained that up to 70 percent of the television sets made by the Ekran Production Association in Kuybyshev were rejected each year for their poor quality.[12]

In addition to such long-running concerns, Soviet officials became more and more aware of the inability of their planners and their system to master what in the West we have come to call the new high technology. For example, the age of information technology, video, mini and large-scale computers, biotechnology, word processing, process control, CAD-CAM (Computer Aided Design–Computer Aided Manufacturing), artificial intelligence, copying machines, and robots have yet to come to the Soviet Union in any major way, particularly to its consumer sector. The Soviets occasionally are able to display prototypes of such products, but rarely are such items readily available to consumers or even to industrial manufacturers. Nor is there much to indicate that the situation will change soon. The high-technology products that the Soviets do have, at least in the civilian sector, appear to be falling further and further behind those in the noncommunist world.

I

The phenomena of technological change and the need to keep up with that change are not new, so to some extent the current problems facing the Soviet Union do not differ from those faced by other countries in previous decades. After all, some countries were affected more deeply and sooner than others by the Industrial Revolution of the late eighteenth and early nineteenth centuries. Moreover, the initial innovations of that era were followed by additional innovations spread out over a century and a half.

The impact of improved machine tool production, the steam engine, and the innovations of the Second Industrial Revolution, such as the internal combustion engine, electricity, assembly line production, the telegraph, the telephone, radio, television, and the jet engine have had important economic, social, and political consequences. Take the steam engine, for example. It revolutionized manufacturing and rendered obsolete most of the old methods of production. Not only did businessmen of the day have to master the production of the steam engine; they also had to reorganize their other manufacturing activities to take advantage of the production and transportation opportunities the steam engine brought. With the steam engine, miners could pump out water and thus drill in deeper mines. They could then transport the mined materials on trains and ships powered by steam engines. Equally important, with the coming of the steam engine, it was no longer necessary to restrict manufacturing activities to sites with water power. Moreover, with dependable power, the size of those manufacturing operations could be significantly expanded to take advantage of the economies that came when workers engaged in related activities were located side by side. That eventually led to the large-scale factory and the Second Industrial Revolution.

The advent of the computer and the microprocessor set off the Third Industrial Revolution. Its impact has been equally far-reaching. If anything, the pace of change has accelerated. Thanks to the breakthroughs of the earlier industrial revolutions, news of innovations and new products are now diffused throughout the industrialized world immediately. Although the social changes are not yet clear, the rapidity with which high technology has changed industry and business and the extent of those changes has been breathtaking. Whereas the steam engine worked its way into the economy over the course of several decades, today a single decade will see the birth and death of several virtually new products, as well as three to four generations of a product. For example, just thirty years ago, the Friden electromechanical calculator was considered a marvel of the modern age. With the fancy models, one could multiply and divide without having to worry about whether one had properly aligned the columns. Production of these very expensive machines ceased when electronic desk calculators entered the market. These large electronic machines, which initially cost as much as a thousand dollars, in turn lost favor when Bomar announced the hand-held electronic calculator. Before other manufacturers copied them, Bomar calculators sold for several hundred dollars apiece. Today, banks give away even smaller and more sophisticated calculators.

Computer manufacturers have been afflicted by the same type of size and price "downsizing." The first computers occupied several rooms and were operated with vacuum tubes. Data were compiled on bulky computer cards. The invention of the transistor, integrated circuits, and semiconductor memory chips made it possible to reduce the size and the heat of the hardware, and soon the computer cards became obsolete.

As the computer shrank in size and price and as inventors developed software that simplified computer usage, the use of computers and microprocessors spread rapidly. Whereas initially computers were an end product that performed calculations and provided data, increasingly computers and microprocessors became the innards of other products—machine tools, steel mills, automobile plants, automobiles, and even dishwashers. Robots were no longer limited to imaginative sketches on the pages of *Popular Mechanics*. They found their way disguised as automobile welders and painters to the production floor and assembly lines, at least until they were replaced by more sophisticated models and systems. As a consequence of these developments, today's manufacturers have to concern themselves not only with mastering the operation of computers but also with integrating computers into manufacturing.

Most analysts agree that economic leadership will belong to those countries that can lead the way in high technology. At a minimum a country must stay abreast of what other countries do. This is not an easy task, because the distinguishing feature of high technology is the rapidity with which the technology changes. Even we in the United States have discovered that our innovations have become vulnerable. Sometimes, before a manufacturer can recover his development costs, he faces a challenge in the marketplace from an Asian competitor who has utilized the high-speed transportation and communications system that exists today to master our new technology at considerably less cost.[13] The reproduction of personal computers is one of the more notable instances of this practice, but certainly not the only one.

This ongoing technological revolution has an important consequence for Gorbachev and his effort to implement reform.

For the most part, Gorbachev's predecessors did not have to contend with rapidly changing technology. A decade or two ago, reform meant coping with resistance from entrenched bureaucrats, winning over enterprise managers unwilling to take initiative even if it was offered to them, and compensating for the lack of a viable price and market system that could replace the administrative injunctions issued by the planners and senior ministers. Overcoming such obstacles is no longer enough. Today, even if all these matters were to be resolved, the Soviet Union would probably still find itself a second-class nation, at least in the ability to master high technology. The traditional prescriptions for reform would certainly help, but they are unlikely to be enough to bring the Soviet Union into the high-technology age. In other words, because his predecessors failed to make the changes they should have, Gorbachev's task has become all the more difficult.

II

In a sense, Gorbachev's task might be easier if he were starting anew. His problem is that he must deal with the legacy of the Stalinist approach to economic development. But while the Stalinist model served Stalin reasonably well, it has left a deformed economy today. This is true even though Stalin has been dead for more than three decades and even though his successors have tried to lighten its impact. Gorbachev's predecessors have found, however, that because it so altered the nature of the Russian prerevolutionary economy, the Stalinist model resists change. Stalin concluded that his chief priority was the expansion of heavy industry. To obtain the capital he needed to finance such a program, he decided he would have to rely heavily on the agricultural system. Since at the time agriculture provided approximately 50 percent of the country's GNP compared with only 35 percent for industry, this seemed to be a logical solution. Because the Soviet government repudiated the czarist debt, foreign investors refused to lend new money to the Soviet Union, and Soviet industry was incapable of generating the amount of capital that was needed. In effect, he had no place to turn, and he therefore resolved to collectivize agriculture. By combining peasant fields, he thought, he could not only avail himself of the economies of scale but also, with fewer farms to watch over, more easily supervise them. By rigging the prices against the peasants and assigning high production targets, he sought to extract all the food he could, as cheaply as possible, and use it to feed the growing work force he was building up in the city.

To put these resources taken from agriculture to work as quickly as possible, Stalin introduced central planning. The central planners diverted a disproportionate share of those resources to heavy industry. Under the Stalinist model, only much later would the peasants and proletarians be allowed to improve their access to consumer goods. The first priority was to build up heavy industry.

This strategy worked well. Stalin and his successors found that the central control of the country's resources was a particularly effective way of building up not only the Soviet Union's heavy industry but a very powerful military force as well. Indeed, the Soviet Union was able to commandeer resources for the military much more effectively than could any market economy. Military expenditures consistently exceeded 10 percent of the GNP. Only in a time of war could the market economies respond in like fashion.

While the Stalinist model of development and resource allocation worked well for several decades, by the 1960s, economic growth in the Soviet Union began to falter. Industrial production in several industries actually dropped in the late 1970s, and there was little reason to expect any immediate improvement. The short-run challenges were highlighted by the Soviet economist Abel Aganbegian. Using official Soviet statistics, he dramatically illustrated how, because of past and ongoing reductions in the allocation of resources set aside for capital investment, Soviet growth and productivity slowed from 1971 to 1980.[14] The slowdown continued throughout most of the Eleventh Five-Year Plan, which ended in 1985.

III

Because the Soviet economic system has gone so long without economic reform, Gorbachev's task is particularly complex and challenging. As we shall see, he can make and has made marginal improvements in determining worker incentives and enterprise independence. He has even managed to stimulate an increase in the grain harvest. But it will not be enough for him simply to improve the efficiency of the existing system. He must dig at the root problems, and because the roots have been allowed to run so deep, that entails a fundamental restructuring of the system, something he himself has called for.[15]

If Gorbachev decides to undertake that structural upheaval, he will find it necessary to stand the existing Soviet economic system on its head. For reasons that we will explore in the pages ahead, he will have to reverse completely, and not just in a minor way, the emphasis on heavy industry. That in itself will mean a wrenching transformation, but the impact will not end there. A cutback in the heavy industrial sector will necessarily provoke a parallel contraction in the military sector, because heavy industry is the major source of Soviet armaments. Presumably, such a move presupposes considerable progress in arms control and a reduction in international tensions. A drop in the level of military expenditures from the present 14 to 16 percent of the GNP to below 10 percent or even to 6 percent also assumes acquiesence on the part of the Soviet generals.[16] This well may be difficult to obtain even if a meaningful arms agreement is reached. Generals, whether Soviet or American, seldom applaud demobilization and demilitarization. It is no fun being a general without troops to parade.

Assuming Gorbachev can do the unexpected, and free himself and the Soviet economy from the need to spend so much on heavy industry and the military, he will be in a position to divert the country's resources to light industry and consumer goods. For the first time, Soviet peasants and factory workers will feel like working, because they then will be able to buy something with the rubles they earn for working harder in their fields and factories. Such a transformation will go a long way toward stimulating improved productivity and quality of production. The implementation of such a plan is also a precondition to stimulating the mastery of high-technology production. But more will be needed, especially the decentralization of decision making and investment. Those opposed to a reduction in the size of the army and heavy industry will also oppose any effort to reduce centralization, without which the Soviet Union would be unable to expand its military-industrial structure.

As we shall see in Chapter 7, the upending of all these priorities—long regarded as sacred dogmas—is precisely the strategy that Deng Xiaoping has set for himself in China. It has not been easy for him or China. But if Gorbachev is to undertake the radical transformation of the Soviet economy that he insists is necessary, he will have little choice except to follow in Deng's footsteps. Gorbachev may find himself forced to accept other alternatives, but only if he makes the switch from the Stalinist model of economic development to the Asian model of development will he begin to come to grips with the basic forces that hold the Soviet Union back. However, challenging and traumatic such an effort has been for Deng, it will be even more so for Gorbachev.

IV

We shall begin our study by attempting to explain how the Soviet Union worked its way into such an economic straitjacket. We will consider recent Soviet economic developments, the areas where the Soviet Union has done well and where poorly, as seen in part by the economists within the Soviet Union. We will also review past Soviet efforts at reform and examine in more detail how the Soviet Union has or has not adapted to the age of high technology. Next, we will compare Soviet efforts with those of some of its neighbors, particularly East Germany, Hungary, and China. Except for a pause now and then to appease some conservatives, the Chinese appear to be moving at breakneck speed. The Hungarians are proceeding at a much slower and cautious pace, in part because they worry about the Soviets looking over their shoulder. The East Germans may be moving most slowly of all, at least in terms of radical reform, and for that very reason what they are doing has considerable appeal for many Soviet analysts. We will see what the Soviets have to say about some of these initiatives, particularly those in China. We will discuss at greater length why the Soviet central planning system is so ill suited to the age of the new high technology and how the Soviets have attempted to cope thus far. Finally, we will consider what options Soviet leaders have and how they are likely to respond.

The majority of the countries that have taken to calling themselves revolutionary today find that their institutions are rigid and difficult to change when faced with new conditions. Yet the new high technology demands subtlety and flexibility, if not daring. Even though the mode of production is changing in the developed world, many of the communist nations have been unable to keep up. The irony is evident. Marx may have been correct when he claimed that a change in the mode of production, such as the advent of high technology, necessitates comparable changes in the superstructure. What happens, then, when a society, especially one that continues to regard itself as a revolutionary force, resists or is not fully responsive to those changes? What does that portend for the country's competitive and industrial position in the world, and what does that suggest about the economic, social, and political adjustments the Soviet Union will have to make as it attempts to cope with the new high technology? The attempt to resolve those issues is Gorbachev's challenge.

2

Setting the Stage

In some ways, it is surprising that the Soviet economy should be in serious need of reform. Beginning in the 1930s, the Soviets often reported that their country's industrial growth rose by more than 20 percent a year, the highest rate in the world.[1] Even when recalculated to reflect Western standards and concepts, the statistics made the Soviet economy the envy of the vast majority of the world's economies.[2] This growth was particularly impressive in the 1930s. While countries like the United States were agonizing over the growing number of unemployed workers and bankrupt factories, the Soviet Union moved actively to reduce its own unemployment and construct new factories.

To visitors like Beatrice and Sidney Webb, the British socialists, the Soviets seemed to have solved the curse of the business cycle. Importing comparatively modest amounts of Western technology, the Soviets were able to construct a respectable industrial infrastructure. Whereas prerevolutionary Russia had been regarded as an industrially backward and impoverished country, by World War II the Soviet Union had built up a powerful military arsenal.

Our immediate task is to explain how the Soviet Union managed to achieve such impressive growth and why Stalin's growth model eventually became a fetter rather than a facilitator. In fact, subsequent Soviet leaders have had to concern themselves with undoing much that Stalin took great pride in doing.

I

For some years after Stalin's death, Soviet growth continued at impressive rates. Although there was a gradual decline from the extraordinary pace of the 1930s, the growth in the 1950s was high enough that when Nikita Khrushchev journeyed to the United States in 1959, he had good reason to boast that by 1970 or 1980, at the latest, the Soviet Union would overtake and surpass the United States. Given the record of Soviet growth in the last half of the 1950s, Khrushchev's threats were taken seriously. (See Table 1.) Each year, steel production grew by as much as 9 percent.[3] Production in other major industrial sectors was comparable and often higher.

Production in agriculture paralleled the success in industry. Under Khrushchev's leadership, Soviet farmers reaped the largest grain harvest in Soviet history. Khrushchev decided to

TABLE 1

Average Annual Rates of GNP Growth
in the Soviet Union

Five-Year Period	Average Annual Percentage Growth
1951–1955	5.5
1956–1960	5.9
1961–1965	5.0
1966–1970	5.2
1971–1975	3.7
1976–1980	2.7

SOURCE: U.S. Congress, Joint Economic Committee, *USSR: Measures of Economic Growth, 1950–80* (Washington, D.C.: GPO, 1982), p. 15.

increase incentives for Soviet peasants in existing areas and spent large sums of money to expand grain production into the virgin lands. His gamble paid off. There was reason to believe that grain harvests in the future would be even more promising. In addition, Soviet farmers were setting new records for harvests of industrial crops like cotton.[4]

Increased output, particularly in agriculture, left more goods available to consumers. This was an important improvement. Until Stalin's death, the Soviet consumer fared badly. The losses suffered in World War II did not make Stalin's task any easier, but he was not overly concerned with helping the Soviet consumer. He continued to stress investment in Soviet heavy industry. Under the circumstances, it took until 1952 for Soviet living standards to regain the levels reached in 1939, which were not very high.[5]

Khrushchev was much more supportive of improved living standards. Under his leadership, not only did food sales increase, but so did production of other consumer goods. He also increased housing construction. If compared with similar measures in Western Europe and the United States, the Soviet performance would not be quite so impressive; but, remembering conditions inside the Soviet Union in the early 1950s, Soviet citizens had much to be grateful for, and the future looked even brighter. In my conversations in 1959 and 1960 with Soviet citizens both in and out of the Soviet Union, I was struck by the sense of pride in their government's accomplishments and the feeling that Khrushchev's optimism about the future was not exaggerated. They may have thought he was a bit of a boor, but they sincerely appreciated what he had done for the Soviet population.

Impressive as Soviet economic accomplishments were, it was the growing prowess of the Soviet Union in science and technology that made Khrushchev's challenge to outsiders increasingly plausible. What initially seemed to be bluster soon became believable as the Soviets announced one scientific achievement after another. At first, there was general agreement that some of the early Soviet successes would have been impossible without espionage or other kinds of technological borrowing from the United States.[6] Without such secrets, for example, the Soviets would have had considerably more difficulty producing the atomic bomb and various industrial products, including petrochemicals and even automobiles. The skepticism was shaken when the Soviets went on, without outside help, to produce a hydrogen bomb and similarly sophisticated military weapons and aircraft. But it was the Soviet development of their unmanned and manned Sputniks, first launched on October 4, 1957, that caused the complete reexamination of past assumptions and provoked much alarm in the United States. There was concern that the United States had become number two to the Soviet Union in space and might soon be number two on the ground as well. Some skeptics continued to question whether any of the Soviet claims were true, but others had already begun to calculate mathematically just how long it might be before the Soviet GNP exceeded ours.[7] Admittedly, the Soviets had used some captured German scientists to help them in their space program, but so had the United States, and, unlike the Soviets, the Americans had very little to show for their efforts. Soviet space successes engendered enormous doubts about American technology and spurred a crash program to catch up with Soviet space triumphs and upgrade the American educational system.

Although Soviet economists and bureaucrats continued to complain about shortcomings in the Soviet system, it became harder to ignore Soviet accomplishments. Some foreign specialists began to warn that Soviet industrial successes would soon spill out of the Soviet Union itself and into world markets. The Soviets had already begun to undercut Western petroleum prices in Western Europe and in the Third World. Some alarmed Western oil executives warned that unless Soviet encroachments on Western oil markets were not halted, the Soviets would soon undermine NATO and destroy the Western alliance.[8] Soviet oil production continued to rise relentlessly until, in 1974, the Soviet Union, as Khrushchev had correctly predicted, began to outproduce Saudi Arabia and the United

States and became the largest producer of petroleum in the world.[9] The Soviet Union became the largest producer of steel in 1974 and of natural gas in 1983. By 1970, it was producing more than two machine tools for every one made in the United States. The machine tools may have been standardized and unsophisticated, but some American engineers were convinced that it was only a matter of time before some Soviet machine tools would be dumped in the United States and bankrupt the American machine tool manufacturers.[10] Many American fishermen had already been forced out of business by the massive fishing operations being mounted by the Soviet Union off the American coast. Serviced by large mother ships, Soviet trawlers could fish at sea considerably longer than individually owned and uncoordinated American trawlers. To many observers, this was a sign of the future.

It was evident that by selecting and mastering relatively unsophisticated technologies, the Soviets could take advantage of mass production on a scale beyond that normally achieved by privately owned industry. Because they had no need to concern themselves about bottom-line profit operations, there was some reason to fear that the Soviets might soon drive some American and other Western manufacturers out of business.[11] Even more intimidating was the assumption that if they could master the technology needed for Sputnik, the Soviets would eventually adopt sophisticated technology in their civilian manufacturing operations and use it to enhance their industrial competitiveness. The Soviets had demonstrated that they could master the technology of the day and grow at an impressive rate.

II

Given that the rest of the world during much of this period, particularly the 1930s, was having trouble generating any growth, what explained the Soviet success? Much of the credit goes to Stalin. He insisted on rapid industrial development and concluded that he could not lift the Soviet Union out of the ranks of the economically backward without a fundamental change in its prerevolutionary economic system. As Stalin saw it, the Soviet Union lagged too far behind competitors in Western Europe and the United States. The traditional profit-and-loss incentive system, not to mention the private enterprise system, was incapable of generating the growth in heavy industry and military strength that Stalin and his supporters concluded they had to have. As long as the primary goal of a factory manager was to earn higher profits, the manager would be tempted to produce consumer frills, not industrial fundamentals. That the Soviets were able to grow as fast as they did in the 1930s, 1940s, and 1950s suggests, on the surface at least, that Stalin may have been correct.

Led by Nikolai Bukharin, some Soviet officials countered that Stalin was wrong and that ultimately private agriculture, trade, and the profit-and-loss system would have provided the Soviet Union with the industry that Stalin wanted.[12] As proof, they pointed to the very impressive growth rates of the 1920s. With the end of the civil war in 1921 and Lenin's introduction of the New Economic Policy (NEP), the economy recovered rapidly. Most seemed to agree that, at a minimum, there should be state control of the commanding heights of industry but that if the peasants and small-business men were allowed to respond to a profit-and-loss system, they would continue to increase production and provide for the consumer's well-being.

Despite such arguments, Stalin decided to do away with the private sector and the profit-loss system. As he saw it, the rapid growth in the mid and late 1920s was unusual. After the destruction of World War I and the civil war, it would have been surprising if economic growth had *not* been impressive. Reconstruction almost always produces rapid growth. Normally, one needs only to start the flow of raw materials and other forms of working capital, since much of the current industrial structure had existed before.

Stalin focused on the decades ahead. Once reconstruction was complete, the Soviet Union had to move to the next stage —the formation of new industry. Normal profit/earnings might be high enough to generate additional working-capital funds, but they would be too meager to provide the substantial quantities of capital investment needed to sustain higher levels of industrial growth. New steel mills and machine tool factories, Stalin's high-priority industries, necessitated particularly large capital investments. To Stalin, the existing methods were inadequate for his goals.

To generate the capital he needed and to ensure that the nation's resources would be purposefully used and not squandered, Stalin radically uprooted the existing Soviet way of economic life. Not only did he nationalize all forms of industrial and service activity, but he also decreed that all the Soviet peasants had to turn over their land, livestock, and equipment to newly created collective farms. With the means of production firmly in the state's hands, Stalin could direct investment funds and resources as he saw fit. As promised, this meant an emphasis on heavy industry and a deterioration in the real incomes of workers and peasants.

Had he wanted to, Stalin could have settled for the nationalization of the industrial and agricultural means of production. Many socialists defined socialism as state ownership of the means of production and as a more equitable distribution of wealth. For example, when the British Labour party took over control of the British government after World War II, one of its major goals was state ownership. That, to the Labour party, was the essence of socialism. There was no central planning. But Stalin went beyond state ownership. He replaced the market with a central plan. The plan prescribed for managers what inputs they would use and from where as well as what outputs they would produce and for whom. There would still be prices and cost and profits and losses, but they were now subordinate to and determined by planned orders. Gosplan, the new state planning organization, established yearly and five-year plans for enterprises, republics, and the country as a whole.

In place of the market, with its fine nuances, the Soviets designed a remarkably simple planning system. Instead of profits, the main criterion for success was quantity. That was relatively easy to understand. The more a worker or a manager produced, the better. Moreover, "more" was assumed to be a function of a larger quantity of labor and machinery as well as of increased effort by individual workers and managers. Those who were able to increase production won appropriate recognition, material and nonmaterial, from their superiors. Given the poorly trained work and managerial forces available in the Soviet Union at the time, this was a rather ingenious way to use a large but unskilled labor force to achieve unprecedentedly rapid economic growth.

Frequently, the emphasis on quantity proved to be too simplistic. A standard other than absolute quantity alone ultimately became necessary. Many enterprises produced a diverse collection of goods that did not lend themselves to one overriding index, which could be specified in units like tons or meters. If an enterprise that produced both light and heavy products was assigned a target in tons, it tended to produce only the heavier item and ignore the lighter merchandise, since plan fulfillment normally could more easily be met by concentrating on the production of a few heavy items. In an effort to circumvent such bias, Soviet planners designed a performance measurement system based on the gross value of production measured in rubles. Products, regardless of size or weight, would be added together to determine a firm's ruble output. Thus, for enterprises with a heterogeneous product mix, the higher this year's gross ruble value of output *(valovaia produktsiia),* compared with last year's, the higher their premiums. Known as the VAL system, for short, the gross ruble value of output grew in importance as factories began to produce increasingly heterogeneous menus of production.

While the VAL system had its advantages, it also had its shortcomings. Under the VAL system, just as when they used tons or units as an indicator of success, the managers favored heavy products at the expense of lighter products. The planners apparently neglected to allow for the intricacies of the Soviet pricing system. Pricing in the Soviet Union operates on a cost-plus basis. Given the relative absence of competitive pricing and concerns about finding willing purchasers, the Soviet manager is able to price his goods with full allowance for the cost of his input, regardless of how high that might be. Even more, the Soviet manager actually has an incentive to seek out the most costly raw materials and components available. As factory managers quickly came to realize, under the VAL system the more expensive the inputs, the higher the gross value of output in rubles and the better the managers' performance records. In practice, this has resulted in excessive use of raw materials, and that helps explain the perennial Soviet complaint that products are too heavy and that raw materials are needlessly squandered in the production process.

Viktor G. Afanasyev, the editor in chief of *Pravda,* has provided a common example of how irksome and wasteful the VAL system can be. In a speech on Soviet television, he noted how *Pravda* had come to the aid of the Volga Pipe Mill three times.[13] The mill was producing thin rolled pipe that was equal in strength to thick rolled pipe, but weighed one-half as much. Potentially the switch to such pipe could save the Soviet Union hundreds of millions of rubles and tens of thousands of tons of high quality alloy steel a year. But because the Volga Pipe Mill product sells for less, its VAL was 10 percent less and as a consequence "its wages, reserves, bonuses and all the rest of its rewards to the producers have fallen by 15%, 'fallen,' but in actual fact, its labor productivity has increased."

But VAL's perniciousness does not end there. No one wants to use the Volga Pipe Plant's pipe. Builders refuse to use thin rolled pipe because it is cheap and no construction unit in its right mind will use cheap products because its VAL will also suffer.[14]

But while the disease is widely recognized, no one thus far has been able to do away with the VAL system. Efforts have been made to tie managerial performance to completed sales and to increase competitive pressures among different factories, but despite the best of intentions and even some temporary successes, the VAL system continues to prevail.[15]

The very significant increase in Soviet industrial production over the last several decades makes it hard to dispute the utility of the quantitative approach to industrial growth. Moreover, because in its early days the Soviet economy was so poor, it did not matter all that much, at least initially, that the products were too big or small, colorful or dull, old-fashioned or stylish. Soviet factories and consumers, with rare exceptions, found a use for whatever was produced. If the trucks emerging from the assembly line were too small, the new owner found it expedient to build a larger frame or to barter his smaller truck with someone whose truck was too large. In the early days, with a little ingenuity, something always seemed better than nothing. That is how the Stalin model grew and flourished.

As output grew, an increasing number of officials came to realize that "more" did not necessarily always mean "better." Soviet leaders came to recognize the need for improved quality, methods, and products—which, as the example of the truck indicates, the emphasis on quantity failed to produce.

It also became increasingly necessary to prod the economy to move in a different direction or to break some particularly restrictive bottleneck. Because the Soviet system precluded the use of entrepreneurial profits that serve to stimulate new product and industrial development in the capitalist world, the Soviet leaders found themselves forced to resort more and more to extramarket stimuli like nationwide campaigns. For months at a time, the newspapers and radios would be filled with reverential stories about workers who had set some new output record or managers who had mastered some new technology and soon afterward everyone else would be urged and then ordered to do the same thing.

On October 31, 1935, the coal miner Alexei Stakhanov became the focus of nationwide attention as a coal miner who could produce fourteen times the amount of coal normally produced by fellow miners in one shift.[16] His feat continues to excite Soviet leaders. Gorbachev, for instance, frequently refers to Stakhanov as an example of what Soviet workers can do when properly motivated.[17] What was not publicized, however, was that much of Stakhanov's effort was made possible only because of preliminary preparation by other miners working alongside him. But Stakhanov got all the credit—they got none. Moreover, once Stakhanov could prove that a higher rate of output was feasible, output norms were jacked up without an accompanying increase in pay. Understandably, Stakhanov's fellow miners came to take a less enthusiastic view of his achievements. In fact, in a growing number of instances, in both the mines and the factories where the Stakhanovite model was introduced, other miners and workers began to sabotage the effort. For most Soviet workers, the Stakhanovite movement eventually came to personify worker hostility to a process that was nothing more than a glorified way to ratchet up norms. Gorbachev's resurrection of the movement fifty years later seems to contradict his reformist image. It may yield short-term production gains as a campaign to capture worker attention, but most thoughtful Soviet economists do not recommend it as a means of stimulating the modern-day Soviet worker.

Campaigns are one way to implement change in the Soviet Union, but because one campaign always seems to follow another, frequently urging just the opposite course of action, Soviet managers and workers have become very cynical about the lasting benefits of such an approach. To many managers it often seems that the best strategy is to do nothing. If they wait long enough, the campaign and strategy are likely to shift, and the managers will be in the mainstream again without having to devote what almost always turns out to be wasted effort on some short-term infatuation of a Soviet leader.

III

Of the Soviet leaders, Khrushchev was perhaps the most enthusiastic campaigner. He seemed to shift policies on a yearly schedule. This impetuosity was one reason why he was charged with "having harebrained ideas" when he was thrown out of office in 1964. Since his successors have continued the campaign technique, the secret seems to be that campaigns may be used, but only in moderation and with less frequency. Khrushchev's "sin" was that he was too frenetic and too far-reaching in his efforts. Ultimately, his associates came to yearn for a more sedate, less disruptive leader. In turn, after the near somnolence of Brezhnev, particularly in his later years, the Soviets again sought out an activist in the person of a Yuri Andropov and then a Gorbachev. This shifting of leadership styles is, of course, in itself a form of change by campaign.

Campaigning is not limited to intangible goals. Periodically, Soviet officials will order managers to adhere to some new administrative procedure. Sometimes Soviet managers will be told to concentrate on variables of production, such as tons of production, number of units, labor costs, raw material costs or net normative output (value added), and occasionally even profit.

It is easy to understand why experienced Soviet managers find it difficult to become too enthusiastic about such efforts. True, Gorbachev seems more determined and more far-reaching in his vision than any of his predecessors, but for some, Gorbachev's more recent drive against drunkenness and his call for "the intensification of industry," by which he means retooling, is just an updated version of the same process. The managers can be forgiven for assuming that "this too will pass."

Not only do lower-ranking Soviet officials tend to lose their enthusiasm for campaigns, but campaigning can also be counterproductive. Such a zigzag approach inevitably produces excesses that sooner or later, as in the case of the overenthusiastic planting of corn, lead to cutbacks. At the same time, the near demonic emphasis on a single goal means that complementary processes are neglected (as in the utilization of fertilizer), and thus even the final product may end up as waste. As in the West, when managers use the campaign method, the cynicism of lower-ranking officials is reflected in the callous refrain "What will these geniuses think of next?"

IV

The need to resort to campaigns and the fact that so many campaigns have tended to become ineffective, and even counterproductive, indicated that the Stalinist model had become increasingly inappropriate. The model worked well for several decades, but in time even Soviet economists started to question it. Whatever its initial successes, as early as the 1960s, some began to argue that the Stalinist model had become a fetter on the development of new technologies and methods.[18] Most agreed the Stalinist model had made the Soviet Union a major industrial force. In the late 1930s, it sought to be self-reliant. An economist would say that Stalin's approach emphasized "import substitution"; that is, he tried to reduce imports and produce the goods at home instead. But Stalin went further. In the late 1930s, the Soviet Union sharply reduced both its imports and its exports. The trading doors were opened again during World War II and to the new East European satellites in the late 1940s and the 1950s. But, with relatively few exceptions, trade with the capitalist countries was restricted until the late 1950s.

Despite its accomplishments, however, Stalin's model of development became an impediment for his successors. Some economists today argue that instead of squeezing the peasants through collectivization, building up heavy industry at the expense of agriculture and light industry, and emphasizing import substitution, the preferable strategy is to concentrate on enriching the peasants, promoting light industry (whose products can then be used to stimulate peasants and urban workers), facilitating product innovation, and supporting export expansion. This approach seems to have succeeded well in East Asia. An export-led strategy forces local managers to concentrate on quality and excellence, not just on production. Producing an item of equal quality is not enough; it must also be cheaper or better, which means product enhancement and improved productivity. In contrast, an import substitution approach may easily lead to the neglect of quality and an emphasis instead on quantity, as it did in the Soviet Union.

The impact of Stalin's import substitution approach was compounded by the forced draft manner in which he implemented his program and by his obsession with heavy industry. Heavy industry became such a fetish that even now it often seems all but impossible to shift to an emphasis on consumer goods. Both central planning and heavy industry have taken on all the trappings of sacred objects and have proven highly resistant to meaningful change.

V

As the economy has grown in size and sophistication, the Soviet planning process has naturally become overly complex. Whereas opponents of a state-run economy have warned that it is impossible to have a centrally planned economy without a stifling and ever-expanding bureaucracy, others have argued that an oversized bureaucracy can be avoided if the state system of ownership is accompanied by a system of markets, competitive prices, and the injunction that factory managers maximize profits.[19]

Whether the adoption of such practices will reduce the central-planning bureaucracy has yet to be demonstrated. Despite periodic efforts to reduce bureaucratic power and increase the prerogatives of factory managers, the powers and size of the Soviet central-planning authorities keep expanding. For example, although efforts were made in 1965 to reduce the number of material balances, it increased again.[20] (The material balance accounts are among the planner's main tools for resolving the supply and demand of priority items.) On the basis of these accounts, the planners determine who will produce what quantities of goods using what inputs, and who will receive those goods. According to O. M. Yun, the deputy head of Gosplan's (the state planning commission's) Department for the Improvement of Planning and Economic Incentives, Gosplan in 1983 drew up 2,000 single-product material balances.[21] Just how

many there actually are seems uncertain. Nikolai P. Lebe-
dinsky, a deputy chairman of Gosplan itself, indicated that the
figure was as high as 6,000.[22]

In addition to the higher-priority goods allocated by Gosplan, Gossnab (the State Committee for Material and Technical
Supply) compiles 15,000 material balances, and the various
ministries process up to 50,000 material balances a year for
products with somewhat lower priority. To do all this, Gosplan
alone must handle 7 million documents and make 83 million
calculations annually.[23] In part, the numbers are so large because 50 percent of all the plans are changed each year. Computers do not play an important role in the actual allocation
process, so most of these calculations are made manually, either
on a calculator or, as often as not, on an abacus.

The efforts of Gosplan, Gossnab, and the ministries are only
part of the central bureaucratic process. In addition to the
material balances, Soviet officials must also determine prices.
Despite "a high degree of decentralization" the U.S.S.R. State
Price Committee must still set 200,000 prices each year.[24]

While the planning process becomes encumbered with increasing data and decision-making tasks, Soviet planners find
themselves with a diminishing pool of new entrants in the work
force and of new capital upon which to draw. Because the
birthrate, especially in the western part of the Soviet Union, has
over the years fallen, the flow of workers into the work force
each year is below what it was in previous years. According to
Abel Aganbegian, the country's work force during the Tenth
Five-Year Plan (1976–1980) grew by 11 million people, 3 million of whom went to work in factories.[25] However, as a result
of the drop in the birthrate, only 3 million new employees were
expected to join the work force during the 1981–1985 five-year
plan period, and of those, Aganbegian has pointed out, 2.5
million were to come from Central Asia and Azerbaidzhan,
non-Russian ethnic areas. This means that the bulk of the
population increase will be non-Slav, and the Russians regard
non-Slavs as uninterested in industry and as unwilling to move
to urban industrialized areas in the western part of the Soviet

Union. During the period 1986–1990, Aganbegian has predicted, even fewer new workers will be entering the work force. This decline has important economic implications. Since increments to the work force constituted a source of previous economic growth, this impending shortage must somehow be offset.

One offset would be to increase the rate of capital formation. Like labor, capital stock has also been an important source of Soviet economic growth. But capital investment, too, has been decreasing. Again according to the academician Aganbegian, whereas the capital available for investment for the Tenth Five-Year Plan (1976–1980) increased 32 percent over that for the Ninth Five-Year Plan, capital investment in the Eleventh Five-Year plan was scheduled to grow only 10 percent over that in the preceding five years. The reduction in economic growth has made it harder to set aside resources for capital.[26] Reflecting the slowdown, investment grew by only 2 percent in 1984.[27] Aganbegian has warned that this slowdown could be a serious barrier to increased economic growth.

In addition to declining capital and labor formation, there is the problem that labor productivity has not kept pace with increases in wages. Presumably, this heightens inflationary pressures. According to the economist E. Rusanov, whereas during the last days of Stalin, wages rose only .3 percent for each 1.0 percent increase in productivity, by 1976–1983 wages were rising .9 percent for each 1.0 percent increase in productivity.[28] Moreover, the trend is toward even faster wage increases. In 1982, wages rose almost one-third faster than labor productivity. It was just such a trend that caused Gorbachev to complain that wages have been increasing almost twice as fast as productivity.[29]

As if all of this were not enough cause for alarm about future economic growth, Soviet economists also point to a variety of other shortcomings that are becoming increasingly troublesome. Some are problems of nature. After almost sixty-five years of rapid and often wasteful economic growth, some of the country's best natural-resource deposits have become ex-

hausted. Whereas Soviet energy raw materials once came almost entirely from deposits located west of the Ural Mountains,
today the European part of the Soviet Union accounts for only
9 percent of the Soviet Union's energy output.[30] Siberia and the
Soviet Far East now account for 88 percent of all Soviet energy
output, making energy transportation a much larger portion of
the energy bill. Exploration has also become more costly. Having already exploited much of the most accessible petroleum,
Soviet drillers warned that in 1981–1985 they would have to
spend nine times more on investment to obtain a one-ton increase in oil production than they did in 1976–1980.[31]

It is not only mother but human nature that causes the Soviet
Union problems. During the last years of Brezhnev's administration, the Soviet population became calloused, cynical, and
unresponsive to the continuing exhortations of the party and
the government. Gorbachev seems well aware of how futile
those years were. As he put it, "I have looked through many
resolutions passed during the past 20 years. I do not find they
were mistaken. The slogans and appeals even then were true,
but we did not finish the work."[32] Nonetheless, while recognizing that without action such exhortations fall on deaf ears,
Gorbachev in the same speech reverted to the old pattern, and
at a meeting in the House of Political Education in Khabarovsk,
he found himself telling the crowd, "The main thing needed
now, and I say this to you and ask you: Work, Work, Work!"[33]
What makes this call so surprising is that Gorbachev certainly
knows that such exhortations are futile until living conditions
have improved and until the political and social system has
become more flexible. But so far it remains very rigid—a legacy
of Stalin's approach to economic development, which still ex-
erts a baleful influence.

Another Stalinist legacy is the reluctance of Soviet leaders to
endow enterprise managers with meaningful power. Factory
managers have been and, despite some of the reforms being
proposed, continue to be subject to intense scrutiny. Managerial
controls are deemed necessary not only to prevent managers
from using state-owned resources for frivolous purposes but

also to preclude private usurpation of public resources. Thus, enterprise managers are confronted with a bewildering number of quotas and indices that were intended to guide and control their behavior. Inevitably, some of these controls are at odds with one another or lead to counterproductive results. All too often the means becomes an end in itself. For example, in an effort to prevent managers from granting wages or bonuses that were too high, state planners decreed that the incentive fund for an enterprise would be a function of the number of employees and workplaces in the firm.[34] That limit served to hold down bonuses and even wages, which was the intent, but it also caused managers to build up a needlessly large labor force, which was not.[35] In the same way, the factory managers find that in order to fulfill their plans they must have extra workers around to satisfy worker drafts that are ordered from time to time by local authorities eager to complete local construction or harvest projects.[36] This explains why managers have strongly resisted efforts to reduce the size of their work force.

The great pressure put on managers to fulfill their plan targets has also proven to be economically irrational. For the most part, the failure of subcontractors to deliver promised components is not considered a legitimate excuse for plan underfulfillment. Under the circumstances, Soviet managers have sought to be as self-sufficient as possible, even if that has meant forsaking the economies that come with the division of labor. It is better to perform a task in-house, where it can be controlled, than entrust it to an outside supplier and transporter who cannot be controlled. In the process of becoming self-sufficient, the enterprise plan is more likely to be fulfilled, but costs become higher and the state is the loser. The quest for self-sufficiency is not limited to enterprises. Whole ministries develop the same tendency. Each ministry has its own protected sources of supply, and on occasion one ministry often refuses to deal with other ministries unless ordered to do so by Moscow. Inevitably, this has proven to be wasteful. In the words of G. Popov, the former dean of the Faculty of Economics at Moscow State University, "Everywhere you look you can find more efficient ways of doing things that are not being adopted because they do not fit into the ministries' existing structure.[37] Such behavior not only complicates the production of existing products but also frequently obstructs the introduction of new products and new industries.[38]

VI

Agriculture has its own special problems. Beginning in 1979, the Soviet Union suffered seven bad grain harvests in a row (see Table 2). Whereas before the revolution Russia had frequently exported more grain than anyone else in the world, after the revolution its net grain exports gradually diminished until, in the 1970s, it imported more grain than anyone else in the world (Japan may have imported more than the Soviet Union for the first time in 1984). There were also periodic shortfalls in such basic crops as cotton.

TABLE 2

Soviet Grain Harvests, Exports, and Imports
(millions of metric tons)

Year	Harvest	Export	Import
1950	81	2.9	0.2
1955	104	3.7	0.3
1956	125	3.2	0.5
1957	103	7.4	0.2
1958	135	5.1	0.8
1959	120	7.0	0.3
1960	126	6.8	0.2
1961	131	7.5	0.7
1962	140	7.8	—
1963	108	6.3	3.1
1964	152	3.5	7.3
1965	121	4.3	6.4

Year	Harvest	Export	Import
1966	171	3.6	7.7
1967	148	6.2	2.2
1968	170	5.4	1.6
1969	162	7.2	0.6
1970	187	5.7	2.2
1971	181	8.6	3.5
1972	168	4.6	15.5
1973	223	4.9	23.9
1974	196	7.0	7.1
1975	140	3.6	15.9
1976	224	1.5	20.6
1977	196	2.3*	18.9*
1978	237	2.8*	15.6*
1979	179	0.8*	31.0*
1980	189	0.5*	34.8*
1981	158	0.5*	46.0*
1982	187	0.5*	32.5*
1983	192	0.5*	32.9*
1984	173	1.0*	55.5*
1985	192	1.0*	29.0*
1906	210	1.0*	30.0*

*July to July of following year estimate of Department of Agriculture.

SOURCE: Tsentral'noe statisticheskoe upravlenie, *Narodnoe khoziaistvo SSSR v 1970 gody* (Moscow: Gosstatizdat, 1971), p. 309; 1975, p. 360; 1980, p. 202; 1985, p. 209; Ministerstvo Vneshnei Torgovii, *Vneshniaia torgovlia SSSR v 1976* (Moscow: Statistika, 1977), pp. 30, 42, and earlier editions; U.S. Department of Agriculture, *USSR Situation and Outlook Report* (Washington, D.C.: GPO, May 1986), pp. 13, 14; *Pravda*, January 18, 1987, p. 2.

The reason for the shortfalls is not just poor weather. Soviet peasants have never forgiven the Soviet government for the collectivization of their lands. This may explain why with only about 3 percent of the Soviet Union's arable land, the peasants on their own private plots produce about 60 percent of the Soviet Union's potatoes and honey, over 40 percent of its fruits berries and eggs, and about 30 percent of its milk, meat, and vegetables. Douglas Diamond has estimated that the private plots produce about 25 percent of the Soviet Union's total crop output.[39] These plots account for about 30 percent of the country's total milk and meat output as well. Preference for work on the private plots rather than on the collectively owned land also helps explain why it has been hard to increase grain output. The peasants can earn more working on their private plots than working on the collective lands, where most of the grain is grown.

Whether the cause is poor weather, peasant resentment, or the economic system itself, the sequence of poor harvests is partly responsible for the food shortages and long queues in front of Soviet shops. The same combination of factors explains the fact that milk, dairy product, and fruit consumption per capita, despite the role of private plots, has fallen periodically in recent years.[40] Some Soviet officials rationalize the long lines by arguing that they are a natural consequence of the increase in Soviet wages. Consumers have more money and thus want to buy more. As the economist E. Rusanov has pointed out, from 1970 to 1983, while the wage fund grew by 90 percent, retail sales grew by only 80 percent.[41] In some societies, that would be considered a good sign, but the context of Rusanov's article makes it clear that he does not view it that way—nor do the majority of Soviet economists.[42] Rusanov is partially correct. Although more consumer goods are being produced, consumer incomes have risen even more; as a result, too much money is chasing too few goods. In addition, there are periodic disruptions of production and supply, so even if disposable incomes had not increased, there would be shortages. The problem could be solved at least partly if Soviet authorities dared to raise prices to establish a better market equilibrium. Gorbachev himself seems aware of the problem. Describing his impressions of his visit to Komsomolsk-na-Amure, on the Pacific coast, he began by saying, "I did get the feeling that the wages in Komsomolsk-na-Amure are high, but the question arises: Who needs these wages? If with these wages one cannot satisfy one's reasonable requirements, then the incentive for work is undermined."[43] Some Western economists disagree and argue, not entirely convincingly, that the bulk of savings among Soviet consumers is voluntary, just as in the West.[44]

That all is not well in Soviet collectivized and state agriculture is suggested by numerous signs. In 1985, the state found it necessary, for example, to provide 54.7 billion rubles in subsidies for Soviet agriculture—35.1 billion rubles for meat and milk products alone.[45] Such subsidies are intended to stimulate agricultural production while allowing the state to hold down retail food prices. Bread prices have stayed unchanged since 1955, and the prices of meat, milk, and butter have remained stable since 1962. Price increases in the latter products precipitated bloody riots in 1962 in Novocherkassk. Ever since, Soviet officials have been reluctant to risk another confrontation, although there have been recurring hints since Andropov's reign that prices, even that of bread, might be raised.[46] This also explains why the Soviets do not seem eager to establish the market equilibrium we just mentioned. They would rather have lines than inflation and the possibility of overt protest.

For most Soviet consumers, the subsidization of such basic foods is an important benefit. However, as growing and production costs have increased, the necessity for even larger subsidies has had many unintended side effects. As we saw, because prices are low, the demand for such processed food products has been higher than it would otherwise have been. The peasants, for example, have discovered that it is more profitable for them to sell grain to state procurement agencies at a high price and to feed their livestock not with grain but with the heavily subsidized bread, purchased from bread shops.[47] In Belorussia and Estonia, one of every four families buys food for use as livestock feed.[48] In Turkmenistan, Kirghizia, and the R.S.F.S.R., one out of every seven does. But since the retail price of meat is also heavily subsidized, many peasants carry this misallocation of resources one step further by buying meat in the state meat shops and feeding it to furbearing animals.[49] The state has launched a major campaign against such practices, with posters criticizing those who waste bread and describing bread as a national treasure. In addition, on July 1, 1986 the reselling of bread was formally declared a crime, subject to a 50 to 100 ruble fine.[50] The state has also banned the private possession of furbearing animals.[51]

These measures, however, do not solve the problem. They deal only with the symptoms, not the causes. There continue to be reports of poor-quality bread and of meat shortages. Some peasants and farm managers still find it easier to fulfill their farm quotas by going to the market and buying up such products as butter, milk, and meat and passing them off as their own to the state at the higher wholesale procurement prices.[52] The gap in prices and the profits to be made from the private plots also help explain the many complaints that Soviet peasants spend too much time in the city *kolkhoz* markets or on privately created construction brigades while urban workers, including surgeons and schoolchildren, are drafted to replace them in the fields.[53] What is needed is a major retail price increase so that prices more accurately reflect supply and demand, but given the likely political ramifications, the Soviets have been very cautious about taking such a risky step.

The gap between procurement and retail prices of grain and bread is not the only reason for Soviet agricultural waste. One of the puzzles for foreign observers of the Soviet economy is how there can be such food shortages (even necessitating spot rationing in 1982) when statistics indicate that harvests, even allowing for poor weather now and then, are so much higher than they were in the 1950s and the early 1960s. In those years, when a good harvest was 135 or 140 metric tons, the food lines often seemed to be fewer and shorter than they were in 1982 or 1983, when the harvest was approximately 180 or 190 metric tons. (See Table 2.) Even the 1981 harvest, estimated to be only 158 million tons, was higher, except for that of 1975, than any other harvest before 1966. The population only grew 19 percent between 1966 and 1986, hardly enough to account for the shortages, even with allowance for the diversion of bread and meat to the livestock.

What has not been taken into account, however, is that the size of the harvest in the Soviet Union is not the same as the amount of food available in the stores. The reason for the difference is that an extraordinary share of the typical Soviet harvest is left to rot in the field. According to official statistics and Gorbachev himself, the Soviets lose one-fifth of their gross annual harvest of grain, vegetables, and fruit during harvesting, transporting, storing, and processing.[54] For example, during winter storage, reportedly 25 percent of the potato crop, 20 percent of the grain and sugar beets, and 18 percent of the fruit crop is ruined and never makes its way to the consumer.[55] Some reports indicate that at times 50 percent of the potato crop is left to rot.[56]

Another, more important reason why so much of the crop rots is that Soviet farms lack storage facilities, even for the crops grown on the collectivized and state fields. For example, only 40 percent of all farms in the Soviet Union have a storehouse, and then the building may be used to store cars, not food.[57] Given the severity of Soviet winters, it is no wonder that so much of the crop rots. The absence of nearby storage facilities is explained by the fact that Soviet central planners tend to build fewer but more grandiose storage and processing facilities, a phenomenon the Soviets called gigantomania.[58] Such structures may make the planners and builders look more impressive, but that means fewer can be built with the funds available.

Gigantomania alone does not explain a lack of on-farm storage. Soviet officials are reluctant to place stored grain too near the farmers. During the famine of the 1930s, the peasants looted the stocks, and ever since then the government has been determined to keep such reserves out of the hands of the peasants.

Building fewer and more remote storage facilities has indeed kept the peasants from dipping into state reserves, but it has also made it difficult for them to put that food in storage. Most Soviet farms are located an average of 200 to 300 miles from grain storage facilities and 140 to 150 miles from meatpacking plants.[59] In the United States, such distances would not pose a problem, but even small distances are a serious matter in the Soviet Union because the government has built few roads linking farms to the grain storage and processing centers. According to one report, over 200 district centers and over one-quarter of the state and collective farms in the Soviet Union are not serviced by roads.[60] It is striking to drive through the Russian countryside and see signs indicating the direction to a collective farm, with only a footpath as a link to the main highway. Moreover, the rural roads that have been built generally turn into mud during the spring and fall thaws. No wonder that more than one-half of the country's tractor fleet during such seasons is assigned to the "unproductive work of towing trucks."[61] But there may be waste even when Soviet trucks are able to move on hard-surface roads. Relatively few Soviet tractors and railroad cars are refrigerated, and as a consequence, critics note, as much as one-fifth of the vegetables and fruits shipped may be lost because of lack of refrigeration.[62]

The failure to provide better storage, roads, and equipment seems shortsighted particularly because so much money has been invested in Soviet agriculture. In recent years, the state has allocated 27 percent of the country's total investment to agriculture.[63] The bulk of this money is allocated centrally, and thus the preferences of the peasants are often ignored.

Failure to respond to peasant demand is but one example of how the central authorities and the peasants often seem to be pulling in opposite directions. Since the collectivization of the land, the state has never fully trusted the peasants and vice versa. This distrust explains the failure to build local storage facilities, the continuing restrictions on private plots, and the refusal until 1974 to authorize internal passports for the peasants. Unlike citizens in the West, all Soviet citizens sixteen years or older must have an internal passport to travel within the Soviet Union for more than a day or two. Thus, without an internal passport, Soviet peasants were basically second-class citizens. Even though Soviet peasants now have the right to travel, they do not necessarily have the right to carry their agricultural products with them. The state continues to fear that if given a chance, the peasants will take produce from the collective and state farms and sell it for an illegal profit. Of course, many peasants obtain legal permission to sell the produce of their private plots outside of their local region, and many manage to do it legally. Yet the police carefully monitor such efforts. This tends to inhibit even those who have official permission.

According to complaints from the peasants, the police restrict the movement of goods from areas where they are in surplus to areas where there are shortages and where the prices on the market are higher. New laws decreeing even more restrictions went into effect on July 1, 1986.[64] There are numerous complaints about how the police will rip open bags to see what goods the peasants are transporting.[65] More often than not, this results in needless spoilage and yet more waste.

Abuse and disdain for the peasants can hardly be expected to stimulate them to increase their efforts to produce more. It is hard to see how any significant improvement in agricultural production can ever occur as long as the state seeks to inhibit rather than unleash peasant energies. But any liberalization is unlikely as long as party officials fear that such an unleashing will evoke private rather than social instincts and divert effort from the collective sector.

Agricultural output suffers not only from institutionally generated distortions but also because the Soviet peasants have to work with lower-yielding grains and livestock. This is in part a by-product of a malfunctioning agricultural system and in part a legacy of T. D. Lysenko's destructive influence on biology and plant science.[66] The result is that Soviet cows show a relatively low average milk yield (2,300 kilograms per cow), which means that after the peasants have allocated their grain to feed their relatively unproductive cows, little is left over to feed their beef cattle, which now account for a relatively small percentage of the total herd.[67] Higher milk yields would make it possible to reduce the size of Soviet dairy herds and increase Soviet beef herds. Also, the protein content of Soviet grain supplied to Soviet livestock is relatively low.[68] The Soviets supply their cattle with 24 to 26 centners of feed, which means 7.0 to 8.0 percent protein content per head; other countries supply 40 centners per head, with a protein content of 10.5 to 11.0 percent.

Moreover, because of the country's northern location, it grows relatively little corn, only 3 to 4 percent of the harvest, compared with as much as 60 percent elsewhere. Consequently, the Soviet Union finds it necessary to feed more wheat to its livestock than agronomists think is efficient. Even though the protein in wheat costs 150 percent more than the comparable protein in soybeans, because the Soviet Union is not well located for the production of soybeans, it diverts two-thirds of its wheat from human food to livestock fodder. No wonder it takes the Soviet Union eight tons of grain to produce one ton of meat, whereas in the United States it would take only five tons.[69]

Similarly, because of the lack of incentive and the inadequate storage and equipment, the Soviet Union uses seed wastefully. In 1980, the Soviet Union set aside 16 percent of the harvested crop for seed, whereas the United States had to set aside only 2 percent. Johnson and Brooks have noted that seed and grain concentrates fed to livestock account for almost 10 percent of gross output in the United States, compared with 15 to 20 percent in the Soviet Union.[70] All of this helps explain why the Soviet Union can grow so much wheat and yet must simultaneously import so much grain.[71]

If Soviet agricultural machinery were more reliable, the Soviet peasants would probably be more productive. However, because of poor quality of manufacturing and poor maintenance, Soviet machinery is unreliable. Reportedly, combines break down after 5.7 to 8.7 hours of operation, even though they are supposed to last 300 hours.[72] In late 1981, the Soviet Union had only 2.4 million tractors in working condition, 100,-000 fewer than the number produced in the Soviet Union from 1976 to 1981.[73]

Thus, Soviet agricultural statistics often mask as much as they show. Admittedly, Soviet weather in large areas of the country is not favorable to agriculture. Nonetheless, to say that a Soviet peasant has harvested a bushel of wheat or bred a cow does not necessarily mean that the resulting consumption in the Soviet Union will be the same as it would in the United States or in other Western countries. The same applies to a ton of steel. Soviet agriculture and industry both contain entrenched practices that must be corrected if the Soviet Union is to become a world-class economic competitor. The next chapter considers some of the efforts the Soviets have made to become more efficient and responsive.

3

The Reform Cycle

Where should Gorbachev begin? For about seventy years, the Soviet Union has looked inward and given birth to all manner of distortions and counterproductive reactions. As we saw, the system tends to produce the wrong things for the wrong reasons. Many workers thus work halfheartedly, when they work at all. Why should they bestir themselves when they feel there is relatively little to be gained for hard work? Russians often tell me, "They pretend to pay us, and we pretend to work." Why should one work hard for a high salary when there is relatively little that is attractive to buy with the money earned for work? This situation is a consequence of the decision by Soviet leaders to favor heavy industry over light industry and an emphasis on consumer goods production and the creation of consumer services. It might all have turned out differently if Lenin had broadened his slogan "Communism equals the Soviets plus electrification" to "Communism equals the Soviets plus electrification plus retail shops."

Having discussed why the Stalinist model worked so well initially, we should have a better understanding of the challenge that Gorbachev confronts. We will now examine why the Stalinist legacy is so difficult to remedy. We will also consider more closely what attempts Gorbachev's predecessors made to deal with these problems and what reforms Gorbachev now has in place. This should also provide us with some initial insight into why agricultural reform and increased production of consumer goods are so important as to be almost preconditions to technological growth.

I

Gorbachev faces what Leonard Silk of the *New York Times* has called a gridlock dilemma; each solution requires movement in another sector of the economy, which in turn is precluded by a roadblock somewhere else in the system. For example, one approach might be to order increased production of consumer goods, as Gorbachev did in September 1985.[1] But a call for more goods by itself is unlikely to be enough. Because the system is so distorted, Soviet factories will have a hard time producing quality consumer goods until Soviet workers feel they can put their earnings from such work to use, and that will probably not happen as long as the goods being produced are of poor quality. If he had more and better-quality goods to provide Soviet workers, Gorbachev might induce them to work harder. Even then, however, the quality of what they produce might still suffer because the raw material inputs and the machinery, although newly built, are products of the older era.[2] A conscientious and eager worker will thus still find it difficult to produce a quality product when the machine he works with is poorly built and squanders resources and when the components and processed materials he receives are of poor quality and design. For the same reason, it would not help to purge all the country's planners and managers and replace them with younger and more dedicated ones if the existing infrastructure and incentive system compel the new managers to respond in the same way as did their predecessors.

The result of all this distortion is a disheartening amount of waste and lost opportunity. In a candid speech to party officials in Khabarovsk on July 31, 1986, Gorbachev complained that equipment now being produced and installed in Soviet factories provides a fraction of the productivity that is technically possible.[3] He indicated that this in part explains why as much as 60 percent of the country's industrial capacity is apparently not used and why that which is used is often used inappropriately.

Gorbachev himself has alluded, even if inadvertently, to the gridlock problem he and the Soviet Union face. Addressing petroleum and government officials at the Tyumen oil fields, in Siberia, he tried to ascertain why the Soviet Union had not been able to produce more petroleum.[4] As he explained it, the fault lies only in part with the oil and gas workers. Even when they have the right attitude, they find themselves frustrated by the failure of the machine builders to produce enough high-quality equipment and materials for them to work with. In addition, not enough electricity is available in the region for the workers to operate the equipment once they have it. The infrastructure is inadequate because the construction workers fail to be responsive. This failure stems from the poor quality of the machinery and equipment with which construction workers have to work and from their low morale, which in turn is a response to poor housing and living conditions. For example, there is no movie theater in the region's main urban center of Nizhnevartovsk, a city of 200,000. Furthermore, Gorbachev was told that the usual practice of the region's retail stores is to sell mostly out-of-fashion merchandise that no one would buy in the cosmopolitan centers of Moscow and Leningrad. Finally, Gorbachev criticized the ministries and central planners for failing to anticipate and resolve all these problems. However, the problems are so interdependent that it will be difficult for the planners or Gorbachev himself to remedy one problem without having simultaneously to correct all the others. As the Hungarian economist János Kornai has indicated, it can be done, but only with extraordinary effort.[5] Such interlocking difficulties pervade the system. In a subsequent visit to Vladivostok, Gorbachev found a somewhat similar situation. Addressing the employees of a television factory in the city, he chastised them for producing television sets that "stop working in 13 to 15 minutes."[6] After further complaining, he reminded them, "And you workers in the television plant, you are upset at the way the construction workers build—the roof leaks and so forth." In other words, if you make poor TVs, expect leaky roofs. It is not enough to reform one stage of the process. If better components are somehow obtained, they may be poorly used because the existing industrial equipment and incentive systems are poorly designed, and if better equipment and a better incentive system are brought in, the poor quality of the components may still cause problems. It is a caviar-and-sturgeon puzzle: it is hard to know what, if anything, should come first.

That is not to deny that Soviet workers might be responsive to some unique program of liberalization. Undoubtedly they would be. But it is unlikely, even if they had the best of intentions, that product quality and variety would improve radically and quickly enough for the Soviet Union to be competitive by world standards. After all these years of distortion, the system seems to have lost its self-correcting mechanisms, which tie quantity and output to quality of work.

In other economic systems where there is still a link between quality of work and quality of reward, the threat of economic penalties for poor or inadequate work is usually enough to reorient the system into the desired orbit. But for Gorbachev the distortions are so great that a few nudges alone will not suffice. A radical jolt, like the one administered by Ludwig Erhard in West Germany, after the defeat in World War II, or the even more revolutionary medicine prescribed, as we shall see in Chapter 7, by Deng Xiaoping may be necessary. Indeed, the Soviet system has been so out of kilter for so long that something considerably stronger than what either Erhard or Deng imposed may be required. Even then it would probably take considerably longer for the system to respond properly. Yet, given that Deng's effort in China has evoked considerable opposition among Chinese officials, if stronger medicine were to be prescribed in the Soviet Union, it would in all likelihood prove to be even more disruptive and so create not only economic but also political risks.

Thus far no one in the Soviet Union has been bold enough

to attempt a radical shakeup of the system. Periodically, an economist and sometimes even Gorbachev will propound a potentially far-reaching idea, but for the most part the proposals as well as the actual reforms that have been introduced have been much more modest in scope. We can better gauge the magnitude of Gorbachev's problems and why his proposals so far have been rather limited in scope if we first look at previous efforts to reform the Soviet system and what has come of those initiatives.

II

Most economic reformers in the Soviet Union have attempted to remedy the symptoms of the disease rather than worry about the causes. Few of them dare to step back, as we just did in the preceding pages, and consider the essence of the problem: Why don't the workers and managers work better? Instead, it is usually easier at least conceptually to focus on concrete and apparently soluble manifestations, such as ways to increase production, reduce costs, improve quality and variety, simulate new technology, and facilitate distribution. These are goals all societies seek, even those that are regarded as well run and efficient. The goals take on a greater urgency, however, when the rate of economic growth slows or becomes negative or when a rival country does better.

Soviet interest in economic reform is not something new. Even Stalin would order a periodic reshuffling of production and planning ministries.[7] Shifting responsibility in the chain of command or stressing decentralization for a time and then reintroducing centralization, Stalin believed that such periodic shifts were necessary to ensure that those in authority did not become too complacent or too lax in their ways. Stalin's mischievousness had a certain merit. Business consultants in the West often offer the same advice. A Harvard Business School consultant once admitted that the secret of his success was that he advised highly centralized corporations to decentralize and decentralized ones to centralize. If they heeded his advice, his

clients would easily remedy their most serious shortcomings—
only to develop another set, which would most likely make
them seek more consultation. His only problem was to sort out
which corporations were centralized and which were not.

Reforms of this sort may work well in the short run, but they
do not address the long-run structural problems of Soviet society. For example, price flexibility, self-correcting mechanisms
like bankruptcy, and decentralized capital markets, which
should be used for coping with economic disproportions and
problems, have never been allowed, because to do so would
have been an open admission that the planners had erred. Bankruptcy would mean unemployment and abandoned capital, all
of which would be personally and politically embarrassing,
especially in a society that is going to great lengths to distinguish itself from capitalist societies, where such social disfunc-
tions are taken for granted. Thus, no automatic mechanisms are
available to correct economic mistakes. After a while, the mistakes are simply accepted as inevitable shortcomings, at least
until someone in Moscow notices them and decides it is time
for another campaign.

Unfortunately, the longer this system goes without reform,
the more deeply rooted such distortions are likely to become.
This makes meaningful reform all the more difficult. After a
time, not only ministerial officials but also factory officials, who
would all lose their power, and ultimately even workers, who
would lose their subsidies on food and housing, acquire a stake
in the status quo and have a vested interest in maintaining the
disproportions. Since their status would suffer from any structural reorganization, almost everyone in the society can be
counted on to resist any change. There are strong indications
that the majority of the population has come to oppose anything more than a marginal adjustment in the economy and the
decision-making process. Intellectually, most Soviet citizens
have come to recognize the country's serious need for radical
change, but only if their own role in that reformed economy is
unaffected. Against this background, it is essential that present-
day reformers keep in mind what has already been attempted.

We will here consider two classic reforms: those that affect organizational structures and those that rely on a changing of incentives.

III

The reforms prior to 1960 dealt mostly with organizational change. Initially, the reforms were very far-reaching. Stalin's major restructuring decisions—the collectivization of the land and the introduction of yearly and five-year central plans—both involved major upheavals in daily life. Moreover, collectivization was carried out so brutally that it led to the death of several million peasants, particularly in the Ukraine.

Most of Stalin's subsequent economic reforms involved marginal organizational changes of one sort or another. He did occasionally introduce incentives—for example, when he ordered increased differentiation in wages. In addition, he was very supportive of the Stakhanovite movement, which resulted in considerably higher wages for such "shock workers." But the bulk of his effort concerned the periodic reorganization of various ministries.

One of Stalin's early concerns was to improve coordination efforts among enterprises producing the same product at the same or at subsequent stages of production. To do this, Stalin authorized the formation of syndicates or holding corporations. By linking such enterprises together under one administrative roof, Stalin sought to facilitate interaction among the various units and reduce outside bureaucratic interference. To some extent, he tried to do the same thing in agriculture. After World War II, he first authorized the formation of the *zveno,* or links. These were smaller work units designed to encourage interaction and intergroup peer pressure, which was meant to generate a more enthusiastic approach to work by the members of the link. However, while facilitating smaller work units, at least for a time, Stalin simultaneously began to merge smaller collective farms. By the time of his death, in 1953, the number of collective farms had fallen from 243,500 in 1937 to 93,300.[8] This was done to take advantage of economies of scale and to increase political control. More than anything else, however, Stalin's decision to do away with most market incentives and to institute state ownership of agriculture and centralized state planning in the operation of industry set the basic pattern of both organization and incentives that has lasted until the 1980s.

Even though most of his efforts eventually came to naught, it was Khrushchev who did the most to alter Stalin's model. Khrushchev may have been motivated as much by the desire to displace large numbers of political opponents as by the wish to improve the economy, but in 1957 he took the rash step of abolishing most of the major industrial ministries. This displaced a relatively large number of bureaucrats, many of whom found their way to the 102 regional economic councils, or *sovnarkhozy,* as they were called. The *sovnarkhozy* were established by Khrushchev to provide the regional economic coordination outside Moscow that had previously been the responsibility of the Moscow ministries.

The logic of this move was that economic activity had become too centralized and vertical. A steel mill located in the Donets Basin had to send all its paperwork to the steel ministry in Moscow, even if it wanted only to engage in negotiations with a neighboring coal mine. The steel ministry would then forward the necessary communications to the coal ministry, which in turn would convey the message to the coal mines back in the Donets Basin. Khrushchev reasoned that it would be much more efficient to eliminate the Moscow middlemen and handle all such negotiations on the spot within the borders of the *sovnarkhoz.*

In economic terms, Khrushchev's decision made sense. The need to refer everything to Moscow was wasteful and time-consuming. There seemed to be general enthusiasm among local officials. Of course, this may have been nothing more than the Hawthorne effect. (Experimenters in the Hawthorne works of Western Electric came to realize that plant employees responded well to whatever new experiments were introduced. They ultimately concluded that the nature of the experiment mattered less than the very fact that something new was being tried. The workers responded to the attention they were getting, not to the procedures.) Yet, Khrushchev's reorganization did seem to work, at least for a time.

Eventually, however, the reforms ran into problems. Khrushchev sought not to do away with the central planning process but only to decentralize the implementation of the plan. Of necessity, some functions still had to be performed centrally in Moscow. In place of the abolished ministries, Khrushchev gradually created state committees to handle central functions. These committees, which were few in number, at least in the beginning, turned out to be shrunken versions of the old ministries. Like mushrooms, more and more state committees began to spring up for virtually every type of product, so after a time it was hard to distinguish them from what used to be the ministry. The committees were operating in many instances in the same buildings and with most of the same old faces. In the Soviet Union, as elsewhere, it is often difficult to close down a bureaucratic office. As often as not, it and the staff appear transubstantiated.[9]

Khrushchev was one of the first to discover how difficult it was to tangle with the vested interests of bureaucrats who were creatures of the Stalinist system. Ministries resented their loss of power and their banishment to the provinces. Even though the state committees took over some of the functions previously performed by the ministries, they were not perfect substitutes. In the meantime, dissatisfaction with the *sovnarkhozy* system began to grow. The *sovnarkhozy* were unable to make enough decisions on their own. They found it necessary to continue turning to Moscow. Ultimately, in a rare Politburo coup, party and economic bureaucrats conspired in 1964 to depose Khrushchev because of his various "harebrained ideas." The economic ministries were quickly restored in 1965 by Alexei Kosygin.

To be fair, Khrushchev's experiments were not limited to the *sovnarkhozy* or to economics. He managed to shake up most segments of Soviet society. But the *nomenklatura,* those at high levels of power in both the party and the government whose appointments are closely controlled at the center and who are the beneficiaries of the existing organization, had made their point—that it can be risky to tamper with the status quo.[10]

IV

In addition to reorganization, Khrushchev made the first significant attempt at reforming the prevailing economic incentive system. He did this in May 1964, just before he was deposed. Even though the initiative for such experiments came from below—from some economists like Evsei Liberman and V. Nemchinov—they were explicitly authorized by Khrushchev. In any event, the reforms, which somewhat incorrectly became known as the Liberman reforms, did survive Khrushchev and, indeed, were extended to a large number of firms by Alexei Kosygin, who assumed responsibility for economic affairs after Khrushchev's forced retirement.

Liberman and his colleagues argued that the central plan and the incentive system associated with it had outlived their usefulness. Producing more seldom meant producing better. In fact, it usually resulted in just the opposite. Factory managers found that anything that slowed the production line, whether it was the correction of existing work or the experimentation with new products and production systems, jeopardized managerial and worker bonuses that depended primarily on the quantity of output. (Managerial incentive systems in the United States sometimes produce similar results.) There were such shortages in the economy that poor-quality products were better than no products. This proved to be a shortsighted policy. Although it was assumed that the day for quality would ultimately come, it was not realized that in neglecting quality and feedback this way, the Soviets were building up a flawed industrial infrastructure and locking themselves into a hard-to-break mold.

Liberman and his fellow reformers may not have understood the overall dimensions of the challenge facing them, but they decided they could probably prevent further deterioration by deemphasizing central planning, quantity, and the increase in gross value of output, *valovaia produktsiia* (VAL). Liberman proposed that numerous other targets—such as those for labor productivity, number of workers, wages, production costs, capital saving, capital investment, and new technology—be abolished. The reformers urged, instead, that managers be rewarded for the attainment of such things as profits, sales delivery, and the rate of return on capital targets. This would give the manager more say about the assortment, style, and price of products.

Liberman expected that as the instructions from the center became less important, the manager would look more and more to market signals for guidance. With profits and rate of return as a determinant of bonuses, the manager would conclude that it was in his self-interest to manufacture high-quality products at low cost. Thus, economic signals rather than detailed instructions and impassioned pleading would stimulate efficiency and better efforts. Similarly, the legitimation of rate of return on capital would put pressure on the managers to sell off excessive machinery and inventory. No matter how much profits increased (the numerator), if the manager did nothing to control the expansion of his capital stock (the denominator), the rate of return would not increase as rapidly as it might with tight capital control. As an additional incentive for the manager to economize on the use of his capital stock, the enterprise would have to pay a capital charge (interest) for the use of the capital. The less capital, the lower the capital payments would have to be and the higher the resulting profits for the enterprise.

To provide further interest in earning profits, Liberman proposed, a portion of the profits should go into three separate funds that would directly and indirectly benefit the workers and the enterprise. The first of the funds, the incentive fund, would be used to supplement salaries; the cultural and housing fund would be used to provide better living accommodations for its workers; and the development fund was intended to allow the manager to buy machinery he wanted for the firm rather than accept what the central planners dictated.

Although Liberman had set out the kernel of his ideas as early as 1956, not until May 1964 was any attempt made in the Soviet Union to test them.[11] Then Khrushchev decreed that two factories, the Bolshevichka, a Moscow factory making men's clothing, and Maiak, a Gorky manufacturer of women's dresses, should be evaluated by some criterion other than the quantity of production. As we saw, Khrushchev's ouster did little to dampen the interest in the experiment. Kosygin, who replaced Khrushchev in October 1964, moved rapidly to make the experiment the national norm. By January 1967 approximately 2,500 enterprises had switched to the new incentive system, and by 1970 the reforms applied to all firms.[12] Emboldened by what they saw happening in the Soviet Union, East European and Chinese officials began similar experiments. In Czechoslovakia, the scope of these reforms soon became broader than that of the Soviet reforms.

While in the eyes of many Soviet officials, the Czech reforms seemed to extend too far, the Soviet experiment, though impressive in terms of numbers of firms affected, became less and less meaningful. The authority extended to plant managers was cut back. As long as few firms were involved, no one seemed to care how much power they had. But as the number increased, the ministers and the intermediate officials saw that while the manager was acquiring more authority, their own powers were being eroded, though their responsibilities were not. Thus, the ministers had to account for underfulfilled production targets even if their subordinates had been urged to pay more attention to profit making than plan fulfillment. Not surprisingly, ministerial officials began to impinge more and more on the day-to-day operations of the enterprises. Once again, there were complaints that the ministers were interfering in the enterprises' most minute details. This interference—or "petty tutelage," as it was called—perverted the reform process. Decentralization works only if market signals have real meaning and reflect economic conditions, but the planners and ministers usually seem to have priorities that are not reflected by high prices in the market. To protect their own positions, the planners then would order the enterprises to respond to the planners and ignore the market signals. Such constraints subvert the effect of the market and strip price signals of much of their meaning; this in turn reinforces the critics of decentralization who argue that only the plan can be relied upon to provide proper signals to the state. As one critic puts it, "Without an effective 'outlay containment mechanism,' the decentralization of price formation can lead to disruption of the price system and an overall rise in the price level."[13]

V

Even though it was recognized that the 1965 Kosygin effort provided some initial stimulus to the economy, the reform fell far short of expectations. Indeed, enterprises and ministers continued to treat gross value of output (VAL), not profit, as the key index. An announcement on July 29, 1979, that a new index, net normative output (NNO), would henceforth be the main basis for judging economic performance also had little impact. In effect, this new measurement was an attempt to use what we refer to as value added. Because managers would no longer receive a bonus for utilizing expensive inputs, the expectation was that NNO would stimulate them to use raw materials more efficiently. Unfortunately, NNO was a very difficult index to calculate; when Soviet managers could figure it out, they found they could raise the index by increasing their use of labor. Not unexpectedly, the VAL system remained dominant. Nor was it surprising that much of the economic distortion continued as before.

Because the new performance criterion was unsuccessful in changing managerial behavior, Soviet planners sought other kinds of reform. In October 1967, the Shchekino chemical combine, outside the city of Tula, sought to increase the size of its work force. Soviet officials proposed instead that the Shchekino plant manager do just the opposite—shrink his work force. As an inducement, the officials agreed that the resulting reduction in wages would be divided up so that one-half of the savings would be shared by those workers who were not fired. After some initial resistance, the plan was adopted with impressive results. In two years, even though the work force had been reduced by 1,000 employees, factory output grew by over 80 percent and labor productivity doubled. All of this was achieved with only a 30 percent increase in wages.[14]

Given the general success of the Shchekino experiment, Soviet officials sought to induce other enterprises to do the same thing. By mid-1978, however, only about 1,200 enterprises had complied, and even these elicited many complaints about the less then perfect results.[15] After some initial enthusiasm, the workers often found that they were caught in a trap. Having shown that they could increase production with a smaller labor force and usually without much strain, the workers learned that in the following year they would be pressured to do the same thing again. Encores were more difficult to arrange. Once the workers saw that they might come under pressure to jack up their work norms a second time, they tended to hold back on their initial effort so that they could meet subsequent demands without undue strain.

Resistance to the Shchekino plan came from all directions; this is suggestive of what Gorbachev and his aides are likely to encounter today. Ministry officials quickly realized that a Shchekino-type scheme had its shortcomings. The ministers were upset when they saw that some of their powers had been transferred to the enterprise managers. Managers in the Shchekino system had the power to determine wages and fire workers. In addition, workers in other plants resented the fact that their fellow workers were being paid higher wages than they were. Most upset were the workers who suddenly found themselves unemployed. Layoffs are supposed to happen only in capitalist countries. Admittedly, some of those fired from one shop managed to find another slot for themselves in another section of the same factory, but not everyone was quite so nimble. For the unfortunate, this was a violation of the implicit Soviet social contract that promised all workers employment.

Once Soviet managers discovered that the dividing up and

sharing of the savings in wages was not always as attractive as it first appeared, the Shchekino plan became something to be avoided. They had other reasons for opposing reductions in staff. As we saw in the preceding chapter, managerial salaries and incentive funds depend on the size of the enterprise, as reflected by the size of the workforce.[16] In addition, the incentive bonus for the enterprise is linked to the size of the total wage fund. As we also noted, Soviet managers are called upon regularly to provide labor for special public projects, such as in construction or agriculture. In 1976, for example, it was estimated that urban factories and offices had to divert approximately 750,000 workers from their normal work duties to help with the harvest.[17] Repeated requisitions of this sort make it necessary for the manager to ensure that he has an excess supply of labor on hand at all times. Otherwise the manager will find himself compelled to divert some of his key workers from their essential duties and thus risk plan underfulfillment, and that means no bonuses. In this Catch-22 situation, any attempt to link increased bonuses to the reduction of the size of the work force tends to be more than offset by cuts in the bonuses, cuts that stem from the very reduction of that work force.[18] It is hard to see what, short of some massive assault on the existing system, future economic reformers, including Gorbachev, can do to extract themselves from the morass—more evidence of the economic gridlock that has built up over the years.

VI

Once they saw that changes in the incentive system failed to increase productivity or improve quality, Soviet officials again focused more on organizational reforms. They decided in 1973 that, compared with successful American conglomerates, Soviet enterprises were too limited in scale. By combining a number of related enterprises into what they called *obedenenie,* or syndicates or production associations, much as Stalin did in the 1930s, Soviet authorities hoped they would be able to internalize much of the administrative red tape that had previously preempted so much time and effort from ministry, regional, and enterprise officials. This change would also allow the authorities to benefit from the economies of scale that such integrated operations make available.

The results were disappointing. The production associations turned out to be nothing more than a disguised version of the old, prereform administrative units, called *glavki.* In many instances, the change involved nothing more than calling in a painter to put a new title on the old door. The personnel and their activities did not change. The production associations seemed to be new, but not new enough to cause meaningful change. Some were too big, some were too small, and few of them made effective use of the economies of scale or the improved incentives.[19]

None of these reforms included any provision for attaching meaningful value to prices. Prices were administered by a central price committee and changed rarely. Because they could not increase prices to cover their increased costs and the risks associated with product innovation, enterprise managers had little reason to risk the production of new or improved goods.

Nor were the enterprises given much control over their finances. The enterprise managers knew that if their profits rose too much, the state would probably step in to retrieve the proceeds for the state budget. The director's fund helped a little, but not enough to allow the enterprise manager to build up his own funds to finance the cost of innovations. Even when substantial funds were accumulated, the managers generally found that they were not of much use. The important thing was not money but allocation authorization from Gosplan, which the manager had to have to obtain machinery and materials from other suppliers, whose allocation of output was determined by administrative decree, not by the offering of rubles.

The quest for more innovation was a top priority. Science production associations designed to facilitate the flow of scientific ideas into actual production helped but did not, on the whole, measurably facilitate innovation. The ministries continued to interfere in industry affairs, and the ministers lacked the necessary capital and freedom of maneuvering to be effective. The conversion of Soviet research and development into actual production was not noticeably enhanced.

Although the effort to consolidate was not carried far enough to remedy long-standing administrative and innovative shortcomings, the production associations did become more self-sufficient, at least in terms of relying on suppliers and subcontractors. However, that change was not all to the good. Self-sufficiency facilitated some innovation, but, as we noted in the preceding chapter, it also meant that by becoming more self-reliant, the association denied itself the advantages that enterprises elsewhere derive from the division of labor. Thus, the association sought to produce a product as much as possible within its own doors, in order to reduce its vulnerability to the production and transportation delays of the other associations. A survey of 100 machinery plants revealed that 71 of them produced their own cast iron, 27 their own steel, 57 their own nonferrous castings, 84 their own forgings, and 61 their own clamps.[20] These enterprises and associations tend to become self-sufficient economically. Specialization has become as rare as quality and cheap production.

VII

Like those in industry, experiments in agriculture have been mostly marginal in their impact. The Soviet Union adopted a major agricultural program at the May 1982 plenary session of the Central Committee of the Communist party of the Soviet Union, but this much heralded program offered little in the way of reform. Instead, the emphasis of the New Agricultural Program continued to be on increasing investment in irrigation and drainage and on exhorting the peasants to work harder.

The relatively few experimental reforms in agriculture have been quite modest in scope. For example, beginning in 1981, the "Path of Communism Collective Farm" in the Altai territory adopted what was called a brigade contract system.[21] As proposed by the academician Tatiana Zaslavskaia, this system divided farms into brigades that work as separate units. With these smaller units, the farms that had been losing money soon became profitable. Each brigade signed a contract committing itself to produce a certain amount of a crop on a designated piece of land. The proceeds from the brigade's efforts are allocated to each member of the brigade according to the quantity and quality of work that he or she contributes and as specified by the job qualifications.[22] The brigades are held to ten members; this means that the work units are so small that peer pressure to work hard can be effective.

This brigade contract system was one of the few experiments authorized in the New Agricultural Program of 1982. Apparently based on Zaslavskaia's results in Altai, the May 1982 plenum of the Central Committee of the Communist party decided to extend the experiment to all collective farms.[23] However, the state farms refused to participate, and the bureaucracy generally was unenthusiastic.[24] From their perspective, the contract responsibility system was too complicated and involved too much red tape. For the system to work properly, there has to be a different rate of pay for each brigade and for each worker, depending on their effort and productivity. That in turn necessitates the use of accurate costs and work information, which for the most part does not exist. As of early 1985, the brigade contract system had spread to only a small percentage of Soviet farms.[25] Apparently, the prospect of having to make their own decisions frightened some farm managers who, as Zaslavskaia explained, were "capable only of carrying out orders from above."[26] Zaslavskaia complained that the ministry officials also opposed such an experiment because, if successful, it would mean their jobs had become superfluous.

Even where adopted, the Soviet brigade contract system is not foolproof. Whereas in China the brigades tend to be made up of relatives and family members, in the Soviet Union the brigades are for the most part formed arbitrarily. Unfortunately, the peer pressures in an unrelated group are not as effective as peer pressures in a family.

A natural question is why the Soviet officials seem so reluc-

tant to use the family as the core of the brigade. In fact, Zaslavskaia is one of the few who appears to favor the family-type
brigade.[27] The general reluctance may reflect the fear that brigades made up of families might lead to the decollectivization
of the land, much as it did in China. Soviet leaders have so far
generally opposed the establishment of anything comparable in
scope in the Soviet Union.

Yet, most Soviet agricultural officials do recognize that private incentive is still a powerful force among Soviet peasants.
Since a large percentage of the Soviet crop is grown on a small
percentage of the land, that reality is hard to ignore. The trick,
then, is to harness some of that incentive while holding on to
the principle of collectivization and state ownership. The jug-
gling of these contradictory goals explains as much as anything
the dilemma that Gorbachev, like his predecessors, faces in
trying to reform agriculture.

There is no simple way to balance private incentives and
public ownership. For a time during the early days of collectivization, Stalin apparently assumed he could eliminate all forms
of private farming except for some small private holdings of
livestock.[28] But in the wake of the mass starvation of the early
1930s, Stalin was forced to ease up, and in 1933 the Council of
Peoples' Commissars authorized the creation of small private
gardens.[29] Taking advantage of the new law, the peasants
quickly expanded their private plots until work on the plots
began to detract from work on the collectivized sector. In an
effort to redress the balance, the private plots of about eight
million collective farms were zealously cut back in May 1939,
only to be expanded again a few months later, after the German
invasion of the Soviet Union. Shortly after World War II ended,
the private plots were squeezed again, until 1954, when manda-
tory grain deliveries from private plots were abolished.

This squeeze-and-relax cycle has continued to the present
day. Soviet authorities tend to become more tolerant of private
efforts during agricultural slumps. However, as output increases and the peasants become more assertive, the state begins
to fear for the sanctity of the public sector and restricts the size

and scope of private-plot activities. It also restricts the freedom of peasants and others to sell on the collective farm markets, because the peasants usually utilize collective-sector land and supplies that nominally belong to the collective farm to sustain their own activities. This is illegal. For example, the deputy procurator general of the U.S.S.R., Yu. Feofanov, reported in 1986 that in a number of places approximately one-half of the construction materials being used on personal projects had been stolen from nearby state construction sites.[30] A policy that lets peasants spend more time on private plots leads not only to an increase in theft and embezzlement but also to a growing reluctance on their part to spend the required time working on the collectivized and state farm fields.

Nonetheless, faced since 1979 with a decline in grain harvests, the state has expanded private-plot initiative. In early 1981, individual farmers were allowed to take collectively owned cattle from the collective and state farms and raise them until they were ready for slaughter.[31] In effect, this was a way of increasing the number of the livestock the peasants could raise privately. This measure also acknowledged that the privately tended cattle required much less feed and time before being slaughtered than collectively tended livestock. These new procedures resulted in savings for the state, even though not all the grain fed to the privately tended livestock was obtained legally. Still, it was commonly accepted that a team of two raising livestock for themselves could be expected to produce what five state employees would normally do.[32]

So far, there has been a relatively modest implementation of this putting-out type of livestock raising. Only a few farms in Kazakhstan, Georgia, Uzbekistan, Moldavia, the Crimea, and the Kuban have joined in the experiment.[33] This reflects the Soviet leaders' ambivalence and uncertainty regarding such experiments, and the worry that the private sector will encroach on the public sector persists.

As often happens in the Soviet Union, the experiment to increase peasant prerogatives paralleled an effort that, if successful, will have the opposite effect. Drawing on some experiments in Abasha, Georgia, Talsi, Latvia, and Viljandi, Estonia, that can be traced back as far as 1973, Brezhnev in 1981, as part of his "food program," authorized the formation throughout the Soviet Union of what had come to be called RAPOS (Regional Agro-Industrial Associations).[34] The RAPOs represented an effort to combine the food-growing operations on the farms with food-processing operations in the villages and cities. It was a form of what most economists call vertical integration.

Having been impressed with the efficiency and productivity of agribusiness activity in the United States, Soviet authorities concluded that if they could similarly integrate the food industry with farming, they would reap the same kind of food abundance. But a revamping of organizational structure by itself is not enough to bring Soviet agriculture up to American productivity. Underlying that organizational framework in the United States is a very different incentive, support, and supply system, and there is much less self-sufficiency and more interdependence among suppliers and buyers.

The RAPOs were created at the regional level in order to stimulate local initiative and reduce some of Moscow's power. The expectation was that by integrating farming with food processing, the RAPOs would make decisions on the spot and not turn to Moscow for every answer. To some extent, the RAPOs bore a family resemblance to Nikita Khrushchev's plan for *sovnarkhozy* and decentralization. Since Khrushchev was still out of favor, any such similarity was probably unintended. Whatever the parentage of the RAPOs, it made sense for local units to deal directly with one another rather than through their superiors in Moscow, and there have been hints that the *sovnarkhozy* did make some sense.[35]

However, just as it was not enough even to copy the superficial aspects of the American agricultural system, so it was not enough to expect organizational reform to cure Soviet agricultural shortcomings. Admittedly, the formation of RAPOs did cut into some of the centralized power in Moscow, but they in turn impinged on the effort to increase local peasant prerogatives. New organizations of this sort in the Soviet Union tend to grab all the power they can, particularly when the whole idea is to reduce Moscow's power. It is very difficult to establish a base of power that is real and independent of Moscow and at the same time to expect that new power base to delegate its authority to individual peasant families and other units that are similarly subordinate to the local RAPO. Inevitably, the RAPOs took on "some of the functions and decision making of the farms."[36]

We have seen that the sending of contradictory signals about organization and incentives is more the norm than the exception. Moreover, the practice is not limited to agricultural reform. No sector of the Soviet economy is immune. Bright new or, more appropriately, resurrected ideas are hauled out routinely, tried on a local basis, and just as routinely scrapped. In 1986, for example, Soviet authorities announced, as if it were an ideological breakthrough, that they would allow cooperative trade networks to expand into the cities.[37] The *kolkhozy* (collective farms) and *sovkhozy* (state farms) would then be allowed to take up to 30 percent of what they produced above their plan targets and sell it through the cooperative trade networks and *kolkhoz* markets at higher prices.[38] However, this was not a new measure but something that had been authorized as early as 1959 and that had not proved to be particularly successful. Gorbachev may have better results this time, particularly because some of the farms will be able to set their own prices. Yet, there are already indications of bureaucratic opposition because, as usual, more initiative at the bottom means less power for the bureaucrats at the top.[39] Even more daunting, the higher prices charged for meat sold by the cooperative stores reportedly sparked riots in Minsk in the summer of 1986.

Under the circumstances, it is not surprising that "new" ideas do not generate much enthusiasm. Moreover, reforms tend to be contradictory. Efforts to increase local peasant incentives may be checked by organizational efforts that affect those peasants or by the effort to decentralize. Thus, the emphasis on RAPOs collided with the decision on November 22, 1985, to create a superministry called the Gosagroprom (State Committee for Agricultural Industrial Complex).[40] Reflecting that same faith in the wonders of agribusiness, this new superagency was intended to supersede five traditional agricultural ministries. In addition, the expectation was that, by combining the functions of five ministries into one, the surviving ministry would have too much to do and that it would therefore focus on the big questions and allow the RAPOs and farms to make decisions for themselves. But it is just as likely that the ministry will try to assert itself over the RAPOs and farms and fill any vacuum that temporarily develops. In any event, the initial result was chaos. The reshuffling of the portfolios of five ministries created such confusion that those who survived the consolidation had no idea what their new responsibilities were.

The creation of the State Committee for Agricultural Industrial Complex parallels the the creation of superministries in the industrial sectors, such as the Superministry for Machine Building, and in energy. Undoubtedly, similar organizational confusion affected these new ministries as well. Similar efforts at creating superministries in the past suggest that the prospects for the orderly reassignment of responsibilities and, more important, for the decentralization and delegation of power are not very encouraging.[41]

VIII

As long as the economy continued to grow at a respectable rate, there was no need to worry unduly about Soviet economic growth and technological development. Occasionally, a potentially far-reaching reform would be proposed, but no one felt very alarmed when nothing radical was done and the economy continued on much as it had before. The tone changed, however, during the last four years of Brezhnev's life. As Brezhnev's health began to falter, he could no longer concentrate on most party and government affairs. Even though everyone in the Kremlin was aware that Brezhnev was no longer capable of effective leadership, nothing was done to retire him. In the absence of effective control, the moral fiber and economic vigor of the country also began to collapse, and Soviet society was, according to Gorbachev, hit by a "crisis phenomenon."[42] While the rest of the world struggled to adapt to a new environment of energy shortages and to rapidly moving technological changes, the Soviet Union in its self-imposed isolation not only failed to participate in some of the more meaningful changes but appeared unable even to sustain its old way of doing things.

When the 1979 grain harvest fell by 58 million tons, the largest drop in Soviet history, it seemed at first to be a once-and-for-all blip (see Tables 2 and 3). There appeared to be no reason to panic or to order radical reforms in agriculture. Procedures for dealing with periodic crop failures were already in place. The grain harvest had fallen before—for example, in 1977 and 1975. Admittedly, the drop was larger in 1979, but everyone expected that the grain harvest would recover in the following year. After all, it had almost never dropped for more than two years in a row. Although the harvest did not continue to drop in 1980, it recovered less strongly than had been expected, so the Soviets again had to import large quantities of grain. In 1981, the grain harvest fell again, to 158 million tons. Except for that in 1975, the grain output in 1981 was the lowest since 1967. Given only a slight improvement in 1983 and another drop in 1984, the Soviets suffered through at least six bad harvests in a short period of time. In every instance, the harvest was far below the goal of 235 million tons. Although agricultural imports offset some of the shortfalls, the food situation, particularly the meat supply, deteriorated so rapidly that in 1981 and 1982 it became necessary, as we saw, to reintroduce formal food rationing in at least a dozen major cities.[43]

The grain harvest was not the only part of the 1979 economic decline. For the first time since World War II, the production of steel and of metal-cutting machine tools dropped. During the four-year period 1979–1982, the output of coal and automobiles was similarly affected at different times (see Table 3). Although there was no drop in production, the increase in oil output was only 4 million tons in 1982, compared with as much as 26 million tons in 1978. Unlike the decline in agricultural output,

TABLE 3

Annual Soviet Production Increases

	1975	1976	1977	1978	1979	1980	1981	1982
Electricity (billions of kwh)	63	73	39	52	37	57	30	31
Petroleum (millions of tons)(including gas condensate)	32	29	26	26	14	17	6	4
Gas (billions of m³)	28	32	25	26	35	28	30	36
Coal (millions of tons)	16	11	10	2	−5	−2	−12	14
Steel (millions of tons)	5	4	2	3	−2	−2	1	−2
Metal-cutting machine tools (thousands)	6	1	5	0	−8	−14	−11	−10
Automobiles (thousands)	82	28	41	32	2	13	−3	−17
Grain (millions of tons)	−56	84	−28	41	−58	10	−31	29

SOURCES: Production figures, except for those for metal-cutting machine tools and grain, are taken from the corresponding *Narodnoe khoziaistvo SSSR (Nar. khoz.)* for the appropriate year. Thus, for 1975 the figures come from Tsentral'noe statisticheskoe upravlenie SSR, *Narodnoe khoziaistvo, 1975* (Moscow: Finansy i Statisticheskoe, 1976), pp. 205–7. Also *Nar. khoz.,* 1976, pp. 106–8; 1977, pp. 62–64; 1978, pp. 58, 60; 1979, pp. 76–78; 1980, pp. 68, 79; 1981, pp. 66, 68. The machine tool figures are taken from CIA, *Handbook of Economic Statistics, 1983* (Washington, D.C.: n.p., 1983), p. 163; the grain figures, from *Nar. khoz.,* 1980, pp. 202; 1985, p. 209.

the drop in the production of these various items was not a large one. Nonetheless, the drop came as quite a shock to Soviet planners, who had always prided themselves on the Soviet Union's ability to increase the output of its basic commodities each year. The Soviet Union might have difficulty with innovation and high technology, particularly in the civilian sector, but at least it had always been the master of basic heavy industry.

To some degree, the fall in output had natural causes: some of the richest and most readily accessible resources were being depleted. Yet, natural-resource depletion alone could not explain everything. Some critics became very concerned about what they saw as an erosion of morale and morals. Alcoholism, which has historically been a problem in Russia, seemed to have become even worse. There were even reports of workers' groups organizing to help keep drunken workers from coming to work. The economist Abel Aganbegian has reported, "With the deepest sorrow I noticed drunkenness at the workplace more frequently than before. At several enterprises they have even created special brigades for the purpose of preventing drunkenness and keeping workers from machine tools to prevent accidents."[44] Production was actually higher when they were kept out of the factory than when they were allowed in.

Corruption had become an equally serious problem. There had always been an undercurrent of corruption in the Soviet Union, even in the days of Stalin. After all, in a system of state centralized control, which was operated and directed from Moscow and in which plans were spelled out a year or more in advance, there had to be some mechanism for making adjustments for local and unexpected conditions. Since no institutionalized mechanism for assuring such flexibility existed, it had to be provided informally. Inevitably, if there was to be some give in the system, there usually had to be some take.

By the late 1970s, corruption seemed to have gotten out of hand, and no one seemed to care. After a decade and a half of rule, Brezhnev had adopted a live-and-let-live policy. He and his subordinates rarely dismissed their subordinates. Most assumed, properly so, that once appointed, they would hold on to their offices until death or disability. Under the circumstances, a growing number of officials began to act as if their ministry, their office, or their regional government were just that—theirs. Few questioned the existence of special shops that carried otherwise unavailable goods and that were open only to certain party members. Access to such shops was assumed to be almost a "natural right" of members of the privileged and *nomenklatura* class. Except for occasional criticism in the press, there was for the most part no effective court of appeal. Abuse of power grew as senior-level officials tended to protect their subordinates for fear that without such solidarity their own prerogatives might suffer.[45]

To focus on corruption under Brezhnev is not to imply that other societies or other Soviet governments do not have similar problems, but the scale in Brezhnev's time was enormous and growing. The difference between reality and image was substantial, particularly for a society that emphasizes its virtue and considers itself morally superior to what it insists is the moral rot of capitalism and foreign societies. Increasingly, Soviet newspapers revealed stories about parents who had managed to buy their children admittance to the universities; store managers who had bribed wholesale managers; customers who had paid off store managers; émigrés who had bribed border emigration and customs officials; party officials who had used state funds for travel, privileges, and even the construction of private homes. Some of Brezhnev's former cronies had used their close ties to create little empires out of their regional governments.[46]

As often happened in Third World countries, members of the leaders' own families took advantage of their status. For example, Brezhnev's daughter began to consort with a circus clown who was a well-known diamond smuggler. This alliance persisted although Brezhnev's daughter was married to the deputy head of the national police. Before long, even officers in the Soviet army, the one national institution that had held itself above corruption, began to use army privileges to enhance their own economic well-being. Lower-ranking soldiers would be assigned to build private homes for the senior officers.[47]

Nothing seemed sacred anymore. Educators began to complain that their best students in the 1970s, unlike those in the past, wanted to be salesclerks in retail stores rather than engineers, who had heretofore belonged to one of the most prestigious professions. After some study, the reason for the switch in professions became clear: even though the official pay was low, the opportunities for creative merchandising as a salesclerk offered financial rewards that normally far exceeded those available to an engineer.

IX

For those concerned about these issues, Brezhnev's death, in November 1982, was an event at least four years overdue. His successor, Yuri Andropov, was welcomed with great expectations. Andropov's background as the former head of the KGB made him ideal for a crackdown on the country's rot and corruption. And move he did. Almost immediately, he began to fire ministers and local officials. To break up the cozy arrangements that had taken root, he shuttled police officers, including Brezhnev's son-in-law, who was moved from Moscow to Murmansk, in the northern part of the Soviet Union. That was not exactly Siberia, but it was a reasonable facsimile. In addition, Andropov attacked indiscipline and alcoholism. Bars were raided in the middle of day and managers reprimanded for allowing workers to drink rather than work.

Andropov's return to the basic virtues produced immediate results. As Table 4 indicates, under Andropov's influence, production in most industrial sectors (except petroleum) stopped dropping. A comparison of industrial production in January–February 1983, Andropov's first January–February in control, with that in January–February 1982, Brezhnev's last month in control, shows how striking the transformation was. Whereas output in the vast majority of the major industries dropped in January–February 1982 from the similar months in 1981, a year later, under Andropov, the vast majority of industrial indices showed an increase. Even allowing for the fact that

TABLE 4

Industrial Production Figures
January–February Production as a
Percentage of Preceding January–February

Product	Brezhnev 1982 1981	Andropov 1983 1982	Chernenko 1985 1984	Gorbachev 1986 1985
Electricity	103.4%	103.0%	103.3%	104%
Petroleum (incl. gas condensate)	99.8	102.0	96.3	101
Natural gas	106.4	108.0	109.1	107
Coal	99.3	100.5	98.4	106
Steel	95.6	104.0	92.2	111
Fertilizer	97.7	111.0	98.0	116
Metal-cutting tools	101.5	104.0	103.6	114
Robots	—	147.0	100.0	142
Computer technology	76.8	109.0	110.0	123
Tractors	99.6	102.0	104.0	105
Paper	93.3	108.0	93.7	113
Cement	88.3	113.0	93.7	111
Meat	93.6	106.0	106.3	113
Margarine	100.0	110.0	92.6	108
Watches	100.0	105.0	96.4	108
Radios	98.9	111.0	93.0	106
Television sets	99.9	108.0	100.0	106

SOURCES: Figures are taken from *Ekonomicheskaia gazeta.* For 1982 over 1981: March 1982, no. 12, p. 4; for 1983 over 1982: March 1983, no. 12, p. 4; for 1985 over 1984: March 1985, no. 11, p. 15; for 1986 over 1985: March 1986, no. 12, p. 4.

there may have been more workdays in January–February 1983 than in the comparable period in 1982, the difference was notable. Moreover, the selection of a leader who seemed to care and who was determined to do something served to reawaken feelings of pride and to improve morale. A Soviet journalist explained to me during a visit to Moscow in January 1983, "We are delighted with Andropov. He is forcing us to face up to our problems with candor. There is no more 'hallelujahing.' " Since I had not heard the term before, I asked him to explain. "With Andropov, there is no more 'hallelujah' this or 'hallelujah' that," he said. "We now acknowledge the Soviet Union is not, after all, perfect and that only if we admit to its problems can we solve them."

But is a return to discipline, hard work, and candor enough? To help him decide, Andropov commissioned a series of studies about the Soviet Union's long-run economic needs. From all reports, there was no clear consensus on what course the Soviet economy should take. Some authorities insisted that the Soviet economy was on the right path and that no change was needed. Others boldly argued that the central-planning system developed over the last fifty years had outlived its usefulness and had become an obstacle to further growth. One such study, originally classified, found its way to the West and was published in the *Washington Post* by Dusko Doder, its Moscow correspondent [48] This study by the academician Tatiana Zaslavskaia, who at the time was a section head at the Institute of Economics and Organization of Industrial Production of the Siberian division of the U.S.S.R. Academy of Sciences, argued that the policy of issuing orders from the Moscow center to a managerial and work force of human robots no longer made sense. Unlike their counterparts in the 1930s, workers and managers in the 1970s and 1980s are not fresh off the farm and not newly literate. Today's workers and managers are intelligent, and they welcome the opportunity to show initiative. The circumscribing of their every move with detailed orders from Moscow ensures low-quality and technologically unimaginative production. Tentative as such calls for change by Zaslavskaia and her supporters may have been, they were met with fierce opposition.

There even seemed to be opposition to the very modest reforms announced by Andropov on July 26, 1983. Essentially, he called for more authority for enterprise managers. Introduced in January 1984, these proposals, which have apparently come to serve as the core of the reform process for Gorbachev as well, did not herald a new order. First of all, only two all-republic industrial ministries and three minor republic ministries were involved. The number of ministries involved has increased each year, but little if anything about these proposals was novel, much less revolutionary. Factory managers were urged to take more local initiative but were given little or nothing with which to exercise that initiative. The aborted reforms of 1963–1964 associated with Evsei Liberman had been more far-reaching and imaginative: those experiments, as we saw, authorized factory managers to adjust prices at their discretion. There was none of that here. Little if anything being proposed went beyond what had been attempted twenty years earlier, and in several respects Andropov was actually less forthcoming.

Like the lion that squeaked, the July 26, 1983, pronouncement was hardly what many observers had anticipated. Given all of Andropov's talk about the need for reform, his proposals of July 26 were quite modest. Yet, even then, it was clear that Andropov expected to have a hard time implementing them. At an unusual meeting called by Andropov with what were described as "party veterans of the Central Committee of the Communist party," he sought their support for structural and economic change. Politically, this was a wise thing to do since such apparatchiks had scuttled previous attempts at reform. Given that almost any economic reorganization would affect the jobs and well-being of those very bureaucrats, their resistance was to be expected. In some ways, such personal considerations were more compelling than were the ideological or theoretical implications of less reliance on central planning or more reliance on market mechanisms.

That Andropov had a keen sense of what he was up against became clear two days after his meeting with his ad hoc "party veterans," when Nikolai Baibakov, then chairman of Gosplan, took what was at the time the unprecedented step of calling a press conference to defend the existing system of central planning. In Baibakov's view, central planning and the Soviet economy were doing well enough, thank you. As he put it, while the Soviet Union might increase the authority of the individual enterprises, the government would make sure that central planning would not be weakened but strengthened.[49] Baibakov took issue with those seeking reform: Why should there be change when the existing economic system was "dynamic"? Baibakov claimed, "If you compare our performance with that which is being done in capitalist countries, then I think our indicators look rather good."[50]

Reportedly, some members of the bureaucracy, as well as their opposites—that is, those on the fringe of socialist legitimacy—were pleased to see Andropov die after only fifteen months as general secretary. Some even circulated rumors (most likely, they were only rumors) that Andropov, ill though he was, did not die a natural death but was poisoned by some black marketeers or some disgruntled officeholders whom Andropov had purged. Nonetheless, the bulk of the Soviet Union's population seemed distressed by Andropov's early death. Despite his age and his association with the KGB, he had brought them a sense of hope that the Soviet Union would again find itself. Most Soviets even seemed to welcome the discipline, at least in the short run.

For those seeking fundamental reform, Konstantin Chernenko's subsequent appointment was particularly disappointing. It was as if Brezhnev had been reborn. Chernenko was regarded as nothing more than a briefcase carrier for Brezhnev and had virtually no previous administrative experience. Moreover, he was ill from the start. How could he have the strength to carry out any far-reaching changes? Indeed, the two footmen who spent their lives on either side of Brezhnev, holding him up lest he fall, and who were transferred to holding Andropov when he became ill were quickly reassigned to do the same job for Chernenko.

For the thirteen months that he served as general secretary, Chernenko gave lip service to the implementation of Andropov's reforms, minor as they were. Only with the selection of Gorbachev as Chernenko's successor, in March 1985, did the drive for economic revitalization gather steam again. Initially, that drive involved a strategy almost identical to Andropov's. Given that Gorbachev was Andropov's protégé, this was not surprising. Immediately, Gorbachev reinstituted the crackdown on alcoholism that had been of less concern to Chernenko. And, like his mentor, Gorbachev managed to reinvigorate the economy (see Table 4). Monthly production figures began to increase at a faster pace, just as they had under Andropov.

Even more than Andropov, however, Gorbachev began to stress the need for change. Although in the beginning he hardly ever used the phrase "economic reform" itself, he nonetheless committed himself to "a profound transformation of the economy."[51] This transformation was to come with increased discipline and what he called the "intensification" of industry. By "intensification" he meant retooling and better use of existing plant and equipment. His predecessors had emphasized new plant construction. Gorbachev argued that better discipline and modernized equipment would permit better use of existing facilities.

At first, Gorbachev's strategy was to talk expansively but move moderately. While hinting at more rapid growth and far-reaching change, he seemed to settle for moderate and cosmetic adjustments in the existing system and for continuing purges of inept officeholders from the Brezhnev era. Thus, Gorbachev stated publicly that he had ordered Gosplan to revise its initial draft of the Twelfth Five-Year Plan because the targets for industrial growth were too low.[52] This implied that the national income rates of growth in the Eleventh Five-Year Plan of approximately 3.2 percent were too low. Most observers assumed that, given Gorbachev's exhortations, the Twelfth Five-Year Plan would call for a 4.0 to 4.5 percent annual growth in national income, but the initial goals set up by Gorbachev in the Twelfth Five-Year Plan called for a growth of only 3.5–4.1 percent.[53] After five revisions, he managed to win approval for the upper limits, and while even this will be difficult to reach, it still does not suggest much of an improvement.[54]

As for the revamping of the economy, Gorbachev, like Andropov, seems to have settled for considerably less than some of his earlier statements implied. He apparently has decided not to attempt any radical surgery. Nothing proposed so far would alter the basic economic framework of central planning, investment, and state ownership of the means of production. For example, there was little to indicate any broad move to legitimize the second economy—private services and private manufacturing enterprises outside the realm of central planning. For every experiment in Georgia or Estonia where there is a hint of a semiprivate or cooperative arrangement in which the enterprise is more or less authorized to determine its own work procedures and share of the proceeds, there is still a curbing of private profit-making opportunities. For example, in August 1985 *Izvestiia* ran an article describing the Elektron Radio and TV Repair Association in Tallin, Estonia, which in the spring of 1985 had been authorized to rent out a workshop to a cooperative brigade of workers.[55] After paying a set fee per worker and 30 percent of whatever income it earned, the brigade was authorized to earn as much as it could on its own terms and divide up the remaining proceeds. As might have been predicted, the repair service improved markedly. Instead of a two-week wait for service, there is now usually a one-day wait. Similar experiments have been made in hairdressing in Estonia and in restaurant operation in Georgia, and junk or recycling cooperatives have been approved throughout much of the Soviet Union.[56] The cooperative seems to have become the preferred organizational form for competing with official state enterprises. The Soviet government has also authorized the formation as of May 1, 1987, of private individual and family businesses, particularly those engaged in providing services like sewing and apartment and auto repairs. However, both the private and the cooperative businesses are prohibited from hiring anyone else, and only those not otherwise occupied in the state sector, such as students and pensioners, may work full-time. Regular workers may work in private or cooperative ventures only in their spare time. Moreover, these moves, which might be described as legitimizing some aspects of the underground or second economy in the Soviet Union, were undermined by an October 1985 rule barring the sale of agricultural produce in the collective farm markets of Moscow and Georgia by anyone other than the grower himself. This antitrade philosophy was reinforced by a July 1, 1986, edict banning what was called "unearned" income, which might arise from the selling of someone else's products.[57]

Industrial changes reflect the same contradictory policies. Gorbachev is apparently trying to centralize and decentralize all at the same time. In an effort to transfer more initiative to the enterprise level, important planning powers were transferred in May 1985 to what were at first announced as three major manufacturing entities: the Volga Automotive Plant Association in Togliatti, which makes the Zhiguli; the Elektrovypriamitel' (semiconductor) factory in Saransk; and the Frunze Scientific Production Association in Sumy.[58]

As with earlier reforms, each of these special associations has been assigned a set profit tax for five years. Anything earned above that the association can use to purchase equipment and pay benefits. The goal is to make the enterprise more independent financially. The number of targets assigned has similarly been reduced. Following the example of the Shchekino experiment, which allowed the workers to share the wages saved from the firing of redundant workers, the experimental enterprises are now also being encouraged to reduce their work forces.[59] Similar measures had been introduced several times before, but they had relatively little impact. One of the few new changes was the announcement that the associations will henceforth be able to keep 40 percent of the foreign exchange they earn from the export of their products.[60] This is intended to spark plant workers because they now will have something meaningful to spend their money on. In particular, this concession is to make it possible for them to avail themselves of high technology from the West. The plant managers are also authorized to transfer to their subcontractors and suppliers one-quarter of the hard-currency receipts they are allowed to keep. All indications are that Gorbachev wants this to be the ultimate model for all Soviet industry.[61] However, the initial reports suggest that, regardless of the laws, the banks have been withholding the convertible currency from the enterprises under the same old controls. As has happened so often, the bureaucracy's first concern is to protect its prerogatives, even if reform suffers.

There are also signs that some firms may in the future be given more authority to determine prices. Because this is such an important prerogative and because the consequences are so delicate politically, these steps have so far been tentative. As of 1984, the power to determine temporary markups for the production of light industry was extended to the republic price authorities from the central authorities in Moscow.[62] More important, over 120 light industrial product associations and enterprises were given authority to raise prices up to 30 percent. That may not be enough to meet the basic need for more flexibility, but it does seem to be a step in the right direction.

While such efforts reflect an attempt to decentralize decision-making power, not only are most of the reforms introduced so far reminiscent of past efforts, but the production associations are still bound by rather rigid restraints imposed by the center. The planners and ministers still insist that each enterprise fulfill six major indices, such as profit level and output assortment, which continue to be assigned by central planners.[63] As Alice Gorlin has pointed out, as long as central ministers in Moscow retain such controls, they tend to interfere unduly not only in setting the indices but also in other areas that are theoretically not the concern of the ministries.[64]

To deal with quality concerns, Gorbachev has opted once again for an administrative solution rather than for a radical approach. Instead of calling on market forces to pressure Soviet manufacturers into assuring quality, the Soviet Union announced in late 1986 that as of January 1987 a new unit, the State Acceptance Service, would be charged with ensuring quality at 1,500 associations and enterprises.[65] This State Acceptance Service would become an adjunct of the State Committee for Standards (Gostandart) under the Council of Ministers and would report to the state committee on the work being performed in the factories under its inspection. It will have the power to accept or reject the output of the factory under its supervision. In the past, each enterprise had its own quality inspectors, but these reported to the enterprise managers, who would often pressure the inspectors to accept shoddy work. The new State Acceptance Service hopes to avoid such pressures by removing the inspectors from the control of the enterprise managers and making them accountable to the independent State Committee for Standards. Something similar operates in the military sector and serves to ensure a higher level of quality. But the fact that the procedure works in the military sector is no guarantee that a comparable one will work in the civilian sector, especially if candidates for the new inspector jobs are selected in part, from nominations made by the factory managers. Sooner or later, some inspectors, even if formally accountable to an outside superviser, are apt to find themselves under many of the same pressures to approve quality that led to problems before.

Initially some inspectors seem to have taken themselves very seriously. According to some reports, as much as seventy percent of some factory output has been rejected. The problem is that under the new incentive policy, if factory output is rejected because of its poor quality, the entire workforce will find its salary and bonuses reduced accordingly. Not surprisingly, that can be upsetting, so upsetting in fact that the workers at the massive Kama River Diesel Truck Plant in Brezhnev conducted what an *Izvestiia* article of December 4, 1986, acknowledged to be "a wild demonstration"; nor would it seem that this protest was unique. As has traditionally been the case, the workers were especially irate that they were being blamed for poor quality products when everyone knew that they were being supplied with poor quality components. You can't make durable houses with shoddy bricks.

Based on the above analysis, it is unclear how successful the State Acceptance Service will ultimately be. But if it does succeed, the new State Acceptance Service would seem to represent an enhancement of the bureaucracy and a further effort to take power away from the enterprise and transfer it to the center in Moscow. Equally ominous for those seeking to shift more power from Moscow to the operating level is Gorbachev's apparent determination to establish a small number of superministries, which seems to be an increase in centralization. As we saw, thus far he has created such ministries in agriculture, machine building, and energy development. While this could be an effort to reduce bureaucracy by restricting the superministries to the formation of general guidelines and precluding them from interfering in day-to-day operational matters, there is no guarantee that they will accept this limited role. Indeed, their past behavior gives reason to assume that such superministries, like any bureaucratic organization, will ultimately feel compelled to protect themselves from underfulfillment of the plans and thus begin to impinge on the operations of the enterprises subordinate to them.

Abel Aganbegian has been an outspoken advocate of the superministry concept. Aganbegian first proposed the idea of consolidating the country's ministries into superministries in 1969.[66] His influence is also reflected in his colleague Tatiana Zaslavskaia's proposal to abolish forty or so economic ministries as a means of eliminating the stultifying bureaucracy that has sprung up between the enterprise and the planners.[67] The creation of superministries also bears a strong resemblance to the type of reform adopted by the East Germans.[68] Gorbachev has sought to increase the autonomy of the next-lower economic units as well. In August 1986, a new "basic management unit," a much larger scientific production association, was authorized.[69] It is to be called the "All-Union Scientific Production Association" (VNPO) and, as we shall see in Chapter 6, bears a comradely resemblance to the East German *Kombinat.*[70] Gorbachev has often referred favorably to the East German model.

To the same end, Soviet authorities in early 1986 entrusted eleven institutes of the the Academy of Sciences and eight institutes from various industrial ministries with the actual control of several industrial enterprises. These so-called Inter-branch Scientific Technical Complexes (MNTK) are expected to bring together diverse production activities that would normally fall under the control of different ministries. Since ministries tend to operate vertically, they traditionally resist any coordinating of activities with other ministries on an ongoing basis. The expectation is that this involving of the Academy of Sciences and other prestigious research institutes will lead to improved interaction with industry, which in turn will facilitate technological development. This is part of the effort to eliminate intermediate layers of bureaucracy.

Neither Zaslavskaia nor Aganbegian goes so far as to call for just one superministry like the Supreme Council of the National Economy, which existed from 1917 to 1932. Instead, their vision and apparently Gorbachev's resemble the 1932–1939 arrangement where the functions of the Supreme Council of the National Economy were split up among three ministries,—the Ministry of Light Industry, the Ministry of Heavy Industry, and, strangely enough, the Ministry of the Timber Industry.

X

Because the Soviet reform effort has been so disjointed and uncoordinated and so much a throwback to the past, it might be useful to sketch what seem to be the basic outlines of what we can call the Gorbachev reforms. Since Gorbachev has announced his intention to introduce a series of thirty-eight directives setting forth his proposed changes through the year 1990, this summary may prove to be premature.[71] However, he has done and said enough to make it possible to set out what will probably be the major features of his reform.

In industry, the basic model seems to be the Togliatti-Sumy experiment. As of 1987, several Soviet ministries are to be converted to the new system. If all goes as planned, enterprise managers will have increased financial autonomy. This means that central authorities will be limited as to what they can extract from profitable firms. It also means, however, that unprofitable firms will no longer be able to count on subsidies. All this will be accomplished by setting up a five-year fixed limit on the amount of enterprise and production association profits that will be subject to tax. This should induce them to increase their profits, with the understanding that they will be able to keep whatever extra they earn. The extra proceeds can then be used for special funds for the purchase of equipment, the awarding of bonuses, and the investment in cultural facilities and housing. The manager is also to be given more flexibility in deciding whom he should buy from and whom he should sell to. Moreover, the manager will get increased power to hire, fire, and pay his workers and staff.[72] In some factories, workers will be organized into brigades and asked to contract for the performance of a specified amount of work.[73] The Politburo has ordered that there should be no pay without the production of products that are ultimately sold.[74] Gorbachev has complained that all too often workers are paid even if they produce nothing or if they produce poor-quality products that because of their poor quality find their way immediately to the warehouse.[75] Some experiments have also been authorized that will allow slightly more price flexibility, but for the most part those experiments have not been conducted in manufacturing.[76]

There will be constraints on all of these powers, but there are indications that these powers will be increased if no major abuses arise. This does not mean that the manager can do as he pleases or that this constitutes an end to central planning. There will still be ministries, although fewer than before, and Gorbachev will set basic production goals that the enterprise must fulfill. To stimulate innovation, Scientific Production Associations, as well as the Interbranch Scientific and Technical Complexes (MNTK), are being encouraged to meld together research institutes and production enterprises from different ministries. In addition, as of January 1987, the State Committee for Standards attached to the Council of Ministers in Moscow has been ordered to assign to 1,500 enterprises and associations special quality inspectors who will judge whether production has been to state standards. If they judge it has not, the goods will be declared unacceptable and as a result will not count toward plan fulfillment and bonus payment. Despite such evidence to the contrary, Gorbachev continues to urge that day-to-day interference from Moscow should be curbed. The managers should have more power to make some decisions that they could not make before.

In agriculture, there has been some move to the brigade system of farming and a contract responsibility system. However, for the most part, the experiment has been restricted to the raising of livestock, and the brigades that have been formed tend arbitrarily to link farm workers rather than members of a particular family. In general, the emphasis continues to be on the *kolkhoz* and the *sovkhoz,* not on the family. The goal is to increase the financial independence of the *kolkhozy* and the *sovkhozy.* Anything the farm managers can produce over and above the targets that have been assigned to them, they are encouraged to sell through cooperative stores and the collective farm markets. Gorbachev has again begun to refer to *prodnalog* or a tax in kind.[77] The concept was popularized by Lenin during the NEP (New Economic Policy) period and meant that once the peasant had paid his tax or delivered a set quota to the state, he could utilize whatever else he produced as he saw fit. The *prodnalog* is intended to stimulate production. But, unlike Lenin, Gorbachev has apparently limited the concept of *prodnalog* to the *sovkhozy* and the *kolkhozy;* it does not apply to the individual peasants. In addition, the extra goods produced by the *kolkhozy* and the *sovkhozy* are supposed to be sold first through the cooperative trade network and later through the *kolkhoz* market. Goods sold through the cooperative network can be sold at prices higher than those in the state stores, but that is not the same as a free and unfettered price.

There has been some talk of more private service activity. In another call upon precedent—in this case, Lenin's—several specialists, including the historian Evgenii Ambartsumov, have begun to advocate a return to Lenin's NEP, with its legitimization of the market and small private enterprise.[78] But such proposals have been vigorously attacked by conservatives like E. Bugaev, who staunchly defend central planning.[79]

A compromise seems to have been reached. The preferred form of nonstate activity is to be the cooperative, patterned in part on the junk or recycling cooperatives authorized in August 1986.[80] They can involve from five to fifty people, who will share in the proceeds. As we noted earlier, however, the Soviets have also decided to allow some private activity. On November 19, 1986, the Supreme Soviet voted to allow individuals and families as of May 1, 1987, the right to act as private entrepreneurs in their spare time.[81] The new law specified twenty-nine kinds of private enterprise that would be allowed, mostly service-type activities, but it does permit handicraft, clothing, and shoe manufacturing.

However, this new legislation does not go as far as Lenin's NEP program did. Certain activities, such as the manufacture of medicines and the use of copying machines, are banned. Even more important, the individuals and families involved cannot hire labor to work for them, and they must quit their jobs in state enterprises. They may work privately in their spare time or when they retire. Moreover, the owners of all private businesses are required to register with local authorities and pay taxes on their profits. They are also supposed to obtain all their supplies from Gossnab, the official state supplier, and not from other, private traders. This is a sharp distinction not only from NEP but also from the reforms carried out in other communist countries. In fact, as we noted earlier, a major crackdown was instituted on illegal private service and trade activities on July 1, 1986. That has served to inhibit those activities that are legal.

Reforms affecting external economic activity will be considered in more detail in Chapter 5, but some mention should be made here of a few of the proposals that have been suggested so far. As we saw a few pages ago, enterprises that export have been told they will be able to keep 40 percent of the convertible currency they earn and to spend it as they please. Extending the practice, an effort is under way to decentralize the monopoly functions of the Ministry of Foreign Trade. As of January 1987, approximately twenty individual and seventy industrial enterprises were authorized to negotiate their own export and import arrangements directly with the foreign buyers and sellers.[82] Because the implications of such a step are far-reaching, both ideologically and financially, it is being implemented in a very cautious fashion. In an equally tentative step, Gorbachev and the Politburo have also announced that the U.S.S.R. will begin to authorize joint ventures on Soviet territory.[83] As part of the same effort, the Soviet Union has asked for observer status at the General Agreement on Tariffs and Trade (GATT) meetings and has also hinted that it is interested in joining the International Monetary Fund and the World Bank.

XI

What is striking about this brief review of current Soviet economic reform is that except for some of the proposals dealing with foreign trade and foreign investment, so much of what is being suggested today has a precedent. Almost everything being proposed, including a return to NEP, has already been tried either in the Soviet Union or in Eastern Europe. That includes allowing the enterprises to share in some of the hard currency its exports earn, which has been attempted in several East European countries. Thus, cooperatives, private and family businesses, the brigade system, associations, superministries, and director funds have all had an earlier incarnation. That also is true for the principle of Stakhanovite shock workers, a notion about which Gorbachev has also issued some fond words. In fact, that so much of what is now being proposed has been tried before without particular success suggests just how difficult Gorbachev's task is. There might have been more visible success if contradictory experiments had not been introduced simultaneously. It is hard to generate enthusiasm when the "true economic vision" keeps changing so rapidly.

The failure of past economic reforms also suggests how deeply entrenched the resistance to change is. A purge of economic administrators and government leaders and an emphasis on discipline does help, but only within limits. The prevailing system seems to resist efforts to reform it, let alone to change its very nature. This has been the experience of Gorbachev's predecessors, and Gorbachev seems to be encountering exactly the same resistance. During a visit to Khabarovsk in July 1986, he vividly complained, "Among us are people who have difficulty grasping the word restructuring [Gorbachev's phrase for reform], and sometimes they have difficulty even pronouncing it."[84] As we will see in the next chapter, the advent of the new high technology has made Gorbachev's challenge, already a difficult one, even more problematic.

4

High Technology and the Soviet Economy

Difficult as it may have been in the past to carry out meaningful economic reform in the Soviet Union, today the task is considerably more challenging. On top of all the old obstacles is a new complication—the need to master or even stay abreast of what has come to be known as the new high technology.

"High technology" is a concept that does not lend itself to precise definition. By their very nature, high-technology products change rapidly. That reflects the many scientists and engineers and the large research and development expenditures associated with their production. In fact, measuring the number of scientists and engineers employed is one of the most accepted methods of judging high technology. To merit the designation "high technology," an industry normally must have a work force composed of at least 2.5 percent scientists and engineers —or 10 percent, if technicians are also included.[1] This, in turn, should reflect expenditures on research and development that are at least 3.5 percent of net sales and, by extension, a high percentage of value added. If the industry is to remain in the ranks of high technology, there must also be a rapid rate of technological development. Not everyone agrees on the list, but among the industries usually considered to be high technology are the following: computers and office equipment, electrical equipment, optical and medical instruments, aircraft, drugs and medicine, plastics and synthetic materials, professional and scientific instruments, engines and turbines, and some types of chemicals.[2]

Obviously, not all categories of the products just enumerated qualify as high technology. Those that do qualify have a distinctive nature that makes developing and producing them an unusual challenge. This is not a challenge unique to the Soviet bloc. The United States, Western Europe, and Japan face the same challenge. But because the Soviet Union is already far behind the West in civilian high technology, its task may be considerably more demanding. Unfortunately for Gorbachev, an increase in the output of traditional goods does not necessarily help in the mastering of new technologies. Moreover while an emphasis on discipline, conformity, and sobriety may, at least until recently, have been a prerequisite for any country seeking world leadership in heavy and medium industry, that is today not enough. In some instances, conformity and discipline may actually be counterproductive for those who want to keep pace in the postindustrial era.

Until shortly after World War II, technology, though not stagnant, was nonetheless slow-moving and relatively simple. Economic growth seldom involved more than the mastery of basic and fairly stable technology and the transfer of that technology to other factories elsewhere in the country. For example, there were relatively few major technological improvements in the steel industry in the 1920s, 1930s, and 1940s. The Soviet Union could buy, copy, or invent processes and products and concentrate on multiplying, instead of on improving or upgrading output and production methods, because technology changed so slowly.

Industrial technology evolved gradually in the mid-1960s but changed markedly in the 1970s and thereafter. This happened not only in the new technologies but even in the technologies used in basic industries. Instead of having life cycles of a decade or more, a growing number of products became obsolete in as little as two to three years. This shortening of the product life cycle meant that, to be competitive, planners and manufacturers could no longer concentrate only on repetitive production or rote expansion. Change and innovation became essential for any industry or industrial complex that sought to be economically competitive.

Mastering new and rapidly changing technology is an aspect of the reform process that most of Gorbachev's predecessors did not have to bother with. But whether emerging new technologies can be quickly absorbed in a centrally controlled economy, even a reformed one, is still an unanswered question. In order to gain a better appreciation of why it has complicated Gorbachev's life, we will discuss the various technological revolutions and consider at length the new challenges the current revolution poses for Gorbachev.

I

Each of the three Industrial Revolutions has been marked by an acceleration in the life and death of industrial technology. The First Industrial Revolution was characterized by the mastery of the steam engine, improvements in transportation, and rapid progress in the textile and leather industries. In the early years of that revolution, change did come with some rapidity —especially if measured against previous industrial change. However, once the initial innovation was mastered, further technological changes in those early industries were more modest. Competition was more a matter of finding cheaper labor, better managerial organization, and other manufacturing economies than one of continuous change in production or product technology.

The Second Industrial Revolution saw the development of heavy industrial products, especially ferrous metallurgy and machine tools, and ultimately the production of heavy consumer goods like automobiles or appliances. The pace of development picked up with time, but most products generally had a technological if not an operating life of a decade or more. Given the relatively slow-moving nature of this technology, manufacturers found that in order to increase sales they had to stress style changes. In the automobile industry strenuous efforts were made to convince consumers that the current year's production model was superior to last year's even though in the vast majority of cases the main change was a differently shaped fender or hood. There were technological changes, but, like those of the First Industrial Revolution, they came relatively slowly; with some notable exceptions, competition for sales thus centered more on style than on technical progress.

The tempo of Innovation quickened again during and after World War II. In areas like radar or atomic energy, some of the early research and development had occurred before World War II. Yet, with each year, especially in the 1960s, the movement seemed to gather speed. One of the biggest breakthroughs was the invention of the transistor in 1947. Prior to this invention, electronic products had to rely on the vacuum tube, which generated a good deal of heat, occupied a considerable amount of space, and consumed relatively large amounts of electricity. The vacuum tube worked well enough in simple products like radios, but the need to work with bulky and hot tubes severely limited the development of more complicated projects. The advent of the transistor helped some, but it was still quite a task to link up a million or so individually wired transistors. However, by 1958, engineers had discovered how to fabricate transistors, resistors, and capacitors out of silicon and put them all onto a simple chip.[3] These chips, the size of a fingernail, did the work that had formerly required a room full of vacuum tubes powered by large electric lines and cooled by large air-conditioning units. The availability of these economical and compact memory chips had an enormous impact and accelerated the technological development of computers.

Work on the first computer was sponsored by the U.S. Army, which was seeking a way to determine the trajectory of its artillery shells with greater accuracy and speed. The motivation behind the Soviet decision to build a computer was much the same—a desire to enhance the capabilities of Soviet military and, later, space work. This suggests that government involvement in technological development for military purposes is not necessarily a bad thing, especially when it comes to the underwriting of basic scientific breakthroughs.

Like the first Soviet models, the first American computers were big and clumsy. ENIAC, the first U.S. electronic computer, was eighty feet long and eight feet high. It weighed thirty tons and had 18,000 vacuum tubes, 70,000 resistors, 10,000 capacitors, and 1,500 relays.[4] Even though today the average desktop computer is ten to a hundred times faster than the ENIAC, the ENIAC could nonetheless calculate in twenty seconds what then required several days of work with mechanical calculating devices.

Parallel advances in computers, transistors, and integrated circuit microchips fed into one another, stimulating further developments. Improvements came at a rapid pace. But here large bureaucracies were not especially well suited for the task of facilitating or implementing innovation. Governments and large corporations often tend to be slow and ponderous. They can perceive a need but often have difficulty in generating the flexibility and speed essential for technological leadership. The more quickly technology moves, the harder it is for large bureaucratic units to keep up and the more imaginative they must become to prevent a clogging of the bureaucratic arteries. More sophisticated and cheaper microchips made it possible to build ever smaller and more powerful computers, so that different manufacturers found themselves racing with one another to introduce new and improved models every year or less. This put a premium on quick decision making and implementation, something centrally controlled governments often find it difficult to do.

As computer size diminished, manufacturers began to use the computer not just as an end product, but as a component in other products. These products in turn often became part of the Third Industrial Revolution. For example, the microchip changed the nature of a vast range of technologies, such as typesetting and printing, that had lain dormant for decades, if not centuries. With computers, machine tools and robots could

be programmed to do a variety of complicated and often onerous tasks more precisely than humans. Computers and machinery incorporating computers even changed the nature of steel
and automobile manufacturing. Newly built plants designed
around these new technologies produce much more precisely,
efficiently, and economically than older plants, whose managers
as recently as the 1960s seldom had to worry about such innovations.

By the late 1970s, computers could be programmed to prepare and facilitate design, engineering, and manufacturing
work. Called computer aided design (CAD) or CAE or CAM,
the process used computers to prepare whole sets of drawings
and blueprints for any number of project variations in a matter
of minutes. Previously, such efforts had taken weeks or months.
This progress in turn accelerated the whole cycle of product
innovation and at the same time reduced the costs of such
efforts.

If the model life and cost of computers kept shrinking, so did
the life of the products and processes that used computers as
components. As a consequence, not only do computers and
other high technology products today have a very short life
cycle, but much of what used to be conventional technology has
now become unconventional technology. As American manufacturers have painfully discovered, even steel mills and automobile factories can become obsolete in five years or less. The
most prosaic processes are now subject to the high-technology
treatment. To keep up with these changes, decision makers
today must be adroit, flexible, and quick, words not normally
used to describe Soviet bureaucracy or industry.

II

It would be arrogant and misleading to insist that only the
American way can assure the quick response time that leadership in the high-technology field necessitates. Certainly, even in
the United States, several different approaches have been utilized. Moreover, large integrated manufacturers and semiguided

economies like those of Japan, Taiwan, and South Korea have managed to respond quickly to technological change. The Asians often seem to adapt technologies more quickly than their American competitors do. While this may be changing slightly, they have so far tended to concentrate on product enhancement rather than on new-product development and invention.

One would think that the managers of a centrally controlled economy would have an easy time introducing new technologies, because all they would have to do is decree their adoption. It sometimes works that way in the military sphere, but generally not in the civilian sector. On the whole, the Soviet economic planning system seems particularly ill suited to meet these new challenges. A closer look at the way high technology has developed in the United States may help illustrate the disadvantages the Soviets have.

A distinguishing feature of the new high-technology revolution in the United States and in other countries is that a large share of new-product development and innovation is the work of small and new start-up corporations. Several researchers have found that small firms generate a much greater "inventive output" per dollar of research and development spending than do their large counterparts.[5] Reflecting the same phenomenon, a Department of Commerce study indicated that 50 percent of the innovations in the United States from World War II to the late 1970s originated in companies with a work force of under 500 employees. Not all of these enterprises were high-technology firms, nor have all of them survived the rigors of competition, but much of the new-product development and high technology came from them. The smallness of such firms suggests that many technological innovators enjoy ease of entry. However, it is a fast life, because there is also ease of exit. Since the product life cycle is only two to three years, high-technology firms must keep inventing new products. The life cycle of firms that do not keep developing can be equally short.

To gain some insight into how rapid the process of formation and growth can be, it is instructive to see how the number of

Fortune 500 companies headquartered in the state of Massachusetts has changed. Massachusetts is a particularly good state to use because in the 1970s it became the site of a very high concentration of high-technology industries. In 1969, there were seven companies in Massachusetts large enough to be counted in the Fortune 500 (see Table 5). Four of those—Raytheon, Polaroid, Kendall, and Cabot—were producing sophisticated products requiring large numbers of scientists and engineers. By 1974, American Biltrite, a maker of parts for shoes (low technology), had fallen from the list, as had Kendall, which was acquired by another company. In 1975, USM, a maker of shoe machinery (low technology), also fell from the list, when it was sold to a Connecticut firm. What is striking, however, is that by 1985, rather than shrinking, the list of those in the Fortune 500 had expanded almost threefold, to include eighteen firms. Equally impressive, most of the high-technology corporations are very young. Digital Equipment, now the second-largest firm in the state, was founded only in 1957; Wang, the fourth-largest, in 1955; and Data General, in 1968. The other high-technology firms, among them Prime Computer and Computervision (a CAD-CAM company), were created in the 1970s, only ten to fifteen years ago.

An example will illustrate how fast-moving life in the high-technology lane can be. In 1985, just after it had made the list for the first time, Computervision, a firm that was only ten years old, found that its products were already being fiercely challenged in the marketplace. As a consequence of falling sales, it was forced to lay off over 1,000 employees, and it dropped from the ranks of the Fortune 500 in 1986. Since this is almost entirely a phenomenon of private enterprise, nothing comparable has ever happened in the Soviet Union. That has undoubtedly spared Soviet workers the anguish that comes from losing their jobs, but it also denies their society some of the products and opportunities that can come only with a willingness to facilitate rapid entry and exit.

Many of the new small firms were founded and flourished at the very time when some of the larger and older-technology

TABLE 5

Fortune 500 Companies
with Headquarters in Massachusetts

1985, 1974, and 1969

Company*

May 1985	May 1974
Raytheon (1922)**	Raytheon (1922)**
Digital Equipment (1957)**	Gillette (1917)
Gillette (1917)	Polaroid (1937)**
Wang Laboratories (1955)**	USM (part of Emhart)
Cabot (1960)**	Norton (1885)
Polaroid (1937)**	Cabot (1960)**
Norton (1885)	Digital Equipment (1957)**
Data General (1968)**	
EG&G (1947)**	
General Cinema (1950)	May (1969)
Idle Wild Foods (1974)	Raytheon (1922)** (under
M/A—Com (1950)**	American Appliance)
Dennison Manuf. (1848)	Gillette (1917)
Prime Computer (1972)**	Polaroid (1937)**
Computervision (1975)**	USM (1899)
Foxboro (1914)**	Kendall (1924)**
Ocean Spray (1930)	Cabot (1960)**
Wyman Gordon (1883)	American Biltrite (1954)

*Companies are listed in the same order of appearance on Fortune 500 list according to highest capital for the year. Year following name is year of founding.
**High technology.

firms found they could not compete. Corporations otherwise as successful as General Electric and RCA, which had produced computers for a time, eventually decided to close down their operations because they could not keep up with the rapid pace of technological change in the field. The operations of General Electric and RCA were ultimately folded into Honeywell's computer operations, but then, as development of the integrated circuit made it possible to miniaturize operations, Honeywell found itself facing competition from Digital Equipment, a firm that started from scratch in 1957, with only three employees, including the president. Honeywell then made a larger machine than Digital, but Digital, even without the resources available to a firm as large as Honeywell, proved to be technologically more innovative. Unable to compete effectively, Honeywell decided to abandon much of its computer production efforts in 1986.

The Western experience suggests that the older and larger the firm, the more cumbersome decision making is likely to be. The larger firm usually has access to larger sums of capital for research, development, and construction. But as the operation grows in size, corporate management finds it necessary to delegate more and more authority. Most corporate managers then decide to institute controls to ensure that this delegated authority is not used in ventures that are too risky.[6] Committees are created and reports to supervisors required, and that inevitably prolongs the response time required for action.

Exxon's experience is a perfect example of how bigness can be a hazard in the era of high technology. In the early 1970s, the Exxon Corporation decided that it would diversify its activities in order to be less dependent on petroleum. Because Exxon had annual profits of five to six billion dollars, it was assumed that if its executives could manage something as large and complex as the multibillion-dollar petroleum and petrochemical business, they could also handle a few hundred million dollars worth of high-technology products. Rather than start from scratch, Exxon began by buying up manufacturers of sophisticated office equipment, such as facsimile machinery, word processors, and electronic typewriters. Although the initial products held enormous promise, research and development slowed down under Exxon's ownership. The operating channels immediately became more and more complex. In 1980 a forty-page organization chart was created to expedite matters; of course, it only complicated them even more.[7] By the fall of 1984, Exxon's efforts in high technology had fallen so far behind that it decided to close down its office systems unit and to write off 500 million dollars worth of investment and ten years worth of effort. Just because Exxon had problems with high technology does not mean that every large organization will have the same difficulty, but it should give Soviet leaders reason to wonder whether they will be any more successful.

This is not to say that when it comes to introducing new products, all small firms necessarily have an advantage. In the drug industry, for example, there are not many small firms, and relatively few drugs have been developed and ultimately sold by start-up firms. Here the large established firms continue to dominate. The contrast between drug manufacturing and computer-related corporations is instructive. A large percentage of the new computer firms are spinoffs from established firms or university-related laboratories. Much of the developmental work was performed somewhere else. In the case of Digital Equipment, for example, the founder of the company, Kenneth Olson, did most of his work at Lincoln Laboratories, an MIT-sponsored facility. In turn, Edson de Castro did his initial work at Digital before breaking away to form his own Data General. Similarly, An Wang did most of his research work in the Harvard computer laboratories. In all three cases, because the development work had already been completed elsewhere, the capital needs of the new corporation were relatively small. For instance, Digital's initial funding came to only $70,000, an equity investment provided by American Research and Development.

Presumably, just as in the computer field, much of the work in the pharmaceutical industry is also done outside of the laboratories of the established drug industries. That is true. The difference is that, unlike the drug industry, the computer field does not have to subject new products to prolonged and rigorous testing under federal government supervision. This testing is expensive. Consequently, in the drug industry, capital is needed not only to finance the early development work but also to sustain the firm while the testing results are completed.

There is no reason why the Soviet effort to master high technology has to duplicate the route we in the United States have taken. However, the American experience strongly suggests that the prevalence of large enterprises in the Soviet Union and the inability to react quickly outside of already existing enterprises is a serious handicap for Soviet technology. As long as the Soviets rely on central planning, they will deny themselves the potential that comes from start-up companies. That need not exclude them from all innovative industries, but it is hard to see how they can ever expect to take the lead in a large number of them. Nor is it just a question of central planning. If the Soviets hope to benefit from small start-up companies, they will presumably have to agree ultimately to permit spontaneous, risky ventures. Notable features of the high-technology revolution in Silicon Valley and in Massachusetts are the riskiness of the innovation and the rapidity with which some of these firms come into and go out of being. Many entrepeneurs have made millions in a short time, which attracts other risk takers, investors, or venture capitalists. This in turn has facilitated the creation of capital markets where the risk takers can sell their stock at a high profit. But it also means losses that can be equally large. This latter aspect of the process may deter central governments from participating in risky enterprises. Big bankruptcies are never pleasant. They are particularly messy when government enterprises are involved because, once such losses become public, they usually spark parliamentary cries for investigation and a scapegoat.

Because the Soviet system makes no provision for such phenomena, we have emphasized how important small and new businesses have been for high technology. But we have largely ignored the fact that some highly successful high-technology corporations, such as Digital Equipment, which even though now large have remained highly innovative. If the Soviets have to forgo the innovation that comes with small start-up companies, they will presumably still be able to avail themselves of the breakthroughs made by corporations like Du Pont, Minnesota Mining and Manufacturing (3M), and some of the drug companies. However, the Soviets cannot assume they will automatically be able to do as well.

The case of IBM illustrates some of the problems a large organization can have as it attempts to overcome some built-in obstacles to radical innovation. It is not just a matter of sclerosis of the decision-making process. Because product innovation threatens vested interests in the corporation, it will often be opposed. For example, a few decades ago Tom Horgan, then an IBM employee, demonstrated to his superiors a process that would have made it possible for IBM to do away with the computer punch card, which at the time was how data was put into the computer. Horgan argued that computers would work better and cheaper with tape inputs. But attractive and innovative as such a product may have been, his superiors at IBM quickly realized that a move to tape could be very costly to IBM. Over the years, IBM had rented out thousands of card-punch and card-reading machines to almost anyone who used an IBM computer, and IBM was collecting hundreds of millions of dollars a year in rental payments. When IBM decided not to turn its back on such a lucrative source of income and stuck instead with the punch card process, Horgan struck off on his own and founded Inforex, one of the first corporations to bypass the computer punch cards process.

Given that such conflicts of interest are inevitable in large, diverse enterprises like IBM, the Soviets may still be able to adopt some of IBM's methods to enhance the development of high technology. For example, to lessen the stultifying effect of committees and oversupervision, IBM and a few other large corporations have experimented with a new organizational approach. On special occasions, they set up what has come to be called a "skunk works." The name was first used to describe a facility set up by the Lockheed Corporation for new-product development. Isolated from the main offices and laboratories of Lockheed, the skunk works was assigned a special team of engineers and a separate budget and instructed to be creative. One result was the U-2 spy plane. In IBM's case, senior management established an independent business unit (IBU) in

Boca Raton, Florida, far removed from IBM's headquarters in Armonk, New York. This unit was freed of almost all control from the center and all traditional IBM procedures and was instructed to develop a small personal computer (PC). Although IBM had been very successful in marketing and producing large computers, it had failed to develop a smaller one and was in danger of falling behind new entrants into the small personal computer field, such as Radio Shack, Atari, and Apple. The fact that a successful IBM PC might impinge on the success of IBM's larger hardware had previously caused some senior executives to drag their feet. By setting up a semi-independent unit, IBM was able to outflank such foot-dragging. General Motors is attempting a similar end run by establishing an all but autonomous unit to produce its new car, the Saturn.

For all their successes, many Japanese enterprises share the same concerns about true innovation. The Japanese have relied heavily on the United States for new ideas. According to one estimate, from 1951 to 1984, the Japanese signed more than 42,000 contracts for the purchase of technology from abroad.[8] And while research and development expenditures in Japan have continued to grow and indeed, as a percentage of sales, now exceed what is being spent in the United States, the Japanese worry that they must do more than build upon and enhance innovation developed elsewhere. No one denies the Japanese mastery of color television and VCR production, but these, along with the semiconductor, were first developed in the United States. Can the Japanese go a step farther and create not only improved products but scientific breakthroughs?

By now it should be clear that those who doubt Japanese capabilities do so at their peril. More often than not, the Japanese seem to confound their skeptics. Yet, however successful Japanese corporations were in the past, they may find it very difficult to make radical technological breakthroughs. Strangely enough, one of the obstacles facing the Japanese is their homogeneity and discipline. Consensus and conformity are more highly valued by the Japanese than by Americans. These qualities are critical for producing high-quality improve-

ments in existing products, but they are not necessarily conducive to product and concept innovation. Diversity and nonconformity are more important, but to the Japanese, except for
some in the artistic community, those qualities are usually
alien.

Innovation is often created by those who are uninhibited and
eager to try something different. That is not to say that because
there is a much greater tolerance for nonconformists in the
United States, our nonconformists will be the first to develop
new products. Nevertheless, an atmosphere that permits lack of
conformity may help facilitate product innovation. Here again,
with its distrust of nonconformity and unconventionality, the
Soviet system militates against experimentation and innovation.

III

How does the preceding analysis relate to Gorbachev and the
tasks he faces? Since the Soviet Union has no set term of office
for its party and state officials or regularized procedure for
changing leadership, the odds are that Gorbachev will still be
the Soviet leader as it moves into the year 2000. In the interim,
we can confidently expect that there will be even more technological change and at a faster pace than we have seen thus far.
This makes it all the more important that the Soviet Union
come to terms with rapid technological innovations. Yet, to the
extent that past mastery of technological change in the noncommunist world is any key to future mastery, it is hard to see
how the Soviet Union will be able to cope. The models set out
for product and process innovation and even enhancement are
very different from what exists in the Soviet Union.

The dominant feature of the Soviet economy is the emphasis
on central planning and, by extension, on the central determination of product mix and the central allocation of resources.
Undoubtedly, some forms of innovation, such as those in the
military sector, flourish under a system of this kind. Thus, when
the Soviets concentrated some of their best talent in well-

financed and -supplied research laboratories, they were able to develop their own computers. The same applies to their effort in space, nuclear weapons, and other special fields like advanced materials.[9] These projects absorb large quantities of talent and resources, and this the Soviets can do reasonably well. They also do exceptional work in theoretical fields like mathematics and some forms of physics. However, because they lack hard currency, many Soviet laboratories do not have the equipment they need to conduct proper experiments. An unusually large proportion of Soviet scientists thus concentrate on abstract questions, where the only equipment they need is a blackboard, something not dependent on the availability of hard currencies. But successful as such efforts may periodically be, the considerable role played by small, independent enterprises and venture capitalists in this Third Industrial Revolution does not exist in the present Soviet system. Indeed, just the opposite conditions exist.

There is a danger that American observers of the Soviet system may be so blinded by their own circumstances that they cannot imagine different models of technological development. Other somewhat planned economies, such as those of Japan, Taiwan, and South Korea, are leaders in advanced technology, but their planning systems are not as centrally determined as the Soviet system. The Asians have been able to combine broad planning with private enterprise. Although their enterprises have many more checks and controls than do large American companies, they nonetheless have provided for a flexibility and speed that are missing from the cumbersome Soviet system.

One of the Soviets' biggest problems is that the planning is so monolithic. The economic system does not provide for a court of appeal. When Gosplan or Gosbank rejects a project, innovators almost never have any other place to go. In the capitalist world, there are usually alternative sources of support, some of which are not deterred by the fact that the would-be entrepreneur has already been turned down by other financiers. Some very important inventions, such as the Xerox process, were denied money by the first investors approached.

Conceivably, some of the economic reform experiments introduced in the last few months of Chernenko's life and enlarged upon by Gorbachev may facilitate the innovation process. Once again, some economists have proposed, as did Liberman in the 1960s, that enterprises be allowed to spend some of their profits on machinery and new procedures that their managers, rather than Gosplan and the ministries, might choose. However, to date, such experiments have not been very successful. As long as Gosplan continues to control most of the economy, it is not money that counts but Gosplan's allocation permits. Moreover, the ministers and others in Moscow continue to interfere, sometimes directly and sometimes subtly, so the enterprise manager is inhibited no matter how innovative he may be.

In addition to interference, the true innovator always faces the risk that his venture may fail. That could involve some substantial costs. In most societies, the innovator will accept those risks because he anticipates that if he succeeds, the rewards will more than compensate him for the risks he takes. In the Soviet Union, the state closely regulates the amount of reward the innovator may claim. In addition, the manager knows that if he halts the production process to introduce a new product or does anything to jeopardize the flow of his existing products, his bonuses will suffer. Therefore, he has little inducement to take the risk. It often seems that the system is designed to discourage rather than to stimulate innovation. Although some experiments have been proposed that will make innovation worth the manager's while, most of them still offer him little compensation. For example, it is unthinkable in communist societies that the monopoly windfall from risk taking should go to the manager. Typically, the Soviet manager can raise prices in order to raise profits but by no more than 30 to 100 percent above the normal profit for existing products.[10] But that is often less impressive than it looks. For example, a producer who sells an existing product for 200 rubles, which includes 20 rubles for profit, may be authorized, when he introduces a new product, to increase prices up to 210 or 220 rubles and thereby raise profits 30 to 40 rubles. Beginning in 1984, some manufacturers of consumer goods products were authorized to raise prices by as much as 50 percent for a period of eighteen months. Twenty-five percent of the light industrial products sold in 1984 were marked up with temporary prices, but few markups exceeded 10 to 15 percent. In fact, "two-thirds of all the temporary markups in light industrial products for adults were 10% or less," not much of an inducement.[11] Given the risks, that helps some, but heretofore that has not proven much of an inducement.

The laboratories in which most Soviet inventions are developed do not usually benefit if the ideas or products they create become profitable. In part, this is a natural consequence of the way laboratories and institutes have been separated from industrial control. Many of the institutes and research laboratories have traditionally been under the jurisdiction of the Academy of Sciences. Very few manufacturing enterprises have developed their own in-house research facilities. There is a further problem, however, in that the award of premiums in the laboratory, and in some cases the factory, has not been contingent on whether the invention is ever put to work, or whether the inventor ever invents anything. The laboratory worker is, in effect, paid just for coming to work. Complaining about how ineffective the whole system was, Gorbachev lamented, "A scientist or inventor has not been producing any inventions at all for ten years, but he gets his pay."[12] Because the laboratory worker does not derive material gain from seeing his invention through the laboratory and out onto the production floor, his interest tends to fade after he has done his initial work in the laboratory. In addition, the rewards to inventors have usually proven to be minimal. Indeed, some economists argue that inventors are actually discouraged from converting their ideas into active production. In the view of V. O. Obukhov, "the inventor . . . is sometimes viewed not as a champion of technological progress but as an annoying hindrance in work and life. And if an enterprise offers to pay him his due compensation for an invention it has put to use, it tries to understate the economic effect in order to reduce the amount of payment. While ostensibly saving money in the interests of the state, the enterprise is in fact hurting the state by impeding the development of inventive work and consequently the acceleration of technological progress."[13]

Moreover, Soviet officials have also acknowledged that Soviet science suffers because all too often talented Soviet engineers and scientists are not only separated from the process of practical application but also deprived of the opportunity to try out their ideas. While such complaints are not unique to the Soviet Union, they seem to be more common there than elsewhere. Because of the fear that he might underfulfill his plan and jeopardize his bonus, the factory manager seems more reluctant to experiment and to test a new process or product than his counterparts elsewhere are. This frustrates good engineers and scientists who welcome a challenge. As we saw, a partial consequence of this situation is that it has become harder to attract good students into engineering.[14] Moreover, a growing number of talented engineers become frustrated at the rejection of their innovative ideas, while "mediocre" colleagues receive praise for designing "old, useless machines."[15]

In order to generate greater interest in invention and the ultimate production of that invention on the part of both the inventor and the enterprise manager, efforts have been made to combine more closely the financial interests of the laboratory with those of the factory. That was one of the main reasons for creating the *obedenenie,* or syndicate, which was described in Chapter 4. By making the laboratory a profit center (or *khozraschet*) under the syndicate, officials expected that the laboratory staff would concentrate on research that would pay off. Similarly, since factory managers would have to cover the cost of the laboratory, they would increase the pressure on the laboratory to come up with products and processes with profit potential. The decision to entrust institutes of the Academy of Sciences with the operation of actual industries (the MNTK referred to in Chapter 4) reflects much the same reasoning. While all of this has helped some, there is general agreement that considerably more must be done to facilitate the movement of ideas from the Soviet laboratory to the production floor.

In fact, some Soviet observers have argued, not entirely facetiously, that the quickest way for Soviet industry to avail itself of a new product is to sell a license for that product to foreign firms. The foreign firms have often been able to put that product into production and export it back to the Soviet Union before the Soviets themselves are able to produce it.[16] Examples of products that have been invented in the Soviet Union but have been produced quicker outside the Soviet Union include continuous casting equipment for steel making, some welding equipment, a dry method of making cement, an antinicotine gum, an aluminum casting process, a process for the coating of titanium nitride, the application of an ultrathin film of diamonds on materials, and a many-linked weaving machine. (Lest we be too smug, we should remember that we have sometimes had similar experiences, although for different reasons. An American company, for example, invented the VCR, but today no VCRs are being produced in the United States itself.)

Given such dramatic evidence of the difficulty of moving technology from the laboratory to the production floor, Soviet economists have devoted considerable attention to discussing how to expedite the process. For one thing, some argue, there should be more material incentives. However, there is always a fear that any meaningful incentives will be too disproportionate with other salaries and will thus open the door for abuse. Moreover, in the Soviet Union, as in the United States, there are too many instances where "product innovations" are nothing more than a repackaging of the old product. Thus, textile manufacturers all too often seek to increase the profit premiums they receive for innovation simply by redesigning their product so that, for example, their "new" suit now has four rather than three buttons.[17] Whereas the market in the United States tends to distinguish between major and trivial innovation, the Soviets, as yet, have no such system.

This ambiguity about delineating and rewarding innovation must be resolved if the Soviets are to do more than copy others and be creative on their own. Yet, even if they can devise such a system, they still will have a hard time compensating for the absence of start-up companies. Theoretically, they should ultimately be able to integrate their laboratories and factories in much the same way as large foreign manufacturers like RCA, General Electric, Du Pont, Philips, and Toshiba. If the Soviets can work out such administrative and incentive problems, they will take a big step forward. But even then, the Soviet Union's inability to derive the benefits that come from private start-up firms means that it must compete with one hand tied behind its back, at least in the field of high technology.

The benefits that small start-up firms can bring are still not widely understood in the Soviet Union. At least there seems to be very little discussion of them. Traditionally, the model for innovation in Soviet eyes has been the large-scale enterprise— patterned, for the most part, after the similar large-scale operations in the capitalist world. Recently, the Soviets have also been attracted by the *Kombinate,* or big industrial combinations of manufacturers producing comparable products, which have been formed in the German Democratic Republic.[18] (See Chapter 6.) The East German experience is referred to over and over again by Soviet officials, because it suggests that the technology can be mastered with only marginal adjustments of the present Soviet system.

On top of everything else, Gorbachev's task is further complicated by some peculiarities of the high-technology phenomena that clash directly with the value system the Soviets have uniquely created for themselves since the Bolshevik Revolution. Unlike the heavy industry of the Second Industrial Revolution, today's high technology is more delicate in nature and more likely to be in need of frequent repair. Services are much more important in high technology than in the basic industries, as is evident in the work profile of most American high-technology firms. For that matter, some high technology, such as software, has much more to do with service-type operations than the production of hardware. Whereas two or three decades ago the work force of a firm like U.S. Steel (now USX) would consist of approximately 60 percent blue-collar workers, in a high-technology company like Wang Laboratories, blue-collar workers constitute only about 30 percent of the work force. The rest will be service-type workers, who include engineers and scientists, as well as repairmen. The problem for the Soviet Union is that service personnel have always been considered to be second-class citizens. What counts in the Soviet Union is production, both industrial and agricultural. Soviet heroic statuary almost always shows the male figure with a hammer and the female with a sickle. That derives largely from the emphasis Marx placed on production. In contrast, service activities were viewed as derivative if not parasitic. It would not do for the heroic Soviet man, even the new one, to stand ten stories high flaunting his abacus or even his calculator. Until service activities are accorded more respect, the Soviets will doubtless not be able to maintain the new technologies once they produce them.[19] As we will see in Chapter 5, they already have a serious problem properly maintaining the high technology they possess, just because they lack the proper manpower, tools, and attitude to service the equipment.

The Soviets' difficulty in providing the necessary servicing facilities highlights yet another dimension of the new high-technology revolution that will complicate the Soviet effort to be a world competitor. The Soviets generally do not do well with labor-intensive work, especially the sort that involves intricate detail and manual dexterity. They do well with big, brute-force, labor-intensive undertakings that involve heavy industry or big construction projects like dams or railroads. But in the new high-technology age, heavy industry and major construction projects have become significantly less important than they were.

This points to a difference between the Soviet Union and the East Asian countries such as Taiwan, South Korea, and Singapore. The people in those countries have traditionally specialized in delicate and labor-intensive work. This has given them an advantage in the production of textiles, but not in heavy industry. The development of microchips and other miniature high-technology products has given rise to the renewed need for labor-intensive work. This explains in large part why the Asian countries, which seemed to have little economic future only two or three decades ago, have recently done so well. It is hard to see how the Soviets can hope to emulate them.

Another problem for the Soviets is that so much of today's technology deals with information and information processing, areas that in the Soviet Union touch on internal security. Anything from copying machines to computers and printers can be viewed as potentially subversive. Such equipment can often be operated as a printing press or used to subvert the state control of communications. This holds for personal computers as well as word processors. In a society that carefully controls typewriters, carbon paper, and typewriter ribbons, the Third Industrial Revolution poses an enormous threat to those who seek to control their society's communications. Soviet authorities have already found it necessary to take special measures to ensure that the computers and copying machines they have are closely supervised. In practice, that means that copying machines are under continuous supervision. Indeed, when I once had access to a copying machine in the office of an American business firm in Moscow, the KGB found out about it and warned the office manager that continued unauthorized use of such equipment might necessitate the removal of that machine. Although this may limit some dissent, such controls can obviously be counterproductive in industry.[20]

The way to stimulate the further development of computers and allied products is to encourage as much use as possible of such equipment. That is the way to generate new ideas and new uses for new products and techniques. Early American work on software and new computers owed much to what we have come to call "hackers" or "computer jocks," people who spend most of their day "playing" with computers. How will the Soviet Union, where computers are literally locked up and their use restricted to authorized personnel, foster that "playing"? Recent reforms in Soviet education now decree that by graduation every Soviet student be computer literate. But how can that order be implemented when only a few classrooms in Moscow actually have computers for their students to use and when the authorities keep them under rigid control? As of mid-1986, only 12 percent of all higher-level students had the chance to work with computers and the Soviet press acknowledged that it was all but impossible for an ordinary citizen to buy his or her own computer in the Soviet Union.[21] It will be 1990 at the earliest before the Soviets expect to be able to produce their own personal computers, and even then they expect to produce only 50,000 a year for use inside the Soviet Union.

As long as the Soviet Union is paranoid about secrecy and control of information, it can probably never do more than follow other nations in computer development, if that. Specialists like Seymour Goodman suggest that the gap between the United States and the Soviet computer industries may actually be growing.[22] After the initial stimulus from the U.S. government, much of the impetus for computer development in the United States came from the commercial sector. Corporate users and manufacturers quickly realized that computer sales would be increased if computers could be made to interact or if several users could share time on a computer that would be too expensive and powerful for one user alone. To do this, however, they required not merely standardized software and programming procedures, something the Soviets have had a hard time getting, but also a phone system that can be readily relied upon to link up computers all over the country and, ultimately, the world.

Not only is the Soviet phone system notorious for its poor quality, but the need for secrecy also impinges on the development of that system. The desire to control communications helps explain why only 23 percent of all urban families and only 7 percent of all rural families have their own phones in the Soviet Union.[23] This forces most Soviet citizens to make their long-distance phone calls in a public booth, often in the local post office. Because of the limited facilities available, those who want to make long-distance phone calls must often place calls as much as a day in advance. This creates inconveniences—and makes it considerably more difficult to plot subversion. The restricting of the number of phones in this manner means, however, that a good way to track down those in power is to find out who has phones. That accounts in part for why Soviet phone books are seldom printed and all but impossible to find.

The lack of phones and phone books epitomizes the pitfalls that mark the Soviet path to the new high technology. The concern for secrecy is certainly not the only reason for the poor phone system. The cost and technology involved are also responsible. Yet, the poor quality of the phone system suggests how much the concern for secrecy impedes any effort to nurture the culture associated with the new high technology.

Altering such policies will not be easy, particularly the concern for secrecy and the distrust of nonconformity. But at least Gorbachev seems to be aware of the need for change. His campaign for *glasnost'*, for example, is a direct assault on the Soviet secrecy fetish, although technology secrets are still treated as sacrosanct. Equally important, Gorbachev has apparently come to realize how conterproductive for technology and innovation the Soviet treatment of its intellectuals has been. The Soviet Union not only demands conformity and discipline, it treats dissidents with contempt; political dissidents in particular are frequently imprisoned or exiled. It is almost as if a CIA mole had infiltrated the Politburo and sought to deny the Soviet Union the use of some of its most creative and imaginative minds. What could be more destructive to the Soviet Union and beneficial to the West than for the Soviet Union to send some of its most brilliant minds into exile, whether to Siberia and Gorky or Tel Aviv, New York, Vermont, or Boston? By adhering to such short-sighted policies, Moscow has enriched our culture, laboratories, and classrooms while depriving its own. Even those creative figures who were not moved physically have often exiled themselves mentally in protest against the Soviet regime.

Soviet thought control seemed to work in the early stages of industrialization, when coercion and compliance could ensure economic development and even some innovation. But Gorbachev has apparently come to realize that such a policy is inappropriate in the age of high technology. To move ahead today —or even to keep up technologically—society must foster openness, originality, and unconventional thought. The problem, Moscow has discovered, is that it is hard to stimulate creativity in the laboratory and factory while suppressing creativity elsewhere in society.

That seems in large part to account for Gorbachev's personal telephone call to Dr. Sakharov and Gorbachev's subsequent invitation to "return to work for the public good." It is also why the great director, Yuri Lyubimov, has been promised that he would have artistic freedom if he returned from the United States to resume direction of the Taganka Theater in Moscow.

IV

Not all Soviet life is ill suited for the high-technology culture. The military and space sectors have done quite well. Soviet accomplishments in space show that Soviet scientists can be imaginative and productive. They have frequently led the way in space and weaponry. But thanks to the release of secret documents detailing the importance of Western technology (particularly that obtained through espionage) to the Soviet military and space programs, we now know that the Soviet Union also relied extensively on outside help.[24] Using documents obtained by French intelligence, a Pentagon/CIA study details how the Soviets seek specific processes and items from specific firms in order to incorporate them in their own industry for military purposes.[25] As examples, the report cites the Soviet acquisition of fiber-optic systems, an infrared radiometer, and documents on fire control radar and ballistic missiles.[26] Nevertheless, we would be deluding ourselves if we thought that the Soviets were incapable of impressive scientific and technological achievements. Unfortunately for the civilian sector, though, most of their accomplishments are limited to the military and space sectors.

It is almost as if the Soviets had a classical dual economy, the kind we generally associate with developing countries. In the Soviet Union, however, it is the civilian sector that tends to be backward and the military sector that is more akin to the advanced economic sectors found elsewhere. Soviet leaders assign to the military and space sectors the best skilled personnel, raw materials, and equipment. The leftovers more often than not find their way to the civilian sector. At a Russian Research Center seminar at Harvard University, Anatol Fedoseyev, who before his defection to the United States headed an important magnetron laboratory in the Soviet Union, described how the civilian work performed in his institute compared to the military work done there.[27] In contrast to his military operation, which provided the radar facilities for the ABM (antiballistic missile system) installed around Moscow, the civilian work concentrated on the production of ice skates and electric grills. The manager of the civilian shop earned a salary one-half that which Fedoseyev earned for working in the military sector. It was also common practice to send the castoffs from the military sector (manpower, raw materials, and output) to the civilian shops. Since there are usually very few products or processes spun off to the civilian sector from the priority sectors, spin-offs from military and space technology are much less common in the Soviet Union than in the United States.

There are exceptions to the general rule. Some civilian research institutes, like the Paton Institute in Kiev, appear to have had no trouble in keeping abreast of and often leading the world in welding technology. Metallurgy and welding have tended to be priority sectors in the Soviet Union. Because the work at the Paton Institute has been outstanding, the institute has been able to sell licenses for many of its processes throughout the world.[28] Those laboratory directors like Boris Y. Paton and Vladimir Deryagin, who works on diamond coating at the Institute of Physical Chemistry in Moscow, are successful because they usually have access to most of the equipment they need, even that which must be imported.[29] This normally makes it possible for them to go beyond theoretical work, where generally the brain and the blackboard are the only instruments available for research, to the area of experimental research where they can actually experiment with products.

It is hard to understand why successful research institutes like Paton are so few in number. Some émigré scientists from the Soviet Union explain that a few Soviet institutes are able to go beyond the confines of the blackboard because they have charismatic directors like the academician Paton. They are not only good scientists in their own right but also good politicians with administrative clout. If need be, they can even gain access to hard currency. All of this enables them to stock their laboratories with the human and material resources that so many others lack and that they must have if they are to test their creativity.

The creativity of the work done at the Paton Institute should be reassuring to Soviet leaders. Institutes like Paton demonstrate that, under the proper leadership and with the proper resources, the Soviet Union can produce cutting-edge research and products. However, it must be noted that, except for their work in diamond coating, those institutes where the Soviets do world-class work are for the most part not in fields of high technology. Paton, after all, deals with metallurgy and welding, where technology changes at a relatively slow pace.

The Soviet Union may have to settle for leadership in less advanced fields. Certainly not everyone, even in the United States or, for that matter, in Japan, can achieve world leadership in integrated circuitry and computers. Moreover, as long as the Soviet Union remains rich in resources like petroleum and natural gas, it can afford to buy or if need be steal somebody else's technology. Indeed, with piecemeal economic reform, the Soviets can probably even anticipate relatively moderate economic growth. However, this growth will most probably be limited to the domain of the old technology, which even by Soviet standards leaves much to be desired.

Some economists have even argued that it is wiser to let others do the development work. As Alexander Gerschenkron noted, there are advantages to being industrially backward.[30] Let someone else make the costly mistakes that come with innovation, then import the latest technology and leapfrog ahead. That seemed to work in an era when technological changes came slowly and generated less change than the computer and microprocessor industries do. But given how the new fast-moving technologies complement one another, it is dangerous to fall too far behind. The Soviet Union runs a danger of becoming caught in what might be called a "systems trap": it is as if the rest of the world had accommodated itself to an AC electrical system while the Soviets were still on DC. Conversion to the AC system requires a complete overhaul, not just the installation of a few AC appliances. The "systems trap" helps explain why the Soviets have had a hard time keeping up with the computer information revolution. Computer use and mastery works best when computers are interactive—that is, when they communicate with one another. But such interaction requires a good communications system, particularly via telephone lines. In turn, an advanced telephone and communications system requires the extensive use of computers in the servicing of that network. But, as we have just seen, neither the computer nor the telephone has flourished in the Soviet environment. Since neither has been properly updated, it is now difficult to bring in one advanced component, because it will be incompatible with the rest of the system. Thus, for either to work, the Soviets must update both their telephones and computers simultaneously, not an easy task.

The same "systems trap" helps explain the Soviet lag in developing a copier industry. Copiers in the Soviet Union are limited in number. Ralph Land of the Rank Xerox Corporation in London estimates that as of 1986 the Soviet Union had only about 50,000 installed copying machines. For those who have looked for and had difficulty finding any, that might seem like a large number, but it is small relative to world production—which in 1987, Land expects, will reach three million units a year. Not only are Soviet copiers limited in number; they are almost all of an early vintage; they are largely mechanically operated, containing few if any of the electronic components that now govern the operation of modern-day copying systems.

These mechanical machines serve Soviet short-run needs very well, because repairs can be made by nonelectronic engineers. However, their dominance means that very few engineers are being trained to deal with machinery with electronic components, and the Soviet Union will probably continue to lag behind in the creation of the support systems for such equipment that exist elsewhere in the world.

There are even those in the CIA who suggest that, in some areas of technological development, the Soviet Union may have fallen too far behind to escape this trap. The Pentagon/CIA study referred to earlier offers a fascinating aside: it suggests that, with time and the explosion of advanced technology, the Soviets may fall so far behind that they will not even be able to rely on reverse engineering. "The USSR's practice of reverse-engineering however may soon run into problems. As US and Japanese ICs [integrated circuits] become more complex, reverse-engineering will require: (A) tracking hundreds of thousands of connections; (B) understanding how they all fit together; (C) mastering the complex processing steps used in production. Thus copying such circuits will require not only much more sophisticated Western equipment but also much more time to duplicate each circuit, causing their overall microelectronics gap with the West to widen."[31]

Of course, it is dangerous to argue that, once in a trap, the Soviets will not be able to escape. After all, several East Asian countries seem to have brought themselves into the microelectronic age with astonishing speed. Admittedly, they were helped with foreign licenses and investment. Without wishing to succumb to too many stereotypes, we can add that the Confucian oriented cultures that stress study, hard work, and diligence may be particularly suited to doing the fine detail work required in microelectronics.

Whatever the explanation, there is no doubt that the Soviet Union will have a difficult time catching up to the rest of the high-technology world. Indeed, its strength seems to lie in the opposite direction. In Marxist terms, it is almost as if the Soviet system and the central plan had become fetters, holding back the Soviet entrance into the high-technology age. As we saw earlier, the Soviet Union's strength has always been in its ability to mobilize large amounts of capital in an economically poor or backward environment year after year, and to invest that capital in basic industries like steel mills and machine tool factories. This worked well for decades because technology was so stable. In fact, as we shall see in Chapter 5, the Soviets have considered "obsolescence" to be an artificial creation of the capitalist world. Foreign businessmen have been struck by the fact that the Soviets use imported equipment as much as two or three times longer than Western managers operate similar equipment. In effect, Soviet managers use one blueprint over and over again. As a number of Soviet economists have acknowledged, this was the essence of the Soviet central-planning system.[32]

Although in Marxist terms the mode of production has changed, the Soviet system has so far not come to grips with the changing pace of technological innovations and services. The failure to adjust has consequences that go beyond purely economic considerations. They also affect the military sphere. Such concerns were seemingly reflected in a May 1984 interview given by the then chief of staff, Nikolai Ogarkov. Quoting Friedrich Engels, Ogarkov pointed out that "nothing is as dependent on economic conditions as an army and navy. Armaments, personnel, organization, tactics, and strategy depend above all on the stage of production achieved at the given moment and on the means of communication. . . . Technological successes, just as soon as they have become applicable and have actually been applied to military affairs, at once—almost forcibly and often against the will of the military command— cause changes and even revolutions in methods of warfare."[33]

Ogarkov went on to note that "during the postwar years, several generations of weapons systems and military hardware have succeeded one another." Moreover, "rapid changes in the development of conventional weapons and the appearance in developed countries of automated reconnaissance-and-strike complexes, long-range, high-precision, remotely controlled weapons, pilotless aircraft, and qualitatively new electronic controls systems are making many types of armaments global and are making it possible to increase sharply (by at least ten times) the strike force of conventional weapons, bringing it close, as it were, to the effectiveness of weapons of mass destruction." Finally, "the rapid development of science and technology in recent years is creating realistic prerequisites for the appearance in the near future of even more destructive and heretofore unknown types of weapons based on new physical principles. Work on these new types of weapons is under way in a number of countries—the United States, for example. Their creation is a reality of the very near future, and it would be a serious mistake not to take this into account right now."

In September, a few months after he gave that interview, Ogarkov was dismissed as chief of staff. There is reason to suspect that his outspoken criticism of Soviet technology for not providing up-to-date weaponry was implicit criticism of the Soviet Politburo for allowing such a situation to develop and that it consequently was an important factor in his dismissal.

One way in which the Soviets might be able to cope with their inability to master the new high technology is to rely on imports of foreign technology. As we shall see in the next chapter, however, without meaningful economic reform, the Soviet Union may be unable to absorb the full benefits of those imports. In other words, the Soviet Union may need economic reform not only to move its own economy ahead but just to utilize effectively the technology that it wants to obtain from others.

5

The Transfer of Technology to the Soviet Union

Given the problems the Soviet Union has had keeping up with technological developments in the rest of the world, it is only natural that it should decide to seek technology from others. Building on the work of others is a universal practice. What is significant about imported technology, however, is not so much that it is utilized but how it is utilized. Do the Soviets use that technology as well as other importers do? How quickly, if at all, is the technology diffused through the system, and is it enhanced in any way?

To obtain answers to such questions, I interviewed Western businessmen who have sold machinery and technology to the U.S.S.R. Their sense about how the Soviets use foreign technology provides insight into how the Soviet economy deals with more sophisticated technologies, which it must do if it is to be revitalized and reformed. An analysis of their views also helps us understand how machinery of all kinds, domestic as well as foreign, is used in the Soviet Union. As we shall see, the answers to the questionnaire revealed some unanticipated paradoxes. Addressing those paradoxes will give us a slightly different perspective on the problems the Soviets will have to resolve.

I

Sovietologists, as we noted, often call the Soviet economy a dual economy. One sector, particularly aviation and most of the military, is highly advanced, while the other, which includes consumer goods and services, is backward and unsophisticated. As I began interviewing businessmen about technology transfer, I quickly came to the conclusion that a somewhat similar dualism should be used to describe the way in which Soviet industry utilizes imported technology. For example, it is clear that Soviet military industry uses the foreign technology it acquires with relative efficiency. That in large part explains why the Department of Defense, the Department of Commerce, and the U.S. Customs Service devote a good portion of their time these days to trying to curb the flow of American high technology to the U.S.S.R. Although the vigilance of some Pentagon officials is often more akin to misplaced zealotry, particularly when many other countries have begun to produce and sell some of the same equipment, there is little doubt that the Soviets have mounted a massive campaign to acquire advanced American technology by hook or by crook, the latter method illustrated by the recent arrests of more than a score of smugglers and spies caught in the act.

Many of the American-made computers and precision instruments destined for the Soviet Union have been confiscated here or in European airports, sometimes moments before they were to be shipped east. Nevertheless, enough equipment has slipped through to permit what some authorities claim is a noticeable enhancement of Soviet military capabilities. Since there are few firsthand reports about the use of Western technology in Soviet military factories, we cannot say for sure just how effectively this equipment has been used, but we do know, for example, that the improved targeting of Soviet missiles followed the acquisition by the Soviets of American-made precision ball-bearing manufacturing equipment. Similarly, soon after the Soviets purchased highly sophisticated machining devices from the Italians, these machines ended up at a large Soviet factory, which immediately thereafter began to produce a brand-new Soviet tank.

Yet, however impressive the Soviet military industry has been in assimilating the Western technology it has bought, borrowed, or stolen, there are nonetheless indications that other important Soviet officials have serious doubts about the value of all the Western technology they have imported.[1] These officials think that it may even be counterproductive. Anatolii Aleksandrov, until late 1986 the president of the Soviet Academy of Sciences, has said, "The blind copying of the latest scientific and technical ideas (or frequently what was the latest) is often what leads to our falling behind."[2] He goes on to complain that imported technology is used badly but that it must be paid for with the export of exhaustible deposits of oil and gas.

It is hard to justify such imports when it is revealed that they are not being used efficiently. At one point, the Ministry of Ferrous Metallurgy had some 1.5 billion rubles worth of imported equipment sitting in crates uninstalled.[3] The Ministry of Petroleum Refinery had 845 million rubles worth of uninstalled imports, along with a tire plant worth 100 million rubles, and the Ministry of Power and Electrification had 40,000 pieces of uninstalled equipment worth 700 million rubles. (See Illustration 1.) Moreover, the Ministry of the Chemical Industry had hundreds of millions of rubles worth of uninstalled equipment. Not all of this uninstalled equipment was imported, but enough of it was that it caused deep concern.[4]

In addition, by importing machinery instead of producing it domestically, several critics argue, Soviet enterprises are denied the research and development support they would otherwise have. What makes this even more distressing, according to Aleksandrov, is that domestically produced equipment is frequently superior to the foreign, imported equipment. Similar thoughts are expressed in an article fittingly entitled "The Hypnosis of Foreign Trademarks."[5] Leonid Brezhnev questioned the reflex action of Soviet managers who the minute they en-

ILLUSTRATION 1

"These imported machines are very expensive. Why aren't they being used?" "They are already obsolete. We want newer equipment."

From *Mushtum* (Tashkent), no. 24, 1985, p. 7. (Courtesy of David Powell)

counter a problem instinctively cry, "Buy foreign technology!" "We must examine," he said, "why we sometimes forget our priorities and spend large sums of money to purchase equipment and technology from foreign countries that we are fully capable of producing ourselves and often at a higher quality."[6] Even Gorbachev has expressed his skepticism. In a speech to the January 1987 Plenum of the Central Committee, he complained, "Purchases of equipment and many other commodities on the capitalist market were excessive and certainly not always justified."

The difference between the Pentagon and the Aleksandrov-Gorbacheve-Brezhnev-reactions may be due to the fact that the Pentagon officials were focusing primarily on halting technology intended for military purposes, whereas Aleksandrov, Brezhnev, and Gorbachev were addressing themselves primarily to nonmilitary activity. Yet, there is a paradox here. At a time when illegal Soviet efforts to obtain Western technology are as intense as ever, some Soviet officials are questioning their overreliance on Western technology.

This questioning of the wisdom of importing so much foreign technology seems to be more than an intellectual exercise. Soviet trade statistics indicate a drop in Western and Japanese machinery imports by the Soviets in at least 1977, 1979, 1980, 1981, 1984, and 1985. While some of these cutbacks were necessitated by the diversion of hard currency for the purchase of grain, the decline is probably also a reflection of the Soviet officials' disappointment with the utilization of Western equipment. In any event, the more skeptical tone of the 1980s marks quite a change from the enthusiastic expectations that Alexei Kosygin, then prime minister, expressed in April 1966 when he concluded, "It is more profitable for us in many cases to buy foreign licenses than to try to work out this or that problem by ourselves."[7]

II

What accounts for such vastly different attitudes toward the value of technology imported into the U.S.S.R.? My survey of a group of Western and Japanese businessmen about how the Soviets use the equipment they buy from the noncommunist world helps explain the change in attitude. The sample was not scientifically designed. Most of those contacted were people I met in the course of past research on Soviet foreign trade or businessmen who have participated in the programs put on by Harvard's Russian Research Center. Normally, many businessmen are reluctant to discuss such matters, because it could jeopardize future trade activities. But because of our past relationships, most of them were willing to share their experience, provided they were not cited directly. A surprisingly large number of these businessmen have had a chance to see the equipment they exported in operation on-site. Almost all of what they saw was being used for nonmilitary purposes. They discussed successful as well as unsuccessful utilization, but their observations confirm that there may be good reason for the Soviet disappointment with Western equipment.

A large majority of the nearly fifty American, Japanese, and West European businessmen interviewed indicated that they were initially stunned to discover how poorly their equipment was being utilized. There are major exceptions to this in the military and other priority sectors, whose uniqueness demonstrates the dual nature of the Soviet economy. However, disappointing as the productivity of this foreign equipment in the civilian sector may be, more often than not, the imported machinery tended ultimately to be more productive than the domestically made machinery. Yet, in most civilian industries, the businessmen interviewed reported, the Soviet use of foreign technology was frequently only on a par with how managers in non-Asian developing countries use that same technology.

The troubles begin at the negotiating stage. Negotiations take an average of two to four times longer than they would in the West. Much of the difficulty arises because until 1987 the Soviet Ministry of Foreign Trade had monopoly control of all trade with the outside world. As we noted in Chapter 3, approximately twenty ministries and close to seventy enterprises were authorized, as of January 1987, to deal directly with foreign buyers and sellers. In the past, most analysts stressed how this monopoly worked to the Soviet advantage by allowing the Soviet Union to play off one potential buyer or seller against competing buyers and sellers, as happened in 1972 when Soviet grain dealers managed to buy large quantities of grain at relatively low prices. The mirror side, however, is that this monopoly was also an enormous disadvantage when the purchase was not a commodity or a standardized machine but a complicated industrial package. Then the monopoly became a bottleneck.

Since the orders for virtually all Soviet imports and exports had to pass through the Ministry of Foreign Trade, the traffic jam was enormous. Even now, however, it is unclear how much the traffic jam has been reduced. Very few foreign trade officials were or are prepared or allowed to show much initiative. And when they do, it may be in response to an illegal payoff in a foreign bank account.[8] It was just such a temptation that led to the firing and jailing in January 1986 of Vladimir Sushkov, who was once the powerful deputy minister of foreign trade as well as the cochairman of the U.S. and U.S.S.R. Trade and Economic Council. To ward off such temptations, extra controls and checks have often been instituted, and that in turn encumbers the process. One English exporter reported that before his contract could be signed, eighteen Soviet officials had to signal their assent. Another Western seller had heard that as recently as 1985 a deputy prime minister insisted on signing all major import orders for all ministries. This is presumably a result of the late Premier Alexei Kosygin's insistence on obtaining performance guarantees from Western manufacturers. According to several accounts, Kosygin was so disappointed with the performance of some imported equipment that for a time he refused to authorize any purchases without such assurances, a refusal that caused additional negotiating delays.

The process is made all the more cumbersome because when the Ministry of Foreign Trade is involved, it is not the ultimate user but only a middleman. Inevitably, the industrial enterprise, the ultimate user, tends to have interests that diverge from those of the Ministry of Foreign Trade. Whereas the ministry worries about hoarding its hard currency, the enterprise treats hard currency as if it were a free good. Since until recently most enterprises have not been allowed to keep the hard currency they earn, or to buy hard currency for the rubles they earn, it often appears that bureaucratic and political considerations are as important in determining the allocation of hard currency as economic calculations. Undoubtedly, the political clout of the late minister of the chemical industry, Leonid Kostandov, helps to explain why his ministry seemed to have an unusually large claim in the share of hard-currency imports. Whereas the chemical industry shares about 8 percent of the Soviet Union's total industrial investment, it has accounted for about 25 percent of all the machinery imported from the hard-currency bloc.[9] Given the Soviet Union's lack of a strong chemical machinery industry, it makes sense to turn to the West for a large share of the new chemical equipment. But the same can be said of many industries. There seems to be little doubt that Kostandov's importance in the Soviet political hierarchy played a critical part in his getting access to hard currency.

Given the nature of the Soviet system and the inconvertibility of the ruble, when Kostandov or any Soviet enterprise obtained hard currency, at least in the past, the ministry or enterprise was in effect spending somebody else's money. Under the circumstances, the enterprise might just as well ask for the most elaborate equipment or factory it could find. For example, in shopping for drilling equipment for the construction of a railroad tunnel in Siberia, the Soviet buyer insisted on purchasing the most sophisticated models available. They demanded, among other features, that the equipment be able to tell the Soviet users the content of the material being drilled. The Western manufacturer suggested that the Soviet contractors buy something simpler. As the exporter put it when I interviewed him, "If they got such a machine, they wouldn't know what to do with all this information."

This propensity to buy the largest and most elaborate equipment available could be called "the extra-large carriage" syndrome. When visiting offices in poor developing countries (and in the Soviet Union as well), I find more often than not that the typewriters they use have an extra-large carriage and several other exotic features. The extra width is almost never used, but there is always the chance it might be, and, in any case, a large carriage typewriter makes the office look more impressive than does a normal typewriter. In the same fashion, industrial equipment orders in the Soviet Union, as well as in the Third World, emphasize the large and impressive. This tendency, referred to earlier, which the Russians call "gigantomania," explains the practice, not unique to the Soviet Union, of ordering impressive banks of industrial robots, which, as the academician Aganbegian has pointed out, may often lead to higher not lower production costs.[10] One respondent observed, "Soviet importers overspecify and underutilize."

While the enterprise is busy seeking ever more impressive and sophisticated equipment, the Ministry of Foreign Trade is bargaining with foreign exporters for a 10 percent discount in price, so that the hard currency it has can be spread around to a larger number of importers. Not surprisingly, their diverging goals necessitate the frequent resubmission of bids to reflect the ever-changing specifications. The need to have two sets of negotiations, East-West and East-East, prolongs the process. Furthermore, until Gorbachev began to complain about the resulting waste, officials in the Ministry of Foreign Trade showed little sense of urgency. One respondent reported how, after several recalculations to resolve differences between the industrial ministry and the Ministry of Foreign Trade, he warned the Soviet negotiators that unless they came to a decision quickly, they would lose a whole year's time. This project involved drilling offshore in frigid waters, and the drilling teams could operate only during the four months of June to September. If they were not ready to move in May, they would lose the whole season and have to wait until the following year. The Soviet officials, with what seemed to be a sense of mischievous pride, responded by urging calm and pointing out to the prospective capitalist exporters that in the Soviet Union "time is not money."

Whether they acknowledge it or not, delays can be very costly, particularly when it comes to importing high technology. Given that the life cycle of today's high technology is only two to three years, that means that it will be difficult for the Soviets to avail themselves of state-of-the-art technology. One of my interviewees reported that, after three years of inconclusive negotiations, he finally told his East European counterparts that while he had originally submitted specifications for the sale of a state-of-the-art factory, he felt duty-bound to report that now, given the delay, his specifications no longer represented state-of-the-art technology. This may explain why the recent president of the Soviet Academy of Sciences, Aleksandrov, takes such a strong stand against the importing of Western technology. "By the time we buy it and put it into operation," he has said, "it has already lost its leading edge."[11] The so-called advantage that the Soviet Union has claimed for its foreign trade monopoly may turn out to be a disadvantage, particularly when it comes to buying complex machines.

Aleksandrov's frustration reflects not only the delays involved in negotiating but also those stemming from the subsequent installation of the equipment. The respondents to my questionnaire reported that it takes the Soviets two to six times longer to complete an installation than it would take in the West. There were many reasons for this. Western exporters complained that even though the purchase was made by a state agency operating in what is advertised as a planned economy, they found that shipments were often held up by Soviet customs officials. In addition, because of an inadequate or absent infrastructure and nonexistent storage facilities, construction delays were the norm. One executive of an American chemical corporation described the Soviet installation of a large chemical reactor they had shipped. In the capitalist world, to be doubly sure there would be no accident, the installer would use two cranes to move the reactor. Because of the shortage of equipment, the Soviets could use only one; in the moving process, the strain was too much, and so the installers dropped and damaged the reactor.

Some exporters depict the Soviet Union as a misplanned, not a planned, economy. One of them reported that a milk plant was installed in an area where there was a shortage of cows; both European and American chemical company executives complained that the petrochemical plants they installed in Tomsk and Omsk were unable to operate because raw materials were not readily available there. Another recalled that shortly after the Soviets publicly announced they had begun to produce digital watches, he received an emergency phone call requesting a rush shipment of thousands of batteries. Apparently, the Soviet producers had not arranged to produce or import the batteries needed to run the digital watches. Equally distressing, because of the failure to provide adequate storage, radar equipment and computers are often left in the open for months at a time.

The premature arrival of imported equipment is a perennial problem because of the Soviet penchant for insisting on rigid contract delivery dates in their formal agreements. Failure to deliver will cost the shippers substantial penalties. My interviewees complained that these schedules are adhered to whether or not the factory sites have been properly prepared. One French exporter shipped all the equipment as scheduled, but it was left outside in its shipping containers for three years. He estimated that, given the rate of construction, it will be left outdoors in the Russian winter for another three years. (See Illustration 2.) Similar tales are recounted in the Soviet press. In one instance, 136 million rubles worth of electronic equipment had to be stored outside because of the unavailability of a warehouse or a completed factory building.[12] In other instances, more than one Western businessman told of how even when a building had been erected in advance, faulty coordination had resulted in its being too small for the machinery it was intended to house. That happened with the foundry at the Kama River Truck Plant, and it has happened elsewhere as well.[13]

Most of those interviewed reported that Soviet manning levels were excessive compared with similar situations in the West. In those instances where manning requirements were predetermined and thereby limited by machinery-operating requirements, the Soviets still showed their penchant for redundancy and employed excessive numbers of auxiliary personnel. Since, as we saw, the bonuses available to the enterprise managers are a function of the size of the work force, it is only natural for managers to seek to overstaff their operations, even if the equipment they use is imported and even if it is designed to use as little labor as possible.

ILLUSTRATION 2

"But where is the equipment that was sent to us?" "Which year are you talking about?"

From *Ekonomicheskaia gazeta*, January 1986, no. 5, p. 11.

Especially perplexing to several exporters was what happened after the Soviets sent specialists overseas to be trained on the equipment before it was imported. More often than not, after their training these people were assigned elsewhere and were never seen working on the equipment for which they had been trained. This was not a universal practice, but at least four of the respondents complained of this misuse of trained personnel. (Those who sell to China and offer to train Chinese specialists report they often face a similar disappearing act.)

Given how poorly the Soviets normally maintain their own, domestically produced equipment, it comes as no surprise to learn that the frequency and duration of breakdowns of imported machinery was greater than in the West. Several businessmen criticized the lack of preventive maintenance. They were struck by the lack, despite warnings, of regular lubrication, and that took a heavy toll on the machinery, particularly on ball bearings. Anticipating such behavior, Soviet officials almost always try to overcompensate by insisting that as much as 25 percent of an order for imported equipment goes for spare parts. This is necessary because, as one respondent observed, a three-year supply of spare parts is exhausted in eighteen months. But it turns out that this is not as large a supply as it might appear, since each importer normally insists on building up his own set of spares. It is too risky to rely on help from others who might be using the same machine. Moreover, in the absence of a central supply house for imported parts, overlapping orders are unavoidable. This makes it necessary to submit numerous small requests for hard currency for additional spare parts. These requests must pass through the bureaucracy, with all its attendant paperwork and delay.

The solution, it would seem, is to build a central supply house. This has been suggested to Soviet authorities by some Western businessmen, but, as one exporter explained, Soviet officials refuse to authorize such a facility because they fear that any parts stored by such a central supply house would immediately disappear into the black market. For that matter, even when a Soviet importer thinks he has redundant stocks of spare parts, it often happens that not only the operating equipment but also the maintenance equipment is cannibalized. Not surprisingly, one respondent insisted that it was better when the Soviets did not repair the imported equipment at all. As he put it, "The more they fix our machinery, the more it breaks down."

The quality of the goods produced by imported machinery has generally been below world standards. In some instances, this has come as a bit of a surprise because to the extent some of these processes are automated, there presumably is not much room for human interference. Yet, when asked to compare quality, an operator of a highly automated bottling plant, who has had considerable experience in the Soviet Union, stated that, on a scale of one to a hundred, the Soviet plant operator earned a sixty to seventy quality rating, compared with a ninety-eight for the United States. A supplier of a glass-manufacturing plant, also highly automated, rated the Soviets a trifle higher, at seventy-five, compared with a hundred for the United

States. Where there was less automation, the ratings were lower. Several respondents indicated, however, that after a time productivity did improve, as the Soviets began to learn more about the operation of the equipment. Nevertheless, before too long this increased productivity from learning tends to be offset by more frequent breakdowns associated with an aging installation.

What is particularly striking about the Soviet use of Western equipment is that, with one or two exceptions, the Soviets do not upgrade the product or process they import. In this they are very unlike the Japanese, who have thrived on taking foreign technology and so enhancing it that they very quickly produce a cheaper and often higher-quality product. They then proceed to export that improved product, often back into the home markets of the original producer—especially the United States. This practice is largely a consequence of the stress the Japanese place on export growth rather than on import substitution. Except for some improvements in computer routines, the businessmen interviewed could think of almost no other examples of Soviet product enhancement.

III

On the basis of all that has been said so far, it would be only natural to assume that the service life of imported equipment in the Soviet Union is comparatively brief. But the opposite is true. The most counterintuitive discovery of the survey is that the Soviets continue to operate imported equipment way beyond the period their noncommunist counterparts do. An exporter of copying machines cited one of the more dramatic examples: a copier model that would in the West normally be used to produce about 2 million copies a year and last for five years would in the Soviet Union be kept in operation for several decades and produce 40 to 50 million copies before being discarded.

Virtually everyone interviewed had a similar case to report. One Japanese exporter was shocked to find a fifty-year-old

machine tool still in operation. Computer manufacturers who
normally expect a computer in the United States to be used five
to eight years found fifteen- or even twenty-year-old computers
operating in the Soviet Union or in Eastern Europe. Bottling
equipment that in the United States has an operating life of five
to ten years is likely to be used for fifty years or more in the
Soviet Union. Only oil equipment manufacturers in this sample
reported that American equipment lasted longer than similar
equipment in the Soviet Union. Given that the vast majority of
imported machinery lasts so much longer in the Soviet Union,
it would appear at first glance that technology transfer is not
so inefficient after all.

Yet, before we leave this section, we need to address one
bothersome contradiction. If the Soviets treat their imported
machinery so poorly and if it breaks down so often, how and
why do they keep it in operation so much longer than their
Western counterparts? We will examine the "why" shortly, but
the "how" is relatively simple. As we noted earlier, Soviet
import orders invariably include extraordinary quantities of
spare parts, which almost always seem to be consumed in record time. In other words, imported machinery lasts for inordi-
nately long periods of time despite recurring breakdowns and
long periods of downtime, because Soviet managers devote
large amounts of labor, spare parts, and money to frequent
repairs. No wonder that operating costs of imported equipment
tend to be very much higher in the Soviet Union than they
would be elsewhere.

IV

Thus far, we have concentrated on the poor use of imports.
Yet, some sectors use imported technology relatively well. An
analysis of these exceptions may provide some insight into why
imported technology is used so inefficiently in the rest of the
economy. As was noted above, technology adopted for the
military sector reportedly yields a higher productivity. It also
seems to have a shorter service life. Some high-priority nonmili-

tary projects, such as the gas turbine compressors needed for the Soviet–West German natural-gas pipeline, were also ordered and installed in record time. According to the exporters interviewed, all of this took place in less time than would be required to purchase and install similar equipment in the United States. However, Soviet planners can classify only so many projects as priority. Nonpriority equipment, whether imported or not, tends to be treated badly and inefficiently. This is a natural consequence of the Soviet economic system, with its irrational pattern of economic indicators, which in the civilian sector at least emphasizes quantity of production rather than quality and tolerates rigid and unresponsive prices.

Such a system discourages innovation. Except in priority and military industries, if the manager does try to innovate, he will have to interrupt his existing production operation. As we saw in the preceding chapter, by doing this, he jeopardizes his effort to fulfill his plan. This might mean he will lose his bonus. At the same time, if he does produce something new, state price controls preclude his charging a significantly higher price for his new product, so there would be little reward for his efforts. Not surprisingly, most managers find it too risky to bother experimenting with anything new or to bear the burden of overseeing the installation and integration of Soviet machinery into a functioning assembly line. It is much easier and safer to pass the job of contractor on to someone else.

Since the manager is penalized for innovation, the best way to bring in new technology is to import a complete turnkey operation that will insure not only high-quality equipment but also proven operating experience and installation. A leading Soviet chemist, the academician Nikolai S. Yenikolopov, has said, "Not long ago we were supposed to set up the large-scale production of a reagent for the preservation of silage and in the long run to increase its production significantly. We have our own, good Soviet process for producing this product. But the director of the plant to which this task was assigned is doing his utmost to get us to buy foreign technology. He has his own logic. If Soviet technology is to be employed, one must first design the production facility, erect the buildings, order the equipment, and see to it that everything arrives and is installed. The director has a large plant in operation, one that requires constant attention. A contract with a foreign firm relieves him of many worries, and his chief concern becomes to ensure that the stipulated terms are strictly fulfilled. The fact that foreign exchange is spent and a whole line of Soviet science is lopped off is 'in somebody else's department.' "[14]

Yenikolopov's criticism makes it clear that those who oppose imports reflect more than a simple concern that the imported equipment tends to function at less than its rated capacity. Apparently, many Soviet officials fear that the Soviet Union may find itself dependent on some imported components and thus vulnerable to political and economic pressure. As the chemist Yenikolopov put it, "Do not purchase foreign technology . . . that makes us dependent on foreign reagents and spare parts." Related to this is the concern—shared, as we saw, by the academician Aleksandrov—that by importing technology from overseas, other Soviet factories will be denied the opportunity to build the machinery themselves, which they must do if they are to master the leading edge of technology.[15]

There is also the concern, often justified, that enterprise managers have an irrational belief that a foreign machine is by definition better. (Some Americans have the same irrational feeling about foreign-made products, especially automobiles.) Soviet critics can readily point to several instances where hard currency was spent on imported technology even though equal or superior technology was available at home.[16] It is clear that a serious effort is being made to hold down the reliance on foreign products.

Given this distrust of foreign interaction and the shortage of hard currency, it is not surprising that, compared with other countries, the Soviet Union with only minor exceptions tends to import only a small percentage of its technology.[17] Of course, the Soviet Union is a large country and should be expected to be more self-sufficient than smaller countries. But this underlying desire for autarchy, combined with a persistent dose of paranoia and distrust of foreigners, undoubtedly serves to complicate the productive life of enterprise managers. Moreover, the task of the factory manager is not made easier by the traditional practice of limiting the foreign seller's access to the equipment after installation. For that matter, many sellers are not even allowed to participate in the installation process. Whatever the reason for this policy, it denies Soviet factories the benefits of postinstallation servicing and updating by the manufacturer.

Such ambivalent feelings about imported technology have done little to facilitate the diffusion of this technology to other factories and sectors. Not only do Soviet importers tend to distrust the foreign exporter but, despite protestations to the contrary, Soviet ministries also distrust one another. When one ministry imports a process or machinery, it seldom shares what it buys with other ministries. Indeed, there sometimes seems to be very little sharing among enterprises within the ministry itself. That is another reason why each enterprise wants to have its own inventory of spare parts.

Foreign businessmen are not the only ones to note that the purchaser of imported technology is usually reluctant to share the technology or spare parts. *Izvestiia* has complained that the unwillingness to share leads to needless duplication as well as to stagnation.[18] Rather than build upon what has been purchased, other enterprises seek to obtain their own technology and go off in their own direction.

The fault lies not only with an ambivalent attitude toward imports but also with inadequate economic incentives and poor planning. The Soviets often boast that a communist system facilitates the spread of technology because there are no parochial private interests trying to prevent others from obtaining access to their processes, as there are in capitalist societies. Yet, the Soviets appear to have less technological interaction and sharing than exists in the West. Aganbegian, among others, has complained about the narrow departmental ethic that prevails.[19] Each ministry seeks to be as independent of the other ministries as possible.

This vertical autonomy has proven to be a major obstacle to the realization of the Soviet Union's high-technology aspirations. Much that is referred to as high technology involves the bringing together of very different sectors of industrial activity. One of the best examples is the marrying of computers to machine tools. But in the Soviet Union the production of such products involves two different and autonomous ministries. It is not that the enterprises within each ministry never interact —they do, but not on an ongoing, take-it-for-granted basis. No wonder the Soviet Union lags behind in the development and production of programmable and computerized machine tools. The new Interbranch Scientific and Technical Complexes (MNTK), being coordinated by the Academy of Sciences and referred to in Chapter 3, are an attempt to overcome such standoffishness. While this clearly indicates an awareness of the nature of the problem, it does not seem to be the proper solution, and so far the results have not been all that promising.

The vertical incompatibility of two different ministries also hinders the importation of technology. Let me cite two examples. One foreign company has proposed a joint venture within the Soviet Union that would have the Western company build an office machine factory that produces primarily for the domestic Soviet market. Knowing that the Soviets will not be enthusiastic about a venture that does not earn hard convertible currency through exports, the Western company has proposed that the construction of this office machine factory for the machine-building ministry should be coordinated with a paper-producing factory under the jurisdiction of the pulp and paper ministry. The Western country is willing to take paper as in-kind payment for its profit in the producing of machines. Not surprisingly, the pulp and paper ministry sees nothing for itself in this and therefore is, at this writing, quite opposed to any such arrangement, despite pressure from Gosplan and the Council of Ministers for it to go along with the idea. In a second example, a Western exporter was asked to bid on a turnkey factory project designed to produce another type of office equipment. He told the Soviets he could build them a turnkey plant similar to those already operating in Europe or in the United States, but he warned that this would not be enough to produce a finished product even though a similar turnkey operation in the West would be able to start production. The difference between such a turnkey operation in the West and one in the Soviet Union is that the importer, Minpriborg (the Ministry of Instrument Manufacturing, Automation Equipment, and Control Systems), lacks the plastic extrusion machinery needed for the buttons and accessories on the machine. The turnkey plant would produce everything else, but in the West the plastic buttons and accessories would be produced by a subcontractor, and there is no such facility under Minpriborg's jurisdiction. Although the Soviet Ministry of Aircraft Industry does have such equipment, because of the vertically integrated and self-sufficient nature of Soviet ministries, the two ministries have relatively few dealings with one another. It would actually be easier for the Minpriborg to build its own plastic extrusion factory, but then it would sit idle 360 days of the year because it would produce all that was needed for the copying machines in the remaining five.

V

The Soviets' schizophrenic attitude toward imports—some believing that only imports can solve Soviet economic problems and others that imports have been an important cause of Soviet technological backwardness—has prevented the Soviet Union from benefiting from technological transfer in the same way that other countries have. The Soviet experience is very different from that of the Japanese, who encourage repeat purchases of technology. As Josef Brada has pointed out in a very insightful essay, the Japanese approach tends to put pressure on the initial purchasers to keep up and to develop their own refinements.[20] By contrast, in the Soviet Union there is no such pressure (again a consequence of the absence of market competition), and so Soviet firms are often able to sit back until the next generation of new technology is available in the West.[21]

For example, when it came time to upgrade the Zhiguli-Lada automobile, which is produced at the Italian-built plant in Togliatti, Soviet automobile manufacturers found it necessary once again to call in outside help. For the design they went to Porsche, and for the engineering they went back to Fiat.

That the staffs at the Togliatti plant and the Ministry of Automotive Industry were not able to do their own upgrading must be disappointing to Soviet planners. After all, the justification for spending so much on foreign technology is that it is to be a shortcut to catching up with Western technology. Presumably, the Soviet importer should be able to move ahead at that point, especially the VAZ plant at Togliatti, which, as we saw in Chapter 3, had been singled out as one of the two or three leading enterprises in the Soviet Union and been put on the new reform principles before anyone else. This is not a very promising sign.

VI

We have yet to explain why, even though in most respects the Soviets have not been able to use Western technology at its full potential, the service life of imported equipment from the West tends to be so much longer than that of similar equipment utilized in the West. There are several possible explanations. For example, because Marx had difficulty dealing with the concept of obsolescence, Soviet theoreticians have been similarly uncomfortable. In recent years, Soviet economists have become more accepting of the notion that obsolescence is not just a bourgeois fantasy and that Soviet planners must eventually allow for it; but for the time being, at least, problems remain. Thus, while obsolescence in the U.S.S.R. has, like abortion, been legalized, so to speak, there is still resistance to it. Therefore, unlike the criteria prevalent in the West, the criterion for the continued use of a machine in the Soviet Union is whether it has fallen apart, not whether something more productive or effective is available. (See Illustration 3.) This uneasiness with the idea of obsolescence is compounded by the fact that access to hard currency for imports is dependent as much on political and other noneconomic as on economic considerations. Because the ultimate user can never be sure whether he will be able to import replacement machinery, he had better use what he has as long as he can, even if continued repairs are necessary. That also explains the large sums spent initially on spare parts.

Impressive as the longer service life of Soviet imported equipment may be, its prolonged use is not necessarily beneficial to the economy. There are serious disadvantages to using outmoded equipment, particularly if this equipment is wasteful of inputs. As one respondent phrased it, "It is like the young mechanic who continues to drive a gas-guzzling 1957 Chevy. He makes all the repairs by hand. Since he bought the car at such a cheap price, and since he lacks the large sum of money

ILLUSTRATION 3

"Why are they sending us new technology when the old still works?"

From *Ekonomicheskaia gazeta*, June 1986, no. 25, p. 24.

necessary to make a more expensive purchase, he calculates that it pays him to spend more money on gasoline than to buy a new car." While the continued use of obsolete machinery makes it possible for the individual Soviet factory manager to operate without access to hard currency for machinery imports, on a macro basis such practices waste the Soviet Union's vast quantities of raw materials. The interests of the individual managers and the overall economy diverge because hard currency is allocated arbitrarily, interest charges are applied imperfectly, and the price system underprices raw materials.

Since it is such an important concept and since the Soviets have such a hard time coming to terms with it, we must try to understand how crucial the recognition of obsolescence is to the whole process of economic reform. It goes beyond the inefficient use of imported equipment. Failure to allow for obsolescence also results in the uneconomical use of domestic equipment. Gorbachev and some of his subordinates have expressed particular concern that even though machinery is newly installed, it all too often incorporates outmoded designs and thus continues to build obsolete concepts into the present production process.[22] This means that it will take even longer for the Soviet Union to upgrade its production processes. As the example of the Zhiguli-Lada suggests, the legacy of Marxism affects not only industrial efficiency but also the final consumer product. If the reform is to succeed, the Soviets will somehow have to find a way to cope with the need to upgrade both industrial and consumer products on a timely basis. In this instance, adherence to Marxist doctrine, even if the Soviets have now recognized that the change is needed, has not served the Soviet Union well.

The impact of Marxist theory goes beyond the Soviets' inability to deal properly with obsolescence. It also helps explain why the Soviets maintain their equipment so poorly. Echoing Marxist thinking, they do not, as we saw, consider service functions important. The low status accorded service personnel also helps explain why those sent to the West for training often end up never servicing the equipment they were trained to deal with. Once these service personnel are sent overseas, their status is upgraded and they quickly escape to a post in a research institute or to some other higher position.

Soviet restrictions on normal foreign travel also account in part for the disappearing act of those trained overseas. According to several respondents, the Soviet officials in charge of selecting the trainees frequently decide to choose their friends rather than those who will actually be doing the work. This may be an odd form of tourism, but it often is the only way many Soviet citizens can travel outside the country.

Considering the different approaches to economic activity, it would be unusual if the Soviets were able to use imported machinery as productively as noncommunist purchasers use that equipment. In the noncommunist industrial world, scarcity and profit making are the ruling principles, and equipment is designed accordingly. The supporting infrastructure is designed to supply efficient, timely, and cheap service. In contrast, because communist countries tend to operate as if communism had brought with it an age of abundance, they place a low explicit value on raw materials and capital. Thus, these goods are used inefficiently. Waste may be verbally criticized, but the incentive system actually promotes it. As long as "scarcity" is a dirty word in the Soviet Union, it is hard to see how the Soviets will be able to use Western technology effectively. Because of the difference in value systems, it is only natural that Soviet machinery does not mesh well with Western machinery. Soviet machinery is bulky, and a low priority is allocated to producing spare parts for domestically manufactured equipment. If a Soviet machine breaks down, it may be simpler to ask for a new one. Equipment produced abroad, however, is very expensive because nothing can be replaced without foreign exchange, which explains why, unlike spare parts for domestic equipment, spare parts for imported machinery (bought with scarce hard currency) are such an important part of the initial transaction. The user must buy the spare parts while he has access to hard currency. However, unlike his Soviet counterpart, who generally finds it unrewarding to produce spare parts, the Western manufacturer finds producing and selling spare parts to be very profitable. He is therefore eager to sell them.

VII

While the *difference* between the two systems helps explain varying results in the civilian sector, it may ironically be the *similarity* of the two military systems that explains why the Soviet use of Western technology in the military sector compares much more favorably to American military use of the same technology. In the Soviet Union as well as in the United States, the military sector receives priority. In effect, military and industrial personnel in both countries act as if there were no scarcity in either military system; both operate on something like a cost-plus basis.

When it comes to industries producing for the military in the United States, as in the Soviet Union, there is normally little need to worry about the discipline of the market. Cost-plus, cost overruns, and the general laxness that the Pentagon seems to have tolerated, if not encouraged, have enabled military producers to charge prices that would never be tolerated in the commerical sectors. The stories about twelve-cent Allen wrenches being sold for $9,609 by General Dynamics and about alignment pins that cost $91 to produce being sold for $9,379 are unfortunately all too common.[23]

Occasionally, the manufacturers justify their higher cost on the basis that some of their products are one-of-a-kind replacements. Typically, however, such costs are the result of the unrestricted charges the military producers are allowed to make. In testimony before Congress, one Pentagon critic reported that the Department of Defense allows military contractors to charge $95 to $3,000 or more per "standard hour" of engineering work—work that in the civilian sector would cost only $35 an hour.[24] Management may then add on an extra $144 in "management overhead" to the military sector.

Confirming such abuses, the chairman of the board of a large manufacturer located in the Boston area explained to me that one of his most important duties was to keep his managers working on military orders away from his managers working in the civilian market. He feared that if exposed to the "no-scarcity ways" of his military managers, his civilian managers would quickly go bankrupt.

Just as in the American military industry, cost considerations are often secondary in Soviet military production. There is considerable evidence that the Soviet military also has its luxury-class ashtrays and coffeepots, not to mention the even more important, cost-plus military hardware. Soviet equipment costs, like those in Soviet civilian industry and those in the American military, are all but impossible to contain and compare because of the absence of any "efficiency" standard.

This priority cost-plus mentality in the Soviet military sector has led to better quality than is found in the Soviet civilian sector, where production standards are lax and resource allocation not important. Yet, there is evidence to suggest that the military sector may be suffering from some of the same maladies as the civilian sector. Thus, while the Soviets have periodically outdone the United States in space and in military hardware, the quality and sophistication of the work suffers by comparison. In a revealing analysis, Louis Lavoie, a military systems analyst at Honeywell, points out that as of December 1982, even though the Soviet Union had launched 2,069 Sputniks into space, compared with only 997 satellites for the United States, by mid-1983 only 5 percent, or 103, of the Soviet satellites were still in orbit compared with 18 percent, or 179, of the American ones.[25] Thus, while imported technology in the Soviet military sector is generally put to better use than it is in the Soviet civilian sector, even there it does not normally match the production in the American military sector, despite some rather intriguing similarities in the way the two military sectors operate and despite Defense Department jitters about the capabilities of Soviet military technology.

VIII

Although in extreme cases, the technology imported from the West may not have functioned at all, more often than not it seems to have outperformed Soviet technology. Econometric studies of the impact of machinery imported from the West are inconclusive.[26] Some of the earlier studies suggested that imported equipment made possible a significant increase in productivity, but more recent work disputes those earlier findings. To say the least, this makes it difficult to reach any definitive conclusions.

Whatever the econometric findings, the Western businessmen I surveyed surprisingly tended to agree that imported technology achieves only about two-thirds of the productivity that the same equipment produces in the capitalist world. But, as we noted earlier, this two-thirds often represents an increase in output and quality over comparable Soviet equipment. That suggests that, despite lost opportunities, importing may nonetheless help improve Soviet productivity and help the Soviets master new technologies. However, as long as scarcity is not recognized as a guiding concept, it is hard to see how the Soviets can import large enough quantities of Western technology and install it fast enough to keep abreast of the outside world.

Aware of the problem, some Soviet officials have begun to argue that if Soviet managers are unable on their own to upgrade their imported machinery, the Soviets should reverse a long-standing policy and allow the creation of joint ventures with foreigners. Theoretically, if there is a true joint venture and true interaction, the foreign partner will seek to transplant Western technological innovation to the Soviet Union on a continuing basis. However, the legalizing of joint ventures would represent a bold ideological departure. It would be a throwback to the 1920s, when foreign investors like Armand Hammer and W. Averell Harriman had manufacturing and mining concessions on Soviet territory. Stalin put an end to such activities in the late 1920s, and until 1986 there was considerable opposition to overturning that decision. The Bendix Corporation offered to enter into a joint venture on Soviet territory in the 1970s to manufacture automotive parts. After considerable discussion in the Politburo itself, the proposal was rejected. More recently, however, provoked in part by what the Hungarians and the Chinese have done, the Soviets have begun to reconsider. Gorbachev himself, for example, on his trip to Vladivostok in July 1986, indicated that joint ventures with the Japanese were something to be encouraged.[27] The Politburo itself formally approved the concept of joint ventures on August 16, 1986.[28] The intent is to start joint ventures first with countries in Eastern Europe and then gradually to branch out to include countries from the capitalist world. In addition to the Japanese, American, West German, Finnish, and French corporations have also been approached by the Soviets about joining such an arrangement. What exactly joint ventures will mean in the Soviet Union, and whether Western managers will be able to set quality standards, hire and fire, import components, operate outside the formal Soviet planning system, have access to domestic inputs, and repatriate profits in convertible currency, remains to be debated, both in and outside the country. There will be substantial ideological and legal difficulties to settle. Many of the same problems have arisen in Hungary and China, and we will discuss them in greater detail in the next two chapters.

The decision to allow joint ventures, if it is fully implemented, would be a method of upgrading Soviet technology on a continuing basis. It would also be a way for Gorbachev to outflank all the bureaucrats who have been resisting his efforts to reform and restructure the domestic economy from within. Such reasoning may also explain why the Soviet Union, after years of criticism, reversed itself and in 1986 began to express an interest in the workings of the General Agreement on Tariffs and Trade (GATT) and why it created an international economics department in the Ministry of Foreign Affairs and the State Foreign Economic Commission which is headed by a deputy chairman of the Council of Ministers.[29] The decision to break the monopoly of the Ministry of Foreign Trade reflects the same reasoning. If enterprises and ministries are allowed to deal with foreign exporters and importers directly, without the Ministry of Foreign Affairs as an intermediary, many of the shortcomings discussed earlier may be eliminated.

In January 1986, an early version of this chapter was discussed and shown to Soviet authorities, including some who were subsequently assigned by Gorbachev to promote Soviet integration into the Western economic world. There is reason to believe that learning the reactions of Western businessmen to the Soviets' use of Western equipment may have had some influence on the debate. The decision to break up the monopoly of the Ministry of Foreign Trade was also helped by the fact that the longtime minister had retired and that many of his former colleagues had been jailed, fired, retired, or subject to audit to determine if they had resisted the temptation that had seduced so many others. Given that Gorbachev has publicly singled out the Ministry of Foreign Trade for its corruption and "negative processes," there could probably not have been a better time to reorganize the ministry.[30]

As we shall see in our examination of the Hungarian and Chinese experiences, breaking up the monopoly of the Ministry of Foreign Affairs has its advantages, but it can also lead to new problems. For example, if individual enterprises can place their own orders, it will be difficult to ensure that the technology purchased is interactive. Even with the monopoly of the Ministry of Foreign Affairs, the Soviets found that they ended up with over 150 different types of computer systems, most of which were not compatible. Presumably, a planned system should prevent such a thing from happening. There is likely to be even more proliferation without the foreign trade monopoly. Moreover, with ministries and enterprises importing on their own, there is a real danger that in the Soviet Union, as in Hungary and China, the balance-of-trade deficit will soar. Admittedly, despite such risks, all such measures, including joining the International Monetary Fund and the World Bank as well as seeking to move the ruble toward hard-currency convertibility, are essential steps Gorbachev must take if he wants to open the windows of the Soviet economic hothouse and expose it to the competitive winds of the West. More and more Soviet officials and economists are coming to recognize that this is a minimum requirement if the Soviet Union is to develop a more competitive economy, more up-to-date equipment, and more efficient production.

By themselves, such initiatives are a step in the right direction, but hardly enough to make a major difference in the way the Soviet Union copes with high technology or even in how it handles the less advanced technologies it imports. Even with unlimited wherewithal, without a far-reaching domestic reform in the whole economic and social system, the Soviets can hardly hope to integrate the foreign technology rapidly enough to be a competitive force in the world economy. They may not be the only ones to fall behind this way, but it must be disappointing to those who before the age of high technology had always assumed that, at the least, imported technology would provide the Soviets with a critical shortcut.

6

Two Roads to Economic Reform: Hungary and the German Democratic Republic

For those who study the communist world, Hungary has always stood out as an anomaly. Except for a bout of revolutionary fervor in 1956, the Hungarians have managed to come to terms with the geopolitical reality of having a common border with the Soviet Union. More than any other East Europeans, the Hungarians, while accepting their major obligations under the Warsaw Pact, share with their neutral and Western neighbors a better standard of living and a more relaxed political domestic environment.

It is not paradise. The Hungarian police still watch over ideology in the press, and some Hungarians continue to suffer because of their political indiscretion.[1] Yet, despite an occasional crackdown, most Hungarians can travel with relative ease to the West and can be relatively free in their thinking— at least by the standards that prevail among their East European neighbors.

This same sense of openness and experimentation exists in the economy, again by the standards that prevail in Eastern Europe. There is no forgetting that Hungary is a communist country, and the state remains very much in control of the economy, but at the same time remarkable liberties have been taken with some of the traditional institutions normally found in a Soviet-type system. Although there are signs that the Hungarian economy and economic reforms are not as vigorous as they once appeared, most Hungarians seem reasonably comfortable with a flourishing system of private trade and services, foreign joint ventures, a thriving voluntary cooperative system unlike the state-mandated cooperatives in the Soviet Union, and a planning mechanism that is sharply circumscribed. Some of these deviations have been adopted by some of Hungary's neighbors, at least on paper. But no other East European country has moved from theory to practice and adopted so many changes in such a thoroughgoing way.

Unlike the Hungarians, the East Germans continue to emphasize central planning and the traditional Stalinist model. They have made several attempts to reform the model, but basically the East Germans seem much less daring and provocative. They have always allowed a small amount of private trade but have avoided joint ventures with foreign investors and have held to the collective farm and to state ownership in industry.

In this chapter we will see how the two differing approaches of Hungary and the German Democratic Republic provide the Soviet Union with contrasting examples of economic reform. What has been the Soviet reaction to some of the more daring Hungarian initiatives? Alternatively, have the Soviets found the German Democratic Republic's more subtle and sophisticated emphasis on central planning and control more to their liking? As the Soviet leaders look about for possible models will they see anything in either Hungary or the German Democratic Republic that they might try to duplicate?

I

Many Hungarians and political scientists would disagree, but in retrospect the bloody 1956 uprising may have been one of the best things that happened to post–World War II Hungary. It left a widespread feeling that, if at all possible, the people of Hungary must never allow such a thing to happen again. In that spirit, they set themselves the task of making the best out of a bad situation. Consequently, the country emerged from its bloodletting in a more constructive way than almost anyone could have anticipated and has gone on to provide a way of life that, whatever its shortcomings, some consider one of the most desirable available in Eastern Europe.

In a pattern common in the communist world, once János Kádár, along with the Soviet troops, had routed the counter-revolutionary opposition and emerged triumphant, he quickly adopted a more conciliatory stance. Even if the rhetoric did not change, the policies did. Other examples of this more accom-modating stance after a bloody confrontation include Lenin's introduction of the New Economic Policy (NEP) after the Kronstadt rebellion in 1921, the decision to hold meat prices constant after the Novocherkassk riots along the Sea of Azov coast in 1962, efforts to reform the Polish economy after the formation of the Solidarity movement, and, most far-reaching of all, the move toward economic reform in Hungary after the 1956 uprising.

Somewhat facetiously, some specialists on the communist world attribute Hungary's comparatively easy and rapid eco-nomic reforms to the fact that labor leaders in Hungary acted like compromising Mensheviks while those in Poland took a Bolshevik extremist perspective. Certainly, that is how the Hungarians explain their willingness to rally around the state after the revolution. They came to realize that suicidal behavior would help neither them nor Hungary. Henceforth, everyone would have to compromise—no one would have everything he wanted, but, with compromise, all would have at least some-thing. Others, with tongue in cheek, note that Hungary's turn away from central planning and toward private initiative and the market was facilitated by the fact that a relatively large number of the country's economists had left the country for the West, particularly for Great Britain. These economists were thus not around to protest the return of the perniciousness of the market system. Finally, the Soviet ambassador in 1956, Yuri Andropov, who oversaw the bringing in of Soviet troops, subsequently did much to support what was from an ideological point of view a set of heretical reforms.

The intellectual origins of the reform go back at least to the 1950s, when several Hungarian economists pointed out the shortcomings of an overreliance on a central plan and suggested that it might make sense to rely more on market forces.[2] This parallels what was apparently somewhat similar but later thinking in the Soviet Union.[3] But nothing much was done in either the Soviet Union or Hungary until after the revolution, when the Hungarians decided to exercise their own initiative. Then, in late 1956, in an effort to revitalize the economy, the party organized an intellectual study group to suggest changes in the economy. Their ideas were to serve as the framework for many of the subsequent reforms.

Not all reforms were a product of the intellectual discussions. In fact, in the rural areas the peasants did not wait for any official decree; after years of resentment, when the revolution came in 1956, they simply took matters into their own hands. Like the Russian peasants, the Hungarian peasants were forced into collective farms shortly after the Hungarian communists came to power in 1949. Like those in the Soviet Union, the Hungarian peasants also resented having their land taken over by the state. The payments they received for the compulsory deliveries they made to the state often did not cover their costs of production.[4] Taking advantage of the confusion that followed in the wake of the uprising in 1956, large numbers of peasants abandoned the collective farms and resumed their private farming operations. Unfettered by the burdens of the collective farm, they saw their harvests increase.

Rather than reimpose the collective farm on the growing number of liberated peasants, the Hungarian government, in the spirit of reconciliation, decided to recognize a fait accompli and abolish the compulsory production and delivery operations. To motivate the peasants to work harder, they introduced more favorable prices and voluntary contracts. Once the government had consolidated its powers, it moved to reimpose a sort of collective agriculture, but in a way designed to appeal more to the peasants. Between 1959 and 1962, Hungary's peasants were pressured to join either collective or cooperative farms, but they were given considerable flexibility regarding the type of unit they could join. Moreover, they were compensated for the land and property taken from them, something unheard of in the communist world. They were also allowed to retain some of the livestock, as well as reasonably large private plots. In addition, the peasants discovered they could actually pick their own farm chairman, and within a few years the vote was conducted by secret ballot. In the communist world, this was unique.

The peasant came to discover that the cooperative farms really were cooperative and not just the recipients of orders from the Ministry of Agriculture. None of this is to suggest that the reform process was a smooth one or that there were no retreats now and then. But despite occasional setbacks, the general move was toward the relaxation of controls and the unleashing of peasant energies. Moreover, many of the initiatives in agriculture continued to come from the grass roots, not from the center.

The Hungarians generated most of their output on their unique cooperative farms, a reflection of how important the cooperative form of farming had become. Largely as a result of an amalgamation of smaller units, the 4,204 cooperative farms that existed in 1960 had been reduced to only 1,320 in the early 1980s.[5] However, these 1,320 farms produced almost two-thirds of the country's agricultural output. By contrast, the state farms produced only about 20 percent of the agricultural gross output.[6]

The cooperative farms are generally considered to be more productive than the state farms. Purely private farms accounted for the remainder of the output, although their share of output has generally been declining.[7] Private farmers often work closely with the state units, contracting with them to raise livestock in particular.[8]

Most everyone agrees that Hungary's agricultural reforms have been highly successful. Grain output increased at an annual rate of 3.5 percent between 1971 and 1980.[9] Meat production grew at a slightly lower rate, but enough to provide a significant surplus for export.[10] About one-third of the country's agricultural output and almost two-thirds of its processed foods are exported.[11] In fact, agricultural products are one of Hungary's main exports to both the East and the West, and account for about 25 percent of Hungary's total export earnings.[12] Hungary is a major exporter of food to the Soviet Union, including many products the Soviet Union pays for in hard currency.[13]

II

The success of the reforms in agriculture set off pressure for similar initiatives in the industrial sector and in central planning in general. As we will see, this seems to be a characteristic of the reform process in other communist systems as well. Successes in agriculture led a number of economists to call for a reduction in the role of central planning. Shortly after the 1956 revolution, a few Hungarian economists began to sketch out their views of what they thought should be done to stimulate the economy. Their interest in reform grew particularly intense after Evsei Liberman's proposals for reform were published in *Pravda* in September 1962.[14] If a Soviet economist could call for greater reliance on economic mechanisms like profits, interest rates, and prices, the Hungarians could do the same.

While Soviet interest in reform quickly peaked and then subsided, the Hungarian interest continued to grow. The Hungarians were not even diverted by the overeager reform efforts of the Czechoslovakians and by the subsequent overreaction of the Soviets in the summer of 1968 to what the Soviets saw as heresy in Czechoslovakia. Reportedly, it was not the economic reform that provoked the Soviet invasion in 1968 as much as what the Soviet Union took to be growing softness toward the West and the demands for political reform. The Hungarians held their ground and continued to implement, albeit discreetly, what they called their New Economic Mechanism (NEM), which they launched on January 1, 1968.

NEM was by no means free of controversy or problems. Indeed, from 1973 to 1978 most of the NEM was abandoned. Nonetheless, the reformers introduced some notable changes in the way industrial enterprises operated. For example, prior to 1968, prices served as little more than accounting indicators. The factory manager totaled up the cost of his inputs and added a small amount for profit, and that was the sale price. There was no allowance for shortages or other demand considerations. Under the NEM, a three-tier system of prices was inaugurated. Prices of goods considered to be essential to the economy were set at a fixed level by the government. The prices of goods of slightly lesser importance could fluctuate within a range, and the prices of everything else could fluctuate according to market pressures. In addition, the role of the central plan and the use of delivery targets were downgraded. Enterprises were assigned a general plan, but deviations from plan output targets were no longer a serious offense. Profit maximization became more important than fulfillment of the plans. An effort was made to increase the powers of the enterprise manager and to legitimize activities that had previously been forced underground or into the second economy. Private trade and cooperatives, as well as joint ventures with foreign investors, were legalized. In economic terms, NEM sought to retain macroeconomic powers for the state, while transferring the micro-operations to the operating units.[15]

Much of the early success of the reforms was apparently due to the efforts of the two men put in charge of its implementation, Rezsö Nyers and Jenö Fock.[16] As members of the Politburo, they were well positioned to protect the reforms. Moreover, the success of their efforts in industry made it easier to implement additional reforms in agriculture.

III

The path of reform seemed to be relatively smooth until 1972. The years 1968–1971 have been called "the golden age" of Hungarian economic history.[17] Agricultural output rose, the rate of growth increased, the balance of payments was satisfactory, and living conditions improved. But there was growing anxiety among many of the party elite. Some were upset by what they saw as the fall from ideological purity. They were concerned by the growing trend toward self-gratification and the deemphasis on "nation building." Others were frankly peeved at what they regarded as the erosion of their prerogatives. In November 1972, these conservative forces rallied together and managed to stop the reform.[18] The proponents of reform, such as Nyer, Foch, and Lajos Fehér, were removed from positions of influence.[19] New directives diminished the powers of the enterprise managers, while restoring the powers of the central planners and ministries.[20]

The reformers were dealt another blow by the sudden increase in world oil prices in 1973. Almost no country in the world, Western or Eastern, was able to escape without some economic damage from the explosive inflation that ensued. Hungary was no exception. The chaos of the world economy in the months following October 1973 was hardly the proper environment for economic experimentation. Even though until late 1974 Hungary received most of its petroleum from the Soviet Union at highly subsidized prices, the hike in world oil prices still had a sizable impact on the Hungarian economy. It was not so much that energy prices in Hungary rose but that oil prices in Western Europe did. This caused both recession and inflation in Western Europe. As a consequence, orders for Hungarian products from the hard-currency world fell while prices of imports from the hard-currency world rose. It quickly became apparent that, communist country or not, Hungary was highly vulnerable to inflation.

The impact was not limited to the foreign trade sector. As a rule, communist countries, including the Soviet Union, have a great deal of difficulty generating much of a competitive rivalry among their manufacturers. The problem is compounded for small countries like Hungary, where the market is so limited in size. Most state-run manufacturers there operate on a small scale. By merging many of the smaller enterprises into single units, Hungarian officials reasoned, they could at least benefit from economies of scale and, thus, lower prices. There would be fewer competitors, but the firms seldom competed in price anyway. That explains why the government in the 1960s began to pressure firms to form single producing units. This seemed to make sense because even though there had been little competition, communist countries like Hungary generally had not recorded any significant inflation. But explicit inflation was absent primarily because prices had always been tightly controlled. Once reform led to the relaxation of some price controls, even without the oil crisis, it was all but inevitable that inflation would ensue. Because prices in communist countries, including the Soviet Union, are usually fixed for long periods of time, any decision to allow price fluctuation is an open invitation to raise, not lower, prices. This holds for all communist countries, especially smaller ones, where there seldom is more than one producer of a good. The rise in oil prices only made the situation worse.

The response of the government and party to the inflation of the early 1970s was to retrogress and institute even more price and central-planning controls. Looking back, most analysts argue that the reinstitution of controls was made easier by the fact that during the experiment with NEM much of the pre-1968 institutional framework was left intact, with the industrial ministries and central-planning bureaucracy unaffected. In other words, the central-planning mechanism often continued to interfere much as it had before in many parts of the economy, so it was quite easy to reassert central controls. The economist János Kornai has pointed out that even though enterprises might be told during the NEM to base their decisions on market considerations, as long as the central planners and ministers remained in place, these government bureaucrats would feel tempted or pressured to try to influence the behavior of the factory managers within their jurisdiction.[21] All it took was a hint on the telephone. The managers, in turn, increasingly came to consider it to be in their best interests to pay heed to the hints or veiled orders of the ministry or central-planning officers. This undermined the market's influence, which, in turn, meant that the market signals, to the extent that anyone paid them heed, were distorted and not reflective of what was really happening in the economy.

IV

The suspension of the NEM reforms came at the wrong time. With a return to central planning, factory managers paid even less attention to cost control. Since domestic oil and other raw material prices had not been raised to reflect the new, higher levels that prevailed in the world economy, Hungarian managers, unlike those in market economies, had no economic incentives to reduce their consumption of such products. Hungarian managers knew that if their operations were unprofitable, they could always fall back on the state for subsidies. Hungary had no such thing as bankruptcy. Kornai calls this the "soft budget" constraint, which meant that there were virtually no constraints since, the managers could always count on more funding.[22] This soft-budget constraint led to excessive consumption, which in turn led to increased imports. Since the prices of the goods Hungary was importing (except for those from the Soviet Union) rose twice as rapidly as the prices of the goods it was exporting, this was something Hungary could ill afford.[23]

In the short run, financing a trade deficit did not seem to be a problem. Hungary's import deficit was readily financed by Western banks, which, flush with new deposits from the import earnings of the OPEC oil producers, were eager to lend money to countries like Hungary. As a consequence, the foreign debt of Hungary and its East European allies rose to dangerous levels in the late 1970s.

Amid increasingly serious economic problems, the earlier NEM reforms were reevaluated. In 1977, Hungary once again moved away from central planning and toward an even greater reliance on the market. A new and expanded set of reforms was announced, which was to be implemented between 1979 and 1985.[24] The goal was to create a system that functioned in a more rational and competitive way.

Remembering what had happened before, the reformers were determined to initiate institutional changes that would frustrate those who again might try to interfere from the center and reinstitute central planning.[25] Three of the larger industrial ministries were merged into a single Ministry of Industry, and the ministry staffs were reduced in half.[26] With the smaller staff and more responsibility, it was hoped, the ministry's staff would have no time or inclination to interfere directly in the day-to-day affairs of the enterprise, as they had done before. If all went as planned, the ministry would focus on the big picture and leave the details to the managers on the spot. Undoubtedly, Gorbachev was similarly motivated when he sought to cluster the various ministries that had been dealing with agricultural matters, with machinery production, and with energy development into three umbrella ministries. (See Chapter 3.) Since there are still central government organs in Hungary that supervise some prices and "material supplies" of enterprises, the center still has more influence, both direct and indirect, than most reformers would like, but not as much as before.[27]

To encourage more competition and to hold down price increases, the reformers moved to stimulate Hungarian managers to produce products according to world standards and curb excessive consumption of raw material and imported components. In January 1980 the state introduced a new set of price guidelines designed to increase the influence of the market and diminish the role of administrative forces.[28] At the same time, an effort was made to make Hungarian prices more reflective of the costs and prices that prevailed in the Western world, rather than of those in the communist world, as had traditionally been the case.

Toward the same end, government officials decided to undo some of their past mistakes. Instead of encouraging the merger of industrial enterprises, they split them into smaller and, in theory, competing units.[29] By early 1983, the state had dissolved 26 industrial trusts into 167 enterprises.[30] In addition, new regulations were introduced to stimulate the creation of new businesses, especially cooperatives.[31] Some of these new enterprises were formed by the joint efforts of existing state enterprises, some were the product of local governments, and some took the form of cooperatives or private enterprise activity. As of this writing, although the Soviets seem willing to facilitate the formation of cooperatives, they have been leery of any extensive private activity. We noted earlier that they have authorized private proprietorship ventures by individuals and families but that they will not allow them to hire anyone else. By contrast, as Table 6 indicates, the results in Hungary were

TABLE 6

New Economic Units in Hungary,
1982–1984

		1982	1983	1984
Small enterprises	number	23	204	285
	employment	2,226	19,322	30,048
Small cooperatives	number	145	255	368
	employment	6,014	9,853	16,087
Industrial & service groups	number	477	1,243	2,253
	employment	n.a.	41,396	78,734
Enterprise economic) working groups)	number	2,775	9,192	17,337
	employment	29,331	98,006	196,014
Individual economic) working groups)	number	2,341	4,741	7,397
	employment	11,145	23,667	42,516

SOURCE: Statisztikai Évkönyv 1984, as reprinted in Paul Hare, "Hungary: Internal Economic Developments" (Paper prepared for the NATO conference on Economies of Eastern Europe and Their Foreign Economic Relations, Brussels, April 1986, Mimeographed), p. 14.

impressive, in terms both of number of new firms created and of number of employees involved.[32]

Many of these new ventures were an attempt to legalize and bring into the open private activity that had heretofore been conducted illegally or as part of the second economy. Thus, in 1982, employees of state enterprises were authorized to set up what were called Enterprise Contract Work Associations.[33] These associations, comprising from two to thirty people, were authorized to contract with the enterprise they work with during the day to perform additional work (often the same) for the same enterprise in their free time.[34] In effect, they are being encouraged to moonlight with not only state approval but even state encouragement. This constituted a recognition that since the workers often did such things on their own illegally, it made more sense for the state to have them work in the open by legitimizing their activities. Other, similar independent groups in factories are now authorized. However, unlike the Enterprise Contract Work Associations, these groups are not limited to working for their parent firm. They can work for anyone as independent contractors. Finally, laws regulating private enterprise were liberalized, and it became easier for businessmen to open up new stores and workshops and employ a maximum of three nonfamily members (Kornai reports that the limit is seven) and up to six family members.[35] This policy brought an immediate response. Whereas there were 9,043 private shops in 1970 and about 9,900 in 1979, by 1983 there were 19,945.[36]

Efforts were also made to increase the responsiveness of the banking system. Heretofore, the Hungarian banks, like most banking systems in the communist world, had been highly centralized. Steps were taken in 1979 to decentralize some of the functions that had been concentrated in the Hungarian national bank or its closely held affiliates.[37] In one of these innovations, the money supply and central banking functions of the central bank were separated from the credit banking department. This was done to signal that the granting of loans would no longer be an automatic process for existing firms. Henceforth, borrowers would have to show they had the ability to put the funds to good use. Considerably more radical was the 1979 decision to create the Central European International Bank.[38] This is a joint venture with the Japanese and five West European banks, in which the Hungarians hold only 34 percent of the shares.[39] In effect, the Hungarians have opened up their banking system to foreign interference. In addition, a dozen new financial intermediaries were created between 1980 and 1983 to provide financing for domestic ventures.

In what was the most venturesome, and therefore the most controversial, step, the government authorized the issuance and sale of bonds by enterprises, cooperatives, financial institutions, and local government entities.[40] In effect, the Hungarians have established a bond market.[41] Trading takes place in the security trading room of the National Development Bank, and ordinary Hungarians are allowed to buy and sell.[42] Investors are rewarded with interest from the bond issues. Some Hungarian companies have also issued stock.[43] All such stock issues have so far been purchased by other state enterprises, but if ideological objections can be overcome, it is conceivable that someday individuals will also be able to purchase stock as well as bonds.

All of these measures were designed to induce a higher degree of financial autonomy, concern, and managerial rigor from plant directors. More and more of the enterprises' financing was to come from the enterprises' own operations—that is, from retained earnings, depreciation, and the prospects of future profits, which would determine how attractive the sale of an enterprise's bonds and other public offerings would be. There was to be less use of subsidies from the government. This, in turn, meant that unprofitable firms would have to face the threat of bankruptcy, something heretofore regarded as unthinkable in the communist world. Since bankruptcy has always been treated as a capitalist disease, there was a reluctance to face up to it. Politically, it had always been easier to continue the subsidies than to throw the workers out in the street and abandon the machinery and equipment. However, the Hungarians have now begun to do just that.[44] An official decree on bankruptcy was passed, and the first overt bankruptcy was declared by the Ministry of Finance on August 13, 1984.[45] The Company for Business Machines and Precision Instruments (IGV) was the first company to be formally liquidated.[46] Effective September 1, 1986, a new, more far-reaching bankruptcy law was put on the books.[47] Now the courts, not just administrative authorities, can begin bankruptcy proceedings, and plant managers or their creditors can act through the courts. For many, the very existence of a bankruptcy law works as preventive medicine.[48] It is perhaps the most persuasive way of enforcing hard budgetary constraints on managers who simply assumed that they could always count on budget subsidies for any losses they might incur.[49]

To the extent that such measures are successful, Hungarian industry should become more competitive not only within the country but also in the outside world. But the increase in economic flexibility at home will be of no avail if Hungarian enterprises are still confined within the bounds of the monopoly of the agencies of the Ministry of Foreign Trade. For that reason, an effort has been made to cut back some of the monopoly powers of the foreign trade agencies. In 1980, a growing number of large enterprises were authorized to deal directly with foreign buyers and sellers, without the intervention of the foreign trade organizations.[50] This is something that it took the Soviet Union until 1986 even to contemplate. In Hungary, however, by September 1983 over 200 firms had been given these powers. Most smaller enterprises must still go through agencies of the Ministry of Foreign Trade, but there is now considerably more competition among foreign trade agencies than there was.

Realizing that all of these measures would be of no avail without an effort to upgrade the quality of the managers running Hungary's industries, the state decided it was necessary to design new criteria for selecting managers for state enterprises.[51] Drawing on the precedent established in agriculture, where the peasants actually were allowed to select the director of the collective and cooperatives by secret vote rather than by the arbitrary decision of the bureaucrats in Budapest, the government took steps to select industrial managers in a similar process.[52] This would not only give the workers more of a stake in the running of their plant but also increase the managers' independence from the officials in Budapest.[53] Beginning in early 1985, three procedures were established for selecting a manager. If the workers prefer, ministry officials can be asked, as before, to select the manager. According to information reported by the British economist Paul Hare, about 21 percent of the country's state enterprises are still run by managers picked by the state and party officials.[54] In the remaining factories, the managers are selected by the workers. In the smaller factories, all the workers meet together in a workers' assembly —a sort of a town meeting—to pick a manager. About 17 percent of the country's enterprises operate this way. The other 62 percent are managed by an enterprise council elected by the workers. One of the main functions of this council is to choose the enterprise manager.

Another change is that candidates for managerial positions may now nominate themselves. Before, only state authorities could decide who was eligible. Vacancies are now advertised, and candidates are asked to apply. They submit their résumés, and the finalists are then called back for interviews by the workers' council, by the entire assembly, or by state officials.[55] The candidate must sell himself or herself and, among other things, present a long-term business plan.[56] In some cases, the state will make the appointment subject to the approval of the workers' council. In others, the interview is handled by the assembly or council itself. Once selected, the manager will be appointed for a fixed period. Reappointment depends on review and reapproval. Reportedly, there have been several instances where the managers were not reappointed after the expiration of their first term.[57] Overall, these changes are bold and imaginative, and they constitute a significant refinement to the original procedures of 1968.

However, these reforms have not produced the economic results that were anticipated.[58] While economic growth in 1985 slowed, inflation and the trade deficit did not. Moreover, an increased gap in incomes between the rich (the private entrepreneurs and peasants in particular) and a growing number of poor (including those receiving less than a subsistence income) has sparked growing concern.[59] As a result, the opponents of reform have again begun to call for retrenchment.

So far, despite an occasional step backward, the Hungarian approach to reform has been to diminish the role of central planning and to enhance the roles of the market and the market mechanisms. But the future of the reforms is by no means assured. As we saw, the opponents of reform managed to force a retreat in 1972. Although institutional reforms were later adopted that were intended to make retreat more difficult, it would be foolhardy to assume that further retrogression is impossible, particularly if economic conditions deteriorate. Nor have all government bureaucrats given up hope that central planning might rise again. Party and state officials may "enunciate new policies," but at the same time they "interfere with their implementation" by "siphoning off the profits" or by "the expropriation of local tax revenues."[60] Under the circumstances, it is unclear what will happen when the aging János Kádár dies or steps aside. The Hungarian Communist party in March 1985 appointed Károly Németh as the number two man to Kádár, who was then seventy-two.[61] Németh, who has been described as lukewarm toward the economic reforms, was apparently selected for his middle-of-the-road position.[62] Thus, while some in the Politburo, such as Ferenc Havasi, are strongly in favor of the reforms, there are also others, such as Károly Grosz, who is described as a "hard liner."[63] Grosz has lost some power, but he has not lost it all, and efforts in 1986 to curb some of Hungary's cultural freedoms suggest that the reforms' continuation after Kádár is hardly guaranteed.[64]

V

What lessons does the course of economic reform in Hungary hold for the Soviet Union. Discussion with Soviet economists suggests that in recent years the Soviets have been skeptical about their relevance, to say the least. Soviet observers are usually quick to point out the shortcomings of the Hungarian experiment. Thus, during a visit to the International Institute for Economic Problems of the Council of Mutual Economic Assistance (also refered as the Shiryaev Institute, named after the director) in Moscow in early 1986, I was told that, except for agriculture—and even in that realm there was a question—Hungary was generally ill suited as a model for Soviet economic reforms. First, in Hungary, a much smaller country than the Soviet Union, it was much easier to decentralize control. Hungary, with only 11 million people, where "everyone" knew everyone else, was also much easier to control than the Soviet Union, with approximately 280 million people. Moreover, most Hungarians were Hungarians, while the Soviet Union consists of fifteen republics and nearly 200 different nationalities. As one Soviet skeptic told me, "If you think we can delegate and decentralize economic decision making to people like the Uzbeks, Armenians, Georgians, and Lithuanians, you are mistaken. They would create their own private empires."

In particular, the Soviet economists frequently point to Hungary's zero economic growth, its annual inflation rate of 7 to 8 percent, its adverse balance of trade, and what they observe as the poor morale of the Hungarian people.[65] Even in agriculture, conditions are not as good as they look on the surface, the Soviets insisted. These critics claim that if the Hungarians subtracted the hard-currency costs of imports of such things as machinery, pesticides, seeds, and fertilizer, their hard-currency expenditures would exceed their hard-currency earnings from agricultural imports.

To these specialists, the East German model was much more attractive and appropriate. While some Soviet observers do look favorably on what the Hungarians are trying to do, with agriculture, the election of farm and industry managers, and the demonopolizing of the Ministry of Foreign Trade, most are impressed more by what they see as the German Democratic Republic's higher economic growth and its continued use of central planning.[66] When the Soviets look at the German Democratic Republic, they see no inflation, no unemployment, and no bad balance of trade. That, at least, is what appears on the surface. As we discussed earlier, even in the German Democratic Republic the taut central-planning system masks economic distortions, such as overemployment and suppressed inflation. There are no high prices, just long lines and, in some cases, no goods. But the East Germans carry on as if there were no problems. It is reassuring, therefore, for Soviet observers to see that in at least one country central planning and state ownership do seem to work, albeit imperfectly. It may, in fact, be that the East German discipline and work ethic (much of which have survived, despite more than forty years of communist control) is what the Soviets admire.

Even Gorbachev is said to harbor such sentiments. While he has made some approving remarks about what "Hungary and other socialist countries" are doing, he also told a Hungarian audience that the Soviet reform would be based on "the improvement of central planning and full-scale cost accounting."[67] He stressed to the Hungarians that the chief yardstick for judging the success of economic reform was whether it led to "the practical strengthening of socialism in all spheres—economic, political, and spiritual."[68] As we will see, this is a very different yardstick from the one used in China by Deng Xiaoping, who cares not what color the cat is but only whether it can catch mice. Reportedly, Gorbachev has been even more explicit about his concern about an overreliance on the market system. Seweryn Bialer and Joan Afferica cite a speech Gorbachev was said to have made in late 1985 to a gathering of East European communist officials: "Many of you see the solution to your problems in resorting to market mechanisms in place of central planning. Some of you look at the market as a lifesaver for your economies. But comrades, you should not think about lifesavers, but about the ship, and the ship is socialism."[69] Even if these were not his exact words, Gorbachev in other pronouncements has expressed very similar sentiments so he has undoubtedly caught the attention of Hungarian reformers and given them some cause for reflection.

What is it that Gorbachev and other Soviet officials find so attractive about the East Germans' achievement? Again, it is hard to tell whether what has happened in East Germany is due to the fact that German workmanship is involved, or that the West Germans have agreed to compensate for East German shortcomings, or that the East Germans have indeed discovered a way of making central planning work. It may be a combination of all three. If so, this means the East German system cannot be easily duplicated elsewhere.

In fact, Western calculations of the growth of net material product per capita in both Hungary and the German Democratic Republic (GDR) do not show much difference. From 1965 to 1975, Hungary grew faster.[70] Thereafter, East Germany grew faster, but the difference in growth was not significant.[71] Conditions deteriorated markedly in Hungary in 1985, and that may be the source of much of the unfavorable comparison; over the long run, though, actual German growth has not been that much more impressive than Hungary's.

When it comes to the institutional features of the East German economy, almost all Soviet observers refer favorably to the recently created *Kombinate*. The *Kombinate* link groups of factories into related production fields. In addition to the production units, the *Kombinate* include research institutes and supplier enterprises. The *Kombinate* also have considerable powers to conduct their own foreign trade activity.[72]

The *Kombinate* became dominant in East Germany in 1979–1980. The Germans had actually created *Kombinate* earlier. In 1973, for example, thirty-seven were already in operation.[73] But the preferred form of industrial organization prior to 1979 was the VVB, or Association of Nationalized Enterprises. The VVBs were created in 1963 as part of the New Economic System under Walter Ulbricht's leadership.[74] While Ulbricht can hardly be considered to be a big reformer, the East Germans, like most of East Europeans at the time, had begun to reexamine the merits of the Stalinist model of tight central control. Like the Hungarians and the Czechs, the East Germans seemed to have taken their signals from the September 9, 1962, *Pravda* article by Evsei Liberman.[75] That the editors of *Pravda* had authorized the publication of such an article seemed to be a sign from Moscow that the East European countries could undertake some cautious experiments on the Soviet economic model. The VVBs in the Liberman spirit were an attempt to diminish some of the center's control and turn it over to organizations more closely associated with the actual producing enterprises.

The VVB system never fully came into its own. Moreover, after what were viewed as the excesses of a decentralized system in Czechoslovakia, the VVB system also became suspect; while it was not abolished, it was critically circumscribed.

By the late 1970s, however, the East German economy began to suffer from the same economic difficulties that had afflicted its neighbors. As the price of raw materials rose faster than what the East Germans could charge for their exports, they found themselves with a growing foreign debt that soon began to threaten the country's ability to obtain further loans. Even though the Germans imported most of their petroleum from the Soviet Union, the second oil shock of 1979 convinced almost everyone that the situation would grow more serious. Gross debt, excluding that owed to West Germany (which totaled approximately $2.0 billion), reached about $9.5 billion, and the debt seemed to be increasing at a rate of 20 percent a year.[76]

As the trade deficit and foreign debt began to mount, the Germans, like their Hungarian allies, decided that some type of additional reform was essential. But, unlike the Hungarians, who opted for decentralization and even more market influence, the Germans sought to make central control and planning more effective. Their solution was to upgrade the *Kombinate*. Factories making similar goods were organized into large *Kombinate*, which were made directly subject to the appropriate ministry.[77] The main difference between the VVB and the *Kombinat* was the inclusion within the *Kombinat* umbrella of research, supply, and foreign trade units. The goal was to stimulate more innovation and foreign trade and reduce the bureaucratic obstacles to such activities that exist within a centralized system.

The *Kombinat* system is very large. As of 1986, there were 132 *Kombinate* operating at the national level. Each had twenty to forty plants and an average of 25,000 workers under its control.[78] Ninety-three *Kombinate* were also created at the regional level. They were generally smaller, having approximately 2,000 workers each.

While the *Kombinat* system seems to work better than the VVB, there are still serious problems of control and coordination. To link the *Kombinate* to the ministry, the directors of the *Kombinate* have also been accorded the post of deputy minister.[79] Not surprisingly, the ministry continues to interfere in the affairs of the *Kombinate*. In an effort to make the *Kombinat* function more as an independent unit, the incentive system was changed in 1984 so that now the *Kombinat* is judged by its net production, net profit, and the production of goods for export and consumption.[80] But this has not been enough to distinguish the work of the factory manager from that of the director of the *Kombinat* and the work of the director of the *Kombinat* from that of the ministry. Further reforms include allowing the firm to build up incentive funds from the above plan profits and trying to increase the influence of "economic levers."[81] But the central planners in East Berlin continue to utilize "material balances," which have always been a means of maintaining central control. In addition, the pricing system is still closely regulated and thus not reflective of changing values. Under these circumstances, any attempt to stress the role of profits is bound to cause distortion as managers also seek to respond to the central planners.[82]

The private sector in the German Democratic Republic does not seem to attract as much attention as its counterpart in Hungary, but the East Germans have been relatively supportive of the private sector. In fact, private trade was never completely abolished.[83] Recently, there has been new interest in private trade, and the number of East German private operations reached a total of 257,000 in 1984. Private businesses in the GDR can hire up to ten employees. The share of private enterprise in the total industrial output is higher in East Germany than in any of the other East European countries except Poland, and the role of the private sector in services and trade exceeds even that of Poland.[84]

East Germany still does not allow joint ventures with foreign companies, however. When the Czechs and Soviets, in August 1986, decided to authorize such activities, the German Democratic Republic (and, of course, Albania) was the only country in Eastern Europe that did not allow such activities.

While German agricultural output began to improve in 1983, and while there has also been an improvement in East Germany's foreign trade balance, what most attracts the Soviets to East Germany is its mastery of technology. But no one knows how far even good German discipline would take the East Germans and their system if they did not have the substantial help of the West Germans. For example, 60 percent of the German Democratic Republic's trade with the West goes to and comes from West Germany.[85] Since the West Germans think of the GDR as still a part of Germany, and therefore not a foreign country, there are no duties or tariffs on East German exports to West Germany, and thus into the Common Market. As it is, the East Germans rely heavily on West German imports of Western technology. This results in a substantial trade imbalance, but the West Germans go a step further and finance that deficit with an interest-free loan.[86] On top of everything else, the West Germans unilaterally transfer over $1 billion a year to the German Democratic Republic in the form of private remittances from relatives in West Germany, as well as payments for services to West Berlin and a quasi-ransom needed to pay for the immigration of a small number of East Germans each year.[87]

VI

Hungary and the German Democratic Republic represent two different revisions of the Stalinist model. So far, both are relatively modest in what they have attempted to do.

The Hungarian approach involves more reinterpretation of ideological norms than does the East German model, but it has not gone as far as the Chinese reforms. To some hard-line Soviet Marxists, China represents the nightmare of what may well happen if a country begins to move away from central planning and toward the market. Moreover, Hungary's economic results, at least in 1985 and 1986, were discouraging. While agricultural output has improved, the relaxation of central control and the toleration, if not encouragement, of private wealth making have led to a significant increase in inequality, or at least monetary inequality. Everyone knows that there has always been inequality in the communist world, but until the Hungarian reforms it was usually masked. It was not so much that monetary incomes were the same or were different but that party leaders had access to special stores and privileges. Now some of the new rich include speculators and private middlemen.

In their effort to improve their operating results, even state enterprises in Hungary have begun to take a harder look at some of society's drones. For the drones, the prospects are not very good. As the Chinese would say, "The Hungarian reforms mean the drones can no longer count on an iron gulash bowl." Alternatively, Marx might warn that if the drones don't work, there will be no job—to each according to his work. Unfortunately, as in any system that begins to rely on the market, it is not only the drones who find themselves unemployed or at a disadvantage. The dismantling of state controls and the discontinuance of subsidies occasionally may affect the hard workers as well as the drones. It is a combination of such factors that explains the very mixed and often negative Soviet response to what is happening in Hungary—one that leads some like Oleg

Bogomolov, the head of the Institute of World Socialist Economic Systems in Moscow, to stress that "it is an error to keep thinking along the lines of a few years ago, namely that it is enough to change prices or to improve some economic mechanism to solve the problem of technological progress. The Hungarian economic reform has produced some positive results but has failed to produce major achievements in that very regard."[88]

Against this background and the fact that East Germany's economic results for 1985 and 1986 were certainly better than Hungary's the East German approach seems to be more attractive to many Soviet officials, especially to those involved with the day-to-day operations of the economy. The GDR's reforms appear to be a relatively painless and costless solution to the Soviet Union's problems. They do not involve major surgery or a dismantling or a downgrading of the central-planning mechanism. They may involve some consolidation of ministries, but the Soviets have done that very well before and have already engaged in some recent consolidations. They may require some reassigning of middle-level bureaucrats, at the *vedomstvo* level, in the bowels of the ministry; but the Soviets have also already done that. In fact, as an experiment the Soviets have already moved close to the *Kombinat* system. As we noted above, in August 1986 they enlarged the Scientific Production Association to bring it closer the *Kombinat* image. Such an approach seems to suit the Soviet aversion to any far-reaching reform. Instead, by following East Germany, the Soviets hope that all they will need is a little tinkering here and a little tinkering there—something the Soviet bureaucracy has developed a special talent for over the years. But such tinkering falls far short of what is needed to reform the economy and absorb advanced technology. If the reforms are to make a difference, the Soviets will have to face up to the dismantling of the bureaucracy, the transfer of power from the center, and the frank acknowledgment of the warts of unemployment, inequality, inefficiency, and the negative balance of trade. Such economic malfunctions are supposed to be afflictions of the capitalist world. The more realistic Soviet analysts know that far-reaching reform will almost inevitably bring these hidden but endemic problems to the surface in their country. The dread of uncorking the Soviet Union's long-suppressed economic and political distortions also helps explain the Soviet reaction to what Deng Xiaoping has attempted to do in China.

7

The Chinese Model and Its Relevance for Soviet Economic Reform

When we speak of twentieth-century revolutions, we invariably refer to a violent move to the left—Lenin's revolution in Russia, Mao's in China, and Castro's in Cuba. All involved a reordering of society and the economic order. Those who were rich and powerful were swept aside or destroyed, and a new class took their place. Shortly thereafter, the new leaders typically declared a campaign to industrialize the country and expressed their intention to push the newly liberated country into the ranks of the economically and militarily powerful. Through the use of central planning, five-year plans, and the collectivization of agriculture, these goals were often achieved, at least in the Soviet Union and China, in a remarkably short span of years. At the same time, the leaders usually embarked on a massive effort to improve public health, raise literacy rates, and enhance living conditions of the very poorest. These measures came at a severe cost, however. Political freedoms were curbed and the economic well-being of the peasants and middle classes exploited in order to expand heavy industry.

When Deng Xiaoping came to power, he pushed through a completely different kind of change. His attempt to dismantle the Stalinist economic and political structure may be just as revolutionary, if not more so, in its impact on the economic and social status quo. But Deng's is basically a peaceful revolution; in the beginning it sought not an increase in heavy industry and military power (at least in the short run) but primarily an increase in the economic well-being of all segments of the population, especially those who were willing to work to enrich themselves.

It may well be that future historians will proclaim Deng the true revolutionary of the twentieth century. It was he who realized that his predecessors had erred when they became fixated with the ideological purity of what they were doing. To Mao, for example, it generally seemed that it was important to have a pure revolution in the abstract sense, even if it came at the cost of a continual improvement in the material well-being of the population. "Poorer but purer" seemed to be his credo. Mao and those like him seemed to have lost sight of their original goal—to improve the livelihood of their people. There was to be a leveling of incomes, but presumably for the bulk of the population that leveling should have meant an economic rise, not a decline or a stagnation, as it turned out to be.

Deng resurrected the original revolutionary goal—to improve the well-being of the masses. As we shall see, he has done a remarkably good job in a relatively short time; however, impressive as his efforts have been, many unknowns remain. Will Deng's revolution survive Deng? Like any revolution, it has caused upheaval; it has admittedly been nonviolent, but it is upheaval nonetheless. Moreover, we must remember that if there has been one dominating feature of Chinese life since the 1949 revolution, it is perhaps the regime's inability to hold to one course for more than a few years. The People's Republic of China has been racked by a continual series of 180-degree flip-flops. Deng's revolution has lasted eight years, a long time by Chinese standards, but Deng is an old man, and as became clear in the reaction to the university student demonstrations in December 1986, there are those who prefer and even seek to restore the old regime. When Deng dies, there will certainly be a difference of views if not a power struggle over the desirability of continuing his work.

To predict the ultimate fate of Deng's reforms is the domain of Chinese specialists; the purpose of this discussion is to see whether the Soviet Union can or might adopt the Chinese model. To do this, we must take an extended look at what the Chinese have done, how they came to do it, how the Soviets have reacted to what the Chinese have accomplished, and whether the Soviets can carry out a similar revolution.

I

While the Soviet Union has not been immune to political power struggles and policy reversals, it has since Stalin's death been spared the more traumatic upheavals that have beset China. In many respects, that is a blessing, but, as we shall see, for those seeking far-reaching economic reform and an escape from the Stalinist model, it may actually be a curse.

China did quite well economically in the years following the establishment of the People's Republic of China and the defeat of the Nationalist government in 1949. Adopting the Stalinist model, Mao launched China's First Five-year Plan in 1953 and collectivized its agriculture in 1955. Until at least 1957, most observers agreed, the economy grew at an impressive rate of about 8 to 10 percent a year.[1] Initially, this growth was balanced so that all sectors grew. This was a relief after the chaos of World War II and the Chinese civil war, and the unification and economic revitalization were welcomed by most of the population. However, under the threat of an American-sponsored invasion from Taiwan and the influence of the Soviet ideology as well as its foreign aid, China increasingly began to emphasize heavy industry at the expense of agriculture and light industry. As Robert Dernberger has reported, "Whereas in 1952, heavy industry accounted for about one-third of total industrial production, by 1977, it accounted for over half."[2] This was the inevitable result of adopting the Stalinist model.

After Stalin's death, in 1953, Mao began to quarrel with the Soviet leadership over who was Stalin's true successor as the leader of the international communist movement. To demonstrate his independence, Mao began to seek new forms of economic organization. Arguing that ideology and revolutionary spirit were as important as economic incentives, if not more so, Mao introduced his Great Leap Forward (1958–1960), by which he sought to establish the ideal "communist society" in one, giant effort. Mao insisted that China could break out of the bonds of conventional economic restraints if only the workers willed it.

Mao's experiment caused great damage to the industrial and agricultural infrastructure, and for the first time since 1949 there was famine in the countryside. In an effort to remedy the damage in 1961, Mao was prevailed upon to return to more traditional economic methods. During this more relaxed period, material incentives replaced ideological exhortation as the driving force for labor. There was a further sharp shift to the left in 1965, as Mao embarked on one of the more destructive episodes in China's long history—the Cultural Revolution. For a whole decade, until shortly after Mao's death, in September 1976, China subjected itself to a terrible period of upheaval and chaos. Those identified with the 1961–1965 economic revivial were denounced for their petty bourgeois stress on material pleasures and economic growth and their deemphasis of ideology. Scientists, engineers, managers, intellectuals, skilled workers, and party officials were shipped off to the countryside to work in the fields or to prison or to death. In effect, the universities were closed down, and anyone with advanced training was suspect. Inevitably, as specialists were cast out and revolutionary enthusiasts and untrained cadres took their places, the economy suffered.[3] According to Robert Dernberger, there was no real increase in per capita food consumption from the mid-1950s to the mid-1970s. He estimates that the per capita disposable income of the peasants rose by a mere 17 yuan ($10) from 1955 to 1977. He further calculates that the real wage of workers and staff from 1957 to 1979 actually fell. Similarly, Nicholas Lardy asserts that, "by 1977–78, rural real income was at best only slightly above the level of 1956–57."[4] All of this explains why it became necessary to import substantial quantities of food. "By 1978 . . . about 40% of China's municipalities were dependent on imported grains and in the 1970's China as a whole became the world's largest importer of major crops such as vegetable oil and cotton."[5] My discussions with Chinese economists substantiate these conclusions.

For Mao, however, there was something more important than economic growth—namely, ideological purity and equality. In particular, he was determined to bridge the gap between the white-collar class and the peasants. What kind of revolution was this if white-collar workers, intellectuals, and party officials were sitting in comfortable offices while the great bulk of the Chinese people were engaged in heavy manual work in the fields, factories, and streets? Given the lack of capital resources, many of China's laborers were often indistinguishable from beasts of burden. Chinese cities were filled with laborers carrying enormous loads on their backs or pushing and pulling them through the streets. If he could not eliminate desk work, Mao was the least determined that white-collar workers and party cadres would come to appreciate the life of the peasant and manual workers. He ordered hundreds of thousands of urban workers and students sent to the fields to work alongside the peasants. In some cases, these intellectuals, office workers, students, and party cadres developed a better appreciation for the rigors of peasant life. In others, however, the gap actually increased, as the peasant came to disdain the ineptness of these forced recruits, who tended to complicate an already difficult rural existence. Just as often, the white-collar workers came to hate what they saw as a primitive way of life. There was a growing consensus, however, among peasants and white-collar workers alike, that the economy was probably better off with the white-collar workers, be they arrogant or humble, in the cities and not on the farms. Admittedly, many of the city folks were drones—the party people, in particular—but exiling them to the farms did nothing for the country's economy.

That the quest for the perfect revolution had come at the expense of the ordinary masses in China gradually became apparent, at least to those not firmly committed to Mao's Gang of Four and to ideological purity. This accounts in part for some relaxation in the Cultural Revolution in 1972 and for the rehabilitation of Deng Xiaoping in 1973. However, the Gang of Four, under the leadership of Mao's wife, Jiang Qing, continued to function in the ideological area, so much so that Deng was purged again in April 1976, as a dangerous rival, when a demonstration for Chou En-lai turned into a demonstration in support of Deng. Shortly thereafter, however, in September 1976, Mao died. With their patron dead, the Gang of Four were arrested the following month, and, not surprisingly, Deng emerged once more in July 1977.

Somewhat unexpectedly, however, a provincial official, Hua Guo-feng, was brought in by Mao just before his death as the heir apparent. In July 1977, Hua became the general secretary of the party. While beholden to Mao, Hua nonetheless recognized the necessity of stopping the economic drift. Following the path of his supporter, Hua sought to reintroduce the Great Leap Forward. In the nationwide campaign that ran from 1977 to mid-1978, Chinese peasants were urged to emulate the Dazhai commune. This was a model collective that stressed the use of a relatively equal work-point system to mark each peasant's contribution to the communal effort. Hua believed that the Dazhai system would mobilize the peasants to work harder, but since everyone ended up with more or less the same number of points, regardless of time or effort, the peasants did not bestir themselves, and agricultural productivity continued to stagnate.

Because the Great Leap Forward had failed the first time around, Hua should have realized in advance that a refurbished version of the Great Leap Forward would probably not do much better the second time. Yet, it is entirely possible that even modest economic improvement would have sufficed, had it not been for what was happening elsewhere in Asia. While China was suffering one convulsion after another, once-impoverished places like Japan, South Korea, Hong Kong, Singapore, and even Taiwan, whose cultures derived from many of the same Confucian values as China's, were experiencing economic transformation, if not miracles. This was not what economic theorists of the 1950s and 1960s had expected to happen. Most of them, from the capitalist as well as the communist world, believed that central planning, centralized investment, and state ownership would bring faster economic growth to an underdeveloped country than would a system relying on the market and private ownership. On the basis of Soviet growth prior to the 1960s, they assumed that the quickest path to growth would be to collectivize agriculture in order to extract as much capital as possible and direct that investment into heavy industry. Because they were adhering to that model, it was expected that North Korea would grow faster than South Korea, China faster than Taiwan, and Vietnam faster than Thailand and Singapore.

By the late 1970s, however, it was clear that just the opposite was happening. Central planning and the Stalinist model were proving to be inferior to more heterogeneous forms of growth. Elsewhere in Asia, instead of being squeezed in a collectivized vise, the peasants prospered as independent cultivators. Their purchasing power sparked the growth of light industry, which increased the markets for heavy industry. That was not the only reason for growth in those areas. The "Gang of Four" countries (South Korea, Taiwan, Singapore, and Hong Kong) plus Japan had predicated much of their growth on an attempt to take advantage of export markets. This is not to imply that the state model was a complete failure or that the Stalinist model brought no economic growth—on the contrary, it brought particularly impressive results in heavy industry for China. But, in comparison with what was happening in so many other countries in Asia, the Stalinist model had proven to be markedly inferior. As several Chinese economists noted during my visit to China in 1979, "What happened? We won World War II, and now we find that it is our neighbors in Asia, even Taiwan, whose economies have flourished."

II

The demonstration effect of what others were doing in Asia gradually began to have an impact in China. There was a general consensus within the leadership that if China was to keep up with its neighbors, it would have to change its ways. With Mao dead and the Gang of Four behind bars, the leaders and experts began to reconsider the viability of the Stalinist model. When during my first visit to China, in December 1979, I was asked to deliver a series of lectures entitled "The U.S.S.R. in the year 2000," I came to realize that what the audiences were really interested in was not the Soviet Union in the year 2000 but China in the year 2000, assuming that it continued to adhere to the Stalinist model.

No one has yet written a definitive history of how China has moved away from the Stalinist model. Many aspects of the reform developed quite independently of one another. This makes it hard to fit Deng's reform into any systematic pattern. Experiments in one part of the country often duplicated, but sometimes contradicted, experiments being carried out in other parts of it. No omniscient body of planners and party people worked out a specific blueprint of "the Chinese economic reform." Often as not, one reform would give rise to another. "Reforms" emerged from here and there—mostly from "there," in provinces and even in remote fields. To an observer who is not a specialist on China, one of the most surprising features of the reform was how spontaneous development in the countryside influenced policy at the center.

What follows is an attempt to piece together what happened, while acknowledging that the actual pattern was more chaotic and less orderly than the description suggests.

Not everyone in China agreed that one of the major preconditions for the reform was Mao's death and the Gang of Four's removal from power. That in itself was not enough, since Mao's successor, Hua Guo-feng, while recognizing a need for an improvement in the country's economic growth, thought it could be done within the existing framework. He did not seem to appreciate, much less encourage, any need for far-reaching economic reforms.

Most China specialists do agree, however, that Deng Xiaoping's return in July 1977 and assumption of power in late 1978 was a critical precondition to the reform. Another was the traumatic nature of the Cultural Revolution, which victimized top officials and ordinary people alike. Yet, for all its destructiveness, the Cultural Revolution had a positive side. It decimated the Communist party's bureaucratic network and forced the leadership to question the worth of a system that gave rise to such a tragedy. It also created a sense of urgency and a determination to make up for those lost years. The bureaucratic network, because it suffered during the Cultural Revolution and because it generally agreed with the need for far-reaching economic reform, did not and could not mount effective resistance.

Given these conditions, China was ready for change. The first steps toward agrarian reform were made spontaneously by a small group of peasants and local officials. Under the communal system that prevailed until the late 1970s, the harvest was shared relatively equally, irrespective of the effort of individual peasants or their families. As a result, hard-working peasants lost their incentive. Why should they work hard when someone else who might not work so hard would end up as the beneficiary of their efforts? Mao thought that ideological exhortation would persuade everyone to work hard and that there would thus be no problem. That may have appealed to some, but not to most.

As a result of the lack of enthusiasm among the peasants in many parts of the country, food was often in short supply. The problem was compounded by the fact that during episodes of ideological hysteria, such as the Great Leap Forward and the Cultural Revolution, the local cadres would find themselves caught up in the fervor. To show that their people shared the same spirit, they would frequently overstate their local harvest (this may explain why official statistics for the period of the

Cultural Revolution appeared to be so impressive).[6] In turn, seeing that the harvest was so high, the state would raise the local delivery quotas, thus often depriving the peasants of essential foods.

When combined with poor weather, this overzealousness by local cadres and footdragging by the peasants caused food shortages in the countryside. The situation grew particularly serious after the chaos of the Great Leap Forward. By 1962, the shortage of food had become so critical that many peasants found it necessary to beg for food.

Concerned about the well-being of the people under his jurisdiction, Zeng Xisheng, the party provincial leader in relatively poor Anhui Province looked about for some way to generate more food production. While on a visit to a remote part of his domain, he discovered a man and his son farming by themselves.[7] Zeng was struck by the fact that by working by and for themselves, they were producing a much higher level of output than many teams in the communes. He decided as an experiment to tie peasant incomes directly to what the peasants produced and to allow the peasants to keep the surplus once they had produced more than an amount contracted for by the peasants and the local authorities. Zeng found that this resulted in a significantly increased harvest. However, despite his success, party officials in Beijing sharply criticized Zeng for permitting what they saw as the restoration of capitalism. To Mao, in particular, socialism meant the commune, with everyone sharing equally "from the same big pot": "To each according to his need." Mao assumed that, given the proper ideological climate, this would be the same as "From each according to his work." Not surprisingly, Mao prevailed. The Dazhai commune became the model for Chinese agriculture. Reportedly, the peasants in Dazhai relied on a system of work points determined by "self-assessment and public discussion to generate more work incentives."[8] In effect, however, everyone ended up with the same number of work points; this did little to motivate them to work harder.

In the late 1970s, economic conditions in Anhui Province

had again become critical. Perennial flooding added to the havoc created by the Cultural Revolution. By 1978, the peasants in Anhui were forced to resume their begging. Out of desperation, a group of peasants in Anhui's Feng Xang County remembered their 1962 experience and reinstituted what came to be called the family responsibility system, where in effect each family farmed for itself.[9]

In March 1978, Wan Li, the new provincial party chairman, decided to seek official permission to authorize the use of a family responsibility system, which emphasized "task rates."[10] Although they were called "task rates," the peasants in Anhui were actually using "household quotas," or contracts under which they committed themselves to deliver a specified level of output. Beyond that, they could produce and sell whatever they wanted.

Approval from Beijing did not come easily. Even though Mao had died, most of the authorities in Beijing were just as opposed as they had been in 1962. The party's Central Committee established a special commission to study the problem, and it recommended that the experiment be terminated.[11] Army officials, in particular, were disturbed that if the system proved to be effective, their troops would go AWOL back to the villages to share in the new economic opportunity. Even the minority that supported the change argued that, to the extent the contract responsibility system had merit, it should be limited to very poor areas for a very brief period of time.[12] Nevertheless, as happens so often with commission reports, the commission was slow in reaching a final decision, and in the interim the family responsibility system spread rapidly to other provinces, including the most populated province, Sichuan.[13]

What had begun out of desperation spread so quickly and the results proved so productive that before the opposition could organize itself, the proponents of the family responsibility system were able to win over some of their opponents. Eventually, enough party leaders changed their minds that at the December 1978 Third Plenum two draft documents were issued that approved the concept that "payment based on output with bonuses for overproduction was within the parameters of the responsibility system."[14] Undoubtedly, Deng's assumption of effective control of the party at this December plenum also helps to explain the adoption of the less dogmatic stance. Even then, however, the family contract and responsibility system was still classified as an experiment, subject alternately to support and to attack. It was only in the summer of 1982 that the reform became official policy. While some criticism continued, a variation of the family responsibility system became the accepted way to do business in the Chinese countryside.[15]

Given the difficulty his predecessor, Zeng Xisheng, had had in 1962, why did Wan Li risk similar punishment in 1978? Wan gambled that, with Mao's death and Deng's rehabilitation, the political and economic climate had changed enough for him to run the risk. However, at the time of Wan's request, Deng had not yet assumed control. Hua Guo-feng still held the posts of prime minister and party chairman and continued to support the traditional Dazhai commune approach. Despite Hua's opposition to a more meaningful incentive system, other voices in Beijing began to call for "payment according to labor."[16] Admittedly, these calls were still in the minority. Nonetheless, Deng's growing power—and his assertion that it mattered not what color the cat was, only that it caught mice—signaled the existence of at least some who favored a more pragmatic attitude. Once they saw that his peasants were starving, Wang hoped that the new pragmatists in Beijing would agree that an increased harvest was more important than ideological purity.

Because it evolved in an uncoordinated fashion, the family contract responsibility system acquired many different variations, reflecting local preferences.[17] Although some of the party ideologues held out against household contracts until 1983, even without formal approval, local authorities began to sign individual contracts as well as family or group contracts.[18] Moreover, while at the local level there was general enthusiasm for the new system, not all regions of the country were as enthusiastic. Some were actually hostile. Many opponents realized that by assigning families to specific plots of land for one, two, or three years, they were breaking up the collectivized common fields of the commune. In addition, as David Zweig has pointed out, communes located in suburban areas of large cities, as well as those heavily dependent on communal public works projects, such as an extensive irrigation system, were often already well off and feared that a collapse of the communal effort would leave them financially worse off. Indeed, communal investment activities have declined sharply.[19] It should also be remembered that Hua Guo-feng continued as prime minister until 1980 and as party chairman until 1981. Even then, although Deng had effectively taken control in December 1978, Hua's presence must have provided some encouragement to those opposed to the change.[20]

Whatever the initial reluctance to move to the family responsibility system, by late 1983 some 94 percent of the peasants had switched. A year later, in October 1984, the figure was 98 percent.[21] Since in early 1980 the total was only about 20 percent, this massive conversion reflected a combination of pressure from party officials to join in and a desire to share in what had become the undeniable increase in peasant well-being.[22] Today, for all intents and purposes, the commune is a thing of the past and most of China's land has been decollectivized. Families, not communes, determine what should be grown, and when and how.

Each family now contracts with local authorities as to what it will grow and which plot of land it will use. Although at one point the household had to contract to deliver a set amount of grain to the state, today the usual procedure is for the family to pay the state an agricultural tax, a contribution for needy villagers, and, in some cases, something for communal projects. Once the family has met these obligations, it can sell the remainder of its crop on the market at whatever price it can obtain.[23]

Initially, there was concern that the three-year contract for the use of the land was too short and would lead to exploitation of the land. Few peasants would be willing to put any capital improvement in the land if they were uncertain about its future use. Since January 1985 the term has been extended from one, two, or three years to fifteen years. In some mountainous areas where the land needs extra tending and care, families can sign contracts for as long as fifty years.[24]

The increase in output after 1978 testifies as much as anything can to how successful the new system has been (see Tables 7 and 8).[25] In fairness, it should also be pointed out that the Chinese government coupled institutional reform with a significant increase in procurement prices for grain. From 1979 to 1982, procurement prices for grain were raised by about 40 percent, which did nothing to dampen peasant incentives.[26]

The combined effect of reform and price increases has transformed Chinese agricultural output. While most people had assumed that agricultural output in China prior to 1978 was already as high as might be expected, a Chinese official explained to me that the increase in yield was due not only to the improved incentive system. In the past, he said, the work brigade would each morning leave the village and assemble in their assigned fields. There they would await the arrival of the brigade chief, who would assign the work tasks for the day. Waiting for him would often waste an hour's time. The transfer of decision making to the family ended the need to wait for the leader's arrival. The peasants now immediately go to the fields and begin their own tasks, which they themselves determine. From 1978, the first year of the reform, through 1983, production of wheat increased annually at a rate of 8.6 percent, rice at 4.3 percent, and cotton at 16.4 percent. From 1981 to 1984, the rate of growth of all agricultural output reached an annual rate of 11 percent.[27] It was particularly important that, unlike most previous increases in the grain harvest, this increase did not come at the cost of a decline in nongrain crops.[28] Output of almost all crops increased.[29]

Somewhat unexpectedly, the grain harvest declined in 1985. Because it is such an important symbol, this caused considera-

TABLE 7

Production of Major Crops in China 1978–1984

[in million tons]

Commodity	1978	1979	1980	1981	1982	1983	1984	Percentage increase 1978–1984
Wheat	53.8	62.7	55.2	59.6	68.5	81.4	87.8	63.2
Rice	136.9	143.8	139.9	144.0	161.6	168.9	178.3	30.2
Coarse grains	79.1	83.1	84.2	80.8	82.7	92.7	96.4	21.9
Cotton	2.2	2.2	2.7	3.0	3.6	4.6	6.3	186.4
Oilseeds[1]	15.8	16.8	19.4	23.6	26.0	27.2	31.0	89.0
Tobacco, flue-cured	1.1	0.8	0.7	1.3	1.8	1.2	1.5	36.4
Sugar crops[2]	23.8	24.6	29.1	36.0	43.6	40.3	47.8	100.8
Total agricultural output[3]	105.7	117.4	119.0	125.3	138.5	149.2	163.3	54.5

[1]Soybeans, cottonseed, peanuts, rapeseed, and sunflower seed.
[2]Sugarcane and sugar beets.
[3]1976 to 1978 average equals 100.

SOURCE: Surls, "China's agriculture," JEC, 1986, p. 338.

TABLE 8

Growth Rate of Area, Yield, and Production in China
1978–1983

[percent per year]

Crop	Production	Area	Yield
Grain:			
Wheat	8.6	−.1	8.7
Rice	4.3	−.8	5.1
Coarse grain	3.3	−1.8	5.2
Potatoes	−1.6	−4.4	2.9
Oilseeds:			
Soybeans	5.2	1.2	4.0
Peanuts	10.7	4.5	6.0
Rapeseed	18.1	7.1	10.2
Sesame	1.6	4.3	−2.6
Cotton	16.4	4.5	11.4
Sugarcane	8.1	3.6	4.4
Sugar beets	27.7	10.4	15.6
Tobacco, flue-cured	1.8	−1.4	3.2
Jute and hemp	−1.3	−11.2	11.2

SOURCE: JEC, *China*, 1986, p. 339.

ble concern.[30] However, food supplies were adequate, and the Chinese were in fact able to export over four million metric tons on a net basis that year, including some to the Soviet Union. The drop in grain output was not a consequence of any souring in the peasants' attitudes toward the reform but a response to the 1985 price increases of other food products. The peasants simply switched to growing more profitable products whose output increased at the expense of grain.

III

Before discussing China's urban and industrial reforms, we should stop to see if any of China's agricultural reforms can be adopted in the Soviet Union. In other words, assuming that he wanted to, could Gorbachev copy any or all of what the Chinese have done? This will also help illustrate why agricultural reform is so important and why it has implications for the Soviet Union's military posture and even its technology.

The first thing to note is that the Soviets have already introduced a form of the family contract system in agriculture.[31] As we saw earlier, experiments have been conducted in the northern Caucasuses, the Gur'evskii oblast of Kazakhstan, Uzbekistan and some mountainous regions of Georgia, Azerbaidzhan, and Armenia, as well as in Latvia and a few limited areas of the Ukraine and the Russian republic. What is striking, however, is how limited the experiment is as of this writing. Admittedly, the experiment in China was also limited in the beginning, but as others began to discover how much more productive the new system could be, the reforms spread rapidly throughout the country. In contrast, for the time being at least, the numbers involved in the Soviet Union are only in the hundreds of thousands. Moreover, the majority of contracts are limited to dealing with livestock only.[32]

That public opinion polls show a lack of enthusiasm for any shift in the agricultural incentive system in the Soviet Union suggests that Gorbachev cannot count on the same kind of pressure for change that existed in China in 1978.[33] After more time and information, some Soviet peasants may become more enthusiastic about the family contract system, but there does not seem to be anything like the grass roots movement for change that occurred in China. Thus, if there is to be any reform, the likelihood is that, unlike that in China, the initiative in the Soviet Union will have to come from the center, not the countryside. Even in China, despite some support, most party officials were reluctant at first to approve what had already taken place. This opposition to change existed even though the party had been battered by the Cultural Revolution and the distress in the countryside. The Soviet Communist party has felt no such pressure. Fear of what might happen and plain inertia make it even less likely that the Soviet leaders will take the initiative to bring the Chinese version of the family responsibility system to the Soviet Union. While there are sure to be costs, they are uncertain of the benefits.

One of the major costs is that if the Soviets adopt a nationwide system of family contracts, not only will it break down the time-honored collective farm but, if successful, the responsibility system will suddenly make the peasants very wealthy. What may be particularly troublesome is that, as in China, peasant wealth may increase significantly faster than proletarian wealth.[34] If this happens, it will generate resentment among those in the cities who remain on a fixed or limited salary system. It will also cause embarrassing questions about who is supposed to benefit more from the revolution, the proletarians or the peasants. Since Soviet peasants constitute only 20 percent of the population, it will be impossible to rationalize the reform, as happened in China, by noting that the peasants constitute the vast bulk of the population. The relatively small percentage of Soviet peasants also means that even if Soviet peasants become enthusiastic about the family contract system, Gorbachev will not be able to assume, as the Chinese leaders do today, that most of the Soviet people support such a change.

Gorbachev also seems determined to hold on to the collectivized and state systems. By contrast, his farm audiences' reaction to some of his ideas suggests that many peasants want to switch to a private system of farming similar to what now exists in China. This was reflected in a speech Gorbachev gave in the Kuban in the Krasnodar region. "The people of Kuban live in what is indeed a land of plenty," he said there, "and as they benefit personally from that, they should remember that they should not embark on the path of grasping the attitudes and psychology of *private ownership.*" But the context of his talk made it evident that the crowd disagreed with Gorbachev. Responding, Gorbachev insisted that the peasants should follow the socialist way. As for those, he added, who are "neglecting the interests of others, who are his fellow workers, especially the working class in town—people like that are not going our way. That's the way it is. I am being open with you. *I can feel that stirs you up!*"[35]

The issue will become even more sensitive if, as in China, the prices of food products are increased because of either a cut in agricultural subsidies or a freeing of retail prices. As we saw, Soviet consumers tend to react rather violently to increases in the prices of their basic foods. Open inflation will constitute a very serious political issue for the Soviet leadership, one that has heretofore been a problem restricted to the capitalist world or to those socialist countries that are beguiled by false promises.

Equally threatening is the prospect that if the peasants are to respond enthusiastically with increased effort to any reform, they must have some assurance that the larger number of rubles they earn will bring them the material goods they desire. This was not done in the 1920s in the Soviet Union and as a consequence the peasants held back their produce and their efforts. Instead, there was what came to be called the scissors crisis. The prices of the goods bought by the peasants increased, while the prices of the goods they sold declined. This embittered the peasants. The harder they worked, the less they were able to buy for their efforts. In reaction, they reduced their efforts and offered less for sale.

Deng did all he could to ensure that the Chinese peasants would not be similarly disappointed. Deng recognized that he not only must increase the quantity of domestic-made appliances that China made available to the peasants but also must make it possible for the peasants to buy new and more desirable products, including construction materials and imported goods.

Gorbachev will have to be similarly supportive of Soviet peasants. That there will have to be a substantial improvement in the kinds of things Soviet peasants can buy is suggested by the fact that, as we saw, despite what is generally considered a relatively low stock of material possessions, Soviet peasants as well as urban residents continue to save a significant portion of their increase in incomes. In 1985, for example, the total amount of savings in Soviet savings banks rose 18.7 billion rubles, while total retail sales in the country rose only 8.1 billion rubles.[36]

Therefore, any effort to whet the Soviet peasant's purchasing appetite and thus his desire for higher income must, of necessity, provide for a significant shift of resources away from heavy industry to light industry and household construction. In China, for example, peasant housing stock increased sevenfold from 1978 to 1983.[37] If such resources are also to be made available to the Soviet peasants, those in control of the economy must make an explicit decision to shift their priorities. The Chinese recognized that, given the general shortage of consumer goods and construction materials in the country, they would have to set aside increased supplies of goods designed specifically for peasant consumption. To do this for any prolonged period would mean a cutback in resources going to heavy industry. Following in the footsteps of their Asian neighbors, the Chinese leaders under Deng decided to do just that and to do it quickly. Whereas in 1979 light industrial production grew at a rate of 9.6 percent, in the following year its rate of growth climbed to 17.4 percent. In sharp contrast, heavy industrial production, which had grown at 7.7 percent in 1979, continued to grow in 1980, but the increase was pared to 1.6 percent.[38] This was the first time in a decade that light industry had grown so much faster than heavy industry.

The deemphasis of heavy industry in order to divert resources to light industry and to provide incentives for the peasants has another effect. Curbing heavy industry inevitably means that military expenditures must also be reduced. Deng was one of the first to recognize this. Back in November 14, 1974, shortly after his first rehabilitation, he met with a delegation of presidents from American universities and told them,

"If we compete with the Soviet Union in atomic bombs, we can all go to meet God. If we make these bombs, we would not have enough food and clothes."[39]

After his second rehabilitation, he moved quickly to implement his ideas. Without seeking a quid pro quo from the Soviets, he moved unilaterally to cut back his military expenditures. He announced in 1985, for example, that China would demobilize a million troops, a cut of 20 percent, and that if the factories producing munitions were to survive, they would have to switch a sizable portion of their production to the civilian and export sectors. Reflecting this shift, the share of civilian products produced by Chinese military industries rose from 10 percent in 1979 to 40 percent in 1985.[40]

Such moves have resulted in a dramatic change in the ratio of China's military expenditures to its GNP. Whereas military expenditures accounted for an estimated 13.2 percent of the GNP in 1973, they had fallen to 8.6 percent of the GNP by 1983, and most observers agree that, given the demobilization of 20 percent of the armed forces and the conversion of much of its armaments industry, the ratio has continued to fall, so that today the ratio of military expenditures to GNP is most likely less than half of what it was a decade and a half ago.[41]

Some of the Chinese generals who oppose this trend have been pacified with the explanation that Deng's decentralization, changed incentive system, and revitalization of agriculture and industry will promote a faster and more technologically oriented economic growth that will make possible more sophisticated military technologies later. In the conservative reaction to the university protests of December 1986, this division of resources away from heavy and military industry came under attack. But for the time being, at least, Deng has undertaken what few other leaders in this century have done—to bring the economic prosperity and technological growth that he wants, he has reduced China's military might relative to other countries' and asked for nothing in return, not even from the Soviet Union, which is still regarded as a potential threat.

China's experience with reform has far-reaching implications for any Soviet attempt at economic reform. It suggests that if Gorbachev is serious, he too will have to provide more for his people. That in turn means a shift in priorities away from heavy industry and toward light industry and agriculture. Even though the peasantry is proportionally smaller in the Soviet Union, Gorbachev must still cater to it because while his main goal is to energize the proletariat, he will not be able to do that until food supplies have radically improved. But if Gorbachev does decide to cut heavy industry in favor of agriculture and light industry, that will seriously affect Soviet military power. Like those in China in 1973, military expenditures in the Soviet Union amount to approximately 14 percent of the GNP; some argue that the percentage is higher.[42] But Soviet authorities apparently feel they must spend that much if they are to keep up with the United States. American military expenditures were about 6.6 percent of the GNP. Since the Soviet GNP is only about 50 to 60 percent of ours, however, the Soviets must spend a considerably larger percentage to match us.[43] Consequently, it is hard to see how the Soviet Union could sustain its military and political domination with something less than a double-digit allocation of resources from the GNP to the military.

Everything we have seen about Soviet behavior makes it unrealistic to expect Gorbachev to declare, as Deng did, that the Soviet Union will slash its military expenditures regardless of what the United States does. Gorbachev may well cut back some, and he undoubtedly will continue to seek accommodation and an arms agreement with the United States that should enable him to cut back a bit, or at least to prevent further escalation. That explains why Gorbachev persists in trying to entice Ronald Reagan into some agreement. However, even if the United States and the Soviet Union do reach some understanding about arms control, it is unlikely to be far-reaching enough for Gorbachev to challenge his generals and cut the military industrial complex by anything comparable to what Deng did unilaterally. The Soviets may not have to go as far as other countries in Asia in using the increase in peasant wealth as an engine for light industry and a more balanced form of economic growth. But if Gorbachev has any intention of unleashing agriculture and light industry in the manner of the Chinese, there will certainly have to be a radical reorientation of priorities, one entailing a sharp drop in military expenditures.

The Soviets would also seem to be at a disadvantage when it comes to using the family as the unit for change. The extended family in China is an enduring and powerful force. Whereas in the Soviet Union the large feudal estate and village *OBSHCHINA* or the collective and state farms have been virtually the only form of land tenure, in China the family unit has been the predominant form of organization in the countryside for hundreds of years. Mao tried to weaken the family and failed. Except for the period of collectivization and communalization, the family or clan has always served as the basic unit of economic activity in the countryside. For that matter, the Chinese family also tends to be the main focus of financial and industrial activity even among the more modernized overseas Chinese. While the family tends to play a greater role in the Soviet Union than it does in many parts of Eastern and Western Europe, it is in no way as important there as it is in China. Moreover, in the Soviet Union, the rural family tends to be strongest in the Central Asian and Moslem parts of the country, where rural families also tend to be larger—comprising an average of 6.0 persons in Uzbekistan and as many as 6.6 in Tadzhikistan.[44] In contrast, the rural family in the Russian republic and the Ukraine tends to be much smaller, averaging approximately 3.4 persons per family. Of course, Chinese units are often not much larger. The Chinese nuclear family units today are sharply limited in size, because of population control, but this can be misleading. The extended Chinese family continues to exercise enormous influence. There is also reason to wonder how enthusiastic the predominantly Slavic leaders in the Politburo will be to promote a policy that will be much more beneficial to the Central Asians than to the Slavs.

Finally, one can question whether a family contract system

in the Soviet Union would be able to generate the spurt in output that it did in China. What attracted so many so quickly to the new system in China was the impressive increase in output. The benefits of the improved harvest were so pronounced that they outweighed whatever material and physical benefits the peasants might have received from the commune and from the collective ownership and working of the land. Several specialists on China have emphasized that the primary difference between the Chinese family responsibility system and the commune was not so much the new land lease or the payment of a limited tax or rent but the new arrangements signaling that the peasant had regained the power to determine his own destiny—whether it was in deciding what he planted, how he lived, or what he wore. These incentives have stimulated the increase in the peasants' productivity. Even then, once the grain harvest fell in 1985 and 1986, some of that initial enthusiasm gave way to opposition.[45]

Even if the Soviets downgraded heavy industry and allowed light industry and services to respond to an unfettered market, unleashing the peasants in the Soviet Union would not necessarily create a similar surge in output. Remember that agriculture in China is primarily labor intensive. At the time of the reform, Chinese peasants relied relatively little on machinery and chemical fertilizers. The initial increase in Chinese output was thus primarily due to harder, longer, and more meaningful work— not to a large influx of capital inputs. Once the process had started and their income began to increase, the peasants did plow back some of what they earned into capital products like chemical fertilizer and agricultural machinery, which increased productivity still more; but even then, most specialists insist, the chief reason for higher agricultural output was the improvement in the quality and quantity of the peasant effort.[46] (See Table 9.)

Soviet agricultural output would also increase if the Soviet peasants applied themselves more intently and intelligently. If nothing else, Soviet peasants would presumably act more decisively in response to weather changes, something that often

TABLE 9

Agricultural Inputs in China
1978–1983

Item	Unit	1978	1979	1980	1981	1982	1983
Draft animals	Million	50.2	50.3	50.9	54.7	58.3	61.3
Chemical fertilizer use[1]	Million tons	8.8	10.9	12.7	13.3	15.1	16.6
Chemical pesticides	Thousand tons	533	537	537	484	457	331
Rural electrical consumption[2]	Billion kilowatt hours	25.3	28.3	32.1	37.0	39.7	43.5
Agricultural machinery	Million horsepower	159.8	181.9	200.5	213.2	225.9	245.0
Machine numbers:							
Tractors, large and medium[3]	Thousand	557	667	745	792	812	841
Tractors, small[3]	Thousand	1,373	1,671	1,874	2,037	2,287	2,750
Combine-harvesters	Thousand	19	23	27	31	34	36
Trucks for agricultural use	Thousand	74	97	138	175	206	275

[1] Nutrient weight.
[2] Includes electrical use by households and in production but excludes consumption by state-owned factories located in rural areas.
[3] Tractors of less than 20 horsepower are classified as small.

SOURCE: Surls, "China's agriculture," JEC, *China*, 1986, p. 340.

does not happen now, because work assignments are prepared centrally. In all likelihood, though, the extent of the increase would not be as proportionately large. Soviet peasants are much more dependent on capital inputs, such as machinery, artificial fertilizer, storage, and transportation. Certainly, Soviet peasants could use what they already have more rationally. Even Gorbachev has complained that 20 percent of the Soviet crop rots in the field.[47]

Improved peasant motivation would undoubtedly reduce some of this waste, but it must be remembered that the bulk of the waste stems from the failure to invest in an adequate farm-to-market road system and an adequate network of grain storage facilities.[48] Because of historical underbuilding, one-quarter of the *kolkhoz* and *sovkhoz* farms in the Russian republic have no roads connecting them with the outside world. No wonder one-half of the country's tractor fleet is assigned primarily to tow the *kolkhoz* and *sovkhoz* trucks mired in the mud. That is not to argue that the Chinese road system is a good one, for it is not. Yet, all of these factors are much more important in the Soviet Union because its weather is much more severe than China's. This means that the growing season and the harvesting season are much more limited in duration and that Soviet peasants must therefore work quickly when the crop is finally ready. They do not have the leisure to wait a day or two to harvest the crop and then move it off the fields.

Increased access to better-quality material possessions might improve the Soviet peasants' work habits. But in all likelihood there would be no immediate increase in the flow of such goods without some prior economic reform in industry. This suggests that any improvement in agricultural output will not come as abruptly in the Soviet Union as it did in China and that it will thus not be as politically attractive either in the Soviet countryside or in Moscow.

Even if the harvest increased, Soviet authorities would have to have the self-discipline to wait patiently until the peasants felt confident enough to market their increased yields voluntarily. While some farms began the reform process as early as

1978, it took until 1981 for Chinese peasants to feel safe and confident enough to sell a substantially higher percentage of their increased output to others. First, given the high elasticity of their own demand, they wanted to satisfy their own repressed needs. In addition, they wanted to be certain that the new policy was not a short-term trick. Only then, when they had satisfied their own appetites and it looked as if there were an abundance of food everywhere, did they decide to release their products for the market. In China, despite improved harvests, the authorities thus had to import increased quantities of grain from 1979 to 1981.[49] It is unclear whether Soviet leaders would have the patience for this and the confidence that the peasants would eventually begin to market more. They certainly did not have such confidence or patience in the 1920s, when they decided to give up on NEP and collectivize the land.

Initial skepticism about the suitability of the Chinese agricultural reform for the Soviet Union may explain, at least in part, why until early 1986 most Soviet sinologists concentrated on the negative aspects of the reform. They stressed that many Chinese peasants did not share in this prosperity and that this led to a significant increase in income inequality. As Soviet writers continue to stress, some peasants remain as poor as before. In other instances, some of this new wealth has come from manipulation, unfair political advantage, or the sale and resale of land that legally belongs to the state, not to the private peasant.[50] To the Soviets, this smacks of kulakization—the kulaks, or wealthy peasants, being a class they did away with at great human and economic cost in the 1930s. To glorify the return of the kulaks would be to suggest that the initial collectivization process may have been a mistake—something most Soviet officials probably do not believe, at least not now. Nor are most Soviet analysts, including those who have nice things to say about the results of the Chinese reform, pleased by the sight of the breakup of the large collectivized landholdings. This negates the economies of scale that come with using machinery over large tracts of land.[51] For the Soviet Union, with its vast fields and abundant stock of farm machinery, such a breakup would strike most Soviet economists as a radical step backward.

Soviet skeptics also emphasize the inflation that has followed a relaxation of price controls.[52] That something similar might result from an attempted Soviet economic reform haunts Soviet officials. Enormous distortions in the economy are inherent in the Stalinist model of centralized planning and its emphasis on heavy industry. Any attempt to relax economic controls over prices and production is sure to unleash pent-up demands. Given that the Soviet model has been in place for at least fifty-five years in the Soviet Union but only thirty-five in China, it seems likely that the inflationary potential would be greater in the Soviet Union than in China.

Many critics in the Soviet Union have pointed to the disregard by the Chinese of desirable social goals, once the reforms began. As the families sought to increase the number of fieldhands at their disposal, they began to disregard population control restraints and violate the guideline of one child per family.[53] Similarly, Soviet critics have complained that it became so profitable to tend one's own field that communal activity like irrigation canal, drain, or road building and land terracing were being neglected.[54] Finally, the growing wealth of some peasants and the fear that peasants would begin to build up their own landholdings in kulak fashion, at the expense of the poor peasants, seemed to cause genuine distress for the Soviets. In focusing on the undeniable problems, Soviet analysts tended to downplay the real accomplishment of the significantly higher output and the general economic improvement for the bulk of the peasantry.

Signs of a more appreciative evaluation began to appear in a number of articles in late 1985 and early 1986. One of the first to hint that the Chinese agricultural reforms might be a useful model for Soviet agriculture was the economist Tatiana Zaslavskaia. While discussing reforms in Soviet agriculture, she referred explicitly to the "collective responsibility family contract system" as a model of what might be done.[55] An even more positive and lauditory article was written by Fedor Burlatskii for *Literaturnaia gazeta* after his visit to China early in the summer of 1986.[56] Just as those before him strained to find only the bad, so he strained himself to overlook or downplay the problems. He told the Chinese during his visit in China in June 1986, before he wrote the article, that his was a minority point of view. We will have another look at Soviet reactions when we discuss economic reforms in Chinese industry, but the new, more sympathetic tone of many Soviet commentators suggests that growing numbers of them feel that comparable reforms in the Soviet Union would be an improvement, at least in agriculture.

If asked for a prediction, we would be tempted to assert that the Chinese model will not serve Soviet conditions, that family farming will not work (at least not work as well), and that it will not appeal as much to Soviet peasants. It is necessary to remember, however, that the Soviet peasants took the initiative in seizing the land from their landlords before the authorities got around to authorizing what was happening in 1917. Similarly, we should not forget that the Soviet peasants responded enthusiastically to the creation of NEP in 1921 and that when the Germans invaded the Ukraine in 1941, many of the joyous peasants welcomed the German invasion because they assumed that the Germans would free them from the yoke of the collective farm. Clearly, the peasants in both instances concluded that they would be better off with private rather than with landlord or communal ownership. Since that was at a time when peasants were more reliant on their own labor and less reliant on capital inputs, the peasants then may have been more eager than they would be now for such a change. Alternatively, the Soviet peasants may welcome a breakup of the collective and state farms with or without a simultaneous increase in farm equipment and supplies. Whatever the proper evaluation about the peasants' response, there is no certainty and even some doubt that a Chinese type of agricultural reform will increase output as impressively as it has in China.

IV

While there is some agreement on the origins of the reform in the Chinese countryside, there is less concensus about the roots of the industrial reforms.[57] Given Deng Xiaoping's pragmatic methods, it is unlikely that he was responding to any theoretical analysis or following any specific blueprint when implementing his urban reforms. In all probability, Deng and his protégés did what seemed logical to them and were not affected by the ideas of "some academic scribbler a few years back."[58] Nevertheless, some Chinese economists began even before the post-Mao era to call for less reliance on state planning and more reliance on market forces and individual incentives. As far back as 1956, for example, the head of the Chinese Institute of Economics, Sun Ye Fang, wrote an article critical of the distortion created by the gross output index, the Chinese version of the Soviet VAL (see Chapter 3).[59]

This is intriguing for Sovietologists because Evsei Liberman was writing much the same thing at the same time. One of his first articles on the subject appeared in June 1956 in *Kommunist,* the Soviet Union's most important ideological journal.[60] It presumably was something more than coincidence that Sun, who had been a student in the Soviet Union many years earlier, had returned that same year to Moscow when Liberman was propounding his ideas. Many Chinese now seem unaware that Liberman wrote about the need for economic reform so early. Even though the Chinese were in 1956 paying close attention to what the Soviets were saying and doing at the time, they insist now that Sun was an original thinker who brought back to Beijing the spirit of de-Stalinization that was then stirring Moscow. They also point to the influence of Chinese economists like Gu Zhun, of the Chinese Institute of Economics, one of the first men to call for an increase in the role of markets. Unlike Sun, who had spent considerable time in the Soviet Union, Gu was an accountant educated in China. Whatever the source of his inspiration, Sun came back to the subject again during the return to more rational economic policies introduced in the aftermath of the Great Leap Forward. In the early 1960s, he repeated his criticism of the distortions in the incentive system. He urged that output be dropped as a success indicator for factory managers and that profits be used instead. Again, there was a strong similarity to what Liberman was writing at the time.[61]

Sun's ideas gave rise to considerable criticism in the mid 1960s, and he and economists were subjected to attack, both intellectually and physically. However, beginning in 1977, Sun was rehabilitated, and he started to write and lecture again.[62] At a speech of his in Sichuan Province on the need for a better incentive system, one member of the audience was Zhao Ziyang, then the head of Sichuan Province and, later, the prime minister of the country. Whether as a result or by coincidence, Zhao began to implement a series of reforms in Sichuan that closely resembled some of Sun's proposals. Zhao's patron, Deng Xiaoping, was soon to use the same model for industrial reform throughout the country.

Another source of ideas for China's reforms was Eastern Europe. The Chinese were particularly interested to learn about reforms in Yugoslavia, Hungary, and Poland. The reformers wanted to hold on to state socialism while enhancing the role of the market. Some Chinese specialists were sent to Eastern Europe to see for themselves what was happening. China also invited specialists on Eastern Europe, such as Wlodzimierz Brus, who before his exile to England had been involved in economic planning in Poland, and his student Cyril Lam of Oxford, both of whom have apparently had a major impact on thinking in China. Ironically, the Chinese seemed to have implemented many of the East European ideas better than the East Europeans had been able to do.

Whatever the source of the idea, party officials in Sichuan were the first to switch to a new incentive system in industry. Beginning in October 1978, Zhao Ziyang increased the autonomy of ten pilot factories in his province and allowed them to retain a specified percentage of their profits. He also increased the bonuses that could be paid to workers for any increase in profits.[63] Initially, enterprises were allowed to retain 15 to 25 percent of any profits that exceeded those spelled out in the plan.[64] Similar experiments were introduced the following year all over the country. Managers were told that the percentage of profits they could keep would be rigidly set for a three-year period. This was done to assure the managers that if they increased their profits, not only the state but also the manager would have a larger amount to spend.[65] In effect, this also became a form of contract responsibility; the manager and workers continued to earn a set amount and, as with the peasants, the more profitable the operation, the more there would be to share after paying the state. Christine Wong points out that Chinese enterprises were by 1984 retaining 85.5 percent of their increased profits.

As happened in agriculture, the pace of reform outran the legitimation of those changes. The Sichuan experiment was also approved at the Third Plenum of the Eleventh Party Congress in December 1978, the same one that authorized the family contract system in agriculture. The decision to spread the reform to other industries in other parts of the country was subsequently reaffirmed in October 1984, at the Third Plenum of the Twelfth Party Congress.[66] In all cases, the emphasis was on stimulating the managers and the workers, like the peasants, to work harder with the knowledge that once a set sum had been put aside for the state, the remainder—or at least a large portion of the remainder—would be for the producers themselves to share. Moreover, within broad limits, they could utilize the residual for consumption or reinvestment.

The emphasis throughout was on increasing the role of the producing unit and on diminishing the role of the state, the party, the plan, and the central planners. There was still a plan, but except for periodic steps backward, the goal was to seek continual shrinkage in the commodities subjected to the plan.[67] Inevitably, this reduced the emphasis not only on planning but on heavy industry as well. The rate of growth of heavy industry has increased somewhat, but generally light industry continues to grow at a faster pace.[68]

By no means were these shifts in policy adopted uniformly. Just as eager reformers often find themselves ahead of the laws that would authorize such changes, so conservative bureaucrats have in many cases continued to oppose them and have attempted to sabotage the new regulations. Many officials, especially local ones, thus still interfere with enterprise operations.[69] In some instances, such encroachment seemed all but inevitable, especially when some of the newly unleashed enterprises began to import new machinery. In 1985, this resulted in an extraordinarily large trade deficit. The central authorities reacted sharply and instituted controls on imports. When prices began to mount and double-digit inflation set in, they also reinstituted price controls.

While some Soviet observers have come to express a better appreciation for what Chinese economic reforms have accomplished, even the more enthusiastic Soviet supporters continue to criticize what they see as the diminution of the role of the central planner and the social and economic excesses that decentralization has brought to China. For example, given their fetish of gigantomania, Soviet observers seem sincerely troubled by not only the tolerance but the actual encouragement of small-scale private enterprise. As they see it, such encouragement is a repudiation of the basic advantage that comes from economies of scale and leads to the proliferation and duplication of resources.[70] That, after all, is exactly what central planning is designed to prevent. How can any socialist state consciously bring back what even bourgeois economists agree is the waste of the marketplace? Kruglov and other critics point out that duplication of output gives rise to the wasteful use of raw materials. As he sees it, this also results in poor quality of output: "Quality is better and also supervised in state-owned large-scale industries."[71]

Soviet critics point out that China's private and decontrolled sector is growing at the expense of heavy industry and central control. Funds that in the Soviet Union would go to heavy industry are diverted in China to increased consumption.[72] To the Soviets, it seemed inevitable that once it curbed the powers of its central planners, China would have a diminished rate of growth in heavy industry and a proliferation of investment projects, resulting in "investment spread."[73] Lack of strong central control has also led to duplication and bottlenecks, particularly in the Chinese transport, energy, and raw material sectors. As *Izvestiia* points out, this overtaxes the system and creates inflation.[74]

In their attack on the growth of the private sector, the Soviets offer evidence to indicate that the waste generated by private enterprise goes beyond a diversion of resources. They have found that private initiatives in several instances have literally cut the underpinnings out, from under state enterprises and crippled their operations.[75] Small-scale Chinese coal mining operations have apparently dug, without checking, into a Hunan state-operated coal mine, cutting off the air ducts of the most important government-operated mine in the region. This is only one example among many that they offer to illustrate the negative effect of private enterprise on state enterprise. *Pravda* points out that the downgrading of central planning and control has set in motion all manner of centrifugal forces. Some provinces are refusing to trade with one another, because they want to keep their products within their home provinces for domestic consumption.[76] Thus, any curb on central planning accentuates financial and regional rivalries and is a particularly sensitive issue for Soviet officials who worry about the loyalty of the various Soviet nationalities and republics.

Despite such shortcomings and an occasional halt or even reversal, the reform process continues. Factories now have the power to hire and fire and some leeway in choosing the source of their supply. Thus, a group of large enterprises, including the Beijing Textile and Dyeing Factory, now have the power on their own to hire and fire workers and to buy their inputs and sell their outputs from and to the sources of their choice. The manager is also allowed and encouraged to utilize his profits after taxes as well as his depreciation allowance to finance his capital investments and to obtain his capital goods in both planned and open markets.[77] In addition, the Chinese are seeking to improve the process for selecting managers. As an experiment, the managers for thirty-two enterprises in Liaoning Province will be selected through an open competition.[78] Prospective candidates may apply to a selection committee, consisting of representatives from the factory as well as of outside specialists. They will judge the candidates on their past record and on the candidates' future plans for the factory. There is a danger that managers selected in this way will sacrifice long-run growth in order to generate high profits in the short run, but those in charge of the experiment seem alert to the dangers. Since profits in the factories that pick their managers in this manner rose sixfold from 1985 to 1986, those responsible for the experiment feel they may have found a way to generate some of the same enthusiasm and sense of participation for industry that the Chinese peasants now have in the rural areas.

Obtaining capital continues to be a problem, however. The Bank of China follows a state plan. According to the directors of some Chinese enterprises, because the bank has no competition, it does more or less as it pleases. This has been a source of considerable conflict and inefficiency.

Some of the more creative managers in China have sought new approaches to resolve their capital needs. With the approval of the state, some enterprises now sell stock to the public and use the proceeds to buy equipment. One of the first enterprises to do that was the Foshan Trust and Investment Company, which had a stock offering in mid-1984. Other enterprises offering their stock for public sale include the Tianquiao Department Store in Beijing and the Yanzhanong Industrial Corporation. The Industrial and Commercial Bank of China, located in Beijing, attempted something similar in August 1986 when it sold $1.5 million in 9 percent bonds to private investors.[79] The Yanzhanong Corporation raised approximately $1.8 million in proceeds from its public stock offering.[80] Each of its shares has a par value of 50 yuan (at the time, $18) and pays an annual net dividend of 13 percent. For now, the stock can be sold only back to Yanzhanong or the Bank of China. Recognizing that this reduces the attractiveness of such investments, some began to call for the reopening of the Shanghai Stock Market. The need became all the more urgent since, as of late September 1986, 749 factories in Shanghai had issued stock.[81] Responding to the pressure, the government authorized the opening of a bond market in Shenyang on August 5, 1986, and of stock markets in Shanghai on September 26, 1986, and in Beijing in January 1987.[82]

Almost as far-reaching as the opening of a bond or stock market is the formation of special interest groups by the managers of some of the larger manufacturing enterprises in China. In Beijing, for example, an association of manufacturers was established in May 1985. It has members from 110 factories. A membership committee evaluates new applicants. In addition to holding theater and social parties for their wives, the managers of these factories meet to discuss common problems and seek meetings with representatives of the government, and even with the Bank of China, to lobby for their interests—more autonomy and better financial arrangements. In Shanghai there are three such groups, including one for younger members—on the order of the Young Presidents Organization in this country, except, of course, that in China they all manage state-owned enterprises. It is significant that the initiative to create such groups came not from the state but from the managers themselves. Normally, in communist societies, particularly in the Soviet Union, there is no such thing as an organization outside the framework of the government, least of all one representing the bosses that in many respects resembles the National Association of Manufacturers.

As far-reaching as many of these initiatives have been, state enterprise in China is still constrained by many of the traditional regulations and procedures that in many ways are the main barriers to more flexible and efficient operation. As of mid-1986, managers of high-priority enterprises still have no control over the setting of their prices. That is still determined by the state. In factories that make goods that are not of the highest priority, such as the Beijing Textile and Dyeing Factory, the manager has somewhat more flexibility, but even he can move his prices only within a 10 percent range assigned by the state. He has, however, a relatively free hand when he decides on the bonuses he wants to disburse to his staff as a result of increased profits. Yet, the base wage he pays remains assigned by the state. Similarly, he must still work through foreign trade organizations of the Ministry of Foreign Trade when he exports and imports. He cannot deal directly on his own with foreign buyers or sellers. He must also follow the state's guidelines regarding the size of his work force and deal with all kinds of subtle and not so subtle interference on a whole range of issues that may attract the interest of the central authorities.

V

Much of what the Chinese are doing in industry fits the outline set up by Liberman in the 1960s. The major difference is that despite an occasional retrenchment Chinese officials continue to support the expansion of enterprise rights. Moreover, in an effort to prod the state sector to take a more competitive stance, Chinese officials have decided to authorize a return to private enterprise and the hiring of employees by the private entrepreneurs. They continue to insist, as did Lenin during the NEP period, that while they would tolerate and even encourage small private trade, manufacturing, and service industries, they will continue to hold on to the commanding heights of industry. It is the private sector the Chinese count on, however, to meet any new demand for service and for greater flexibility in the supply of goods. Party officials expect that by encouraging private operations in the vicinity of state stores, for example, these stores will feel more competitive pressure as to style, services, quality, and prices. That is generally true, except for the prices, which tend to be higher in the private stores but which in part reflect better style, service, and quality.

Given the size of China's population, it is hard to see how Chinese authorities can keep statistical track of the numbers of people engaged in private trade. Many of them are peasants who sell their harvests on a day-to-day basis. In any case, the number of private businessmen and businesswomen, which was reported to be 140,000 in 1978, had increased to 18 million by 1985.[83]

Lenin or no Lenin, for party fundamentalists, the return to private enterprise in China has probably been one of the hardest changes to accept. To keep the phenomenon within bounds, limits were set as to how many employees outside the family a businessman may hire. As of 1986, the limit was set at seven, but, like so much else associated with the reform, the business-men on their own were outpacing what was formally author-ized. For instance, in 1986 I met a department store owner in Beijing who had a work force of fifteen, including a man who works solely as a cashier. Aware that he had pushed his way into forbidden territory, the owner insisted that in hiring such a large work force he was only performing a social service by providing more goods and employing eight people who might otherwise be unemployed. In another instance, one entrepre-neur held himself to seven official employees but by coincidence also had three special assistants who, as far as could be judged, carried out the same functions as the rest of the staff.

Exemplifying the new spirit of innovation, some of these private businessmen have also joined together to share experi-ences and protect their interests. Some of them, after all, have become very wealthy, such as a private businessman I met in Canton whose earnings were ten times the average wage. Natu-rally, he and his fellow businessmen are prone to all kinds of attempts to tap into some of that income. Some of the encroach-ments are legal, some illegal, and some questionable. For exam-ple, local government officials spend a considerable portion of their time thinking up new and imaginative levies to impose on such businessmen—even including, in one instance, a charge for flowers for the city. In other cases there is outright extor-tion. Consequently, in Canton 5,000 of the more successful private businessmen joined together in an association to support one another. When I visited the head of the association in 1986, he was in the process of hiring a lawyer for the association so that the lawyer could represent the members against unfair claims by officials and disgruntled customers. The association also had at its disposal a van and a facility in which to hold meetings.

While some private merchants continually try to push the limits of what is allowed, they still show a certain hesitancy about pushing too far. In the back of the minds of almost all private businessmen I met in China was the concern that, no matter how successful the reforms, they can always be reversed. Reforms have been reversed numerous times before in prerevolutionary as well as in postrevolutionary China. For that matter, they have been reversed in almost every country that adopts communism, as we saw with NEP in the Soviet Union and NEM in Hungary.

If the reforms were to be abolished, one reason would be resentment at the growing inequality in income. This is the inevitable result of allowing private enterprise. The opportunity to break out and earn ten times or more the average income is what motivates the Chinese entrepreneur to take risks. Many others in the society, however, begrudge high incomes made this way. Moreover, entrepreneurs and those who do add to economic growth are not the only ones who have benefited. All of this has attracted adverse Soviet criticism.[84] The Soviets have no objection to wage differentiation that reflects different productivity levels in a factory or between factories. What bothers them is income inequality that stems from private entrepreneurial and speculative activities. To see private shopkeepers and peasants earning three and four times as much as a factory worker in a state enterprise or as a government official or ten to twelve times as much as a Chinese army officer has to be disturbing to true believers in a proletarian society.

Given the burgeoning resentment toward income inequality and private enterprise in general, many officials in China worry that it is dangerous to get too far ahead of what has been authorized. For that reason, relatively few private businessmen have gone into manufacturing. Some with large families could and did. Others, more commonly, have joined together in cooperatives to fill what they saw as gaps in either the quality or the price of the goods being offered.[85] The cooperatives have been particularly successful. In fact, cooperative associations already constitute an important share of all manufacturing activity in the countryside. By late 1985, there were 480,000 "new economic associations" or cooperatives, with 4.2 million employees engaged in industry, construction, transportation, catering, and other services, and some observers have begun to predict that the cooperatives will soon begin to challenge the dominance of the state industrial sector.[86] Yet, if China expects to catch up to its Asian neighbors, at a minimum it will have to loosen the reins on, if not promote, private manufacturing. One of the most notable features of the development of industry in the Chinese cultural sphere—South Korea, Taiwan, Singapore, and Hong Kong—is how, in addition to that of some of the larger conglomerates, most of the industrial growth, especially in export markets, came first from small privately run family firms. Such firms have been a source of export earnings, which are then used to import technology. Equally important in many instances, these small workshops serve as a training ground for what often becomes a producer of more sophisticated technology. Sony and Honda are two of the better-known examples. Such operations have traditionally been an important part of the process of technology transfer, but before they can be of help to China, they must await a change in China's ideology that will permit and even encourage not just cooperatives but also the private sector to move actively into manufacturing and exporting.

Another area where China has shown its willingness to stretch the definition of socialism is that of joint ventures and foreign investment. This was a particularly sensitive reform because in many ways it brings back memories of Western imperialism and foreign exploitation. The humiliations of the era of the open treaty ports, when foreigners went so far as to post signs in a waterfront park along the Shanghai Bund proclaiming that the park was "closed to dogs and Chinamen," will never be forgiven.

By inviting foreign businessmen in as joint or even wholly owned venturers, the authorities in the eyes of some hard-liners seem to be tossing out one of the major gains of the revolution —the reclaiming of the Chinese economy by the Chinese. Many of the reforms, such as private trade, the bond and stock markets, the glorification of the market and the downgrading of the central plan, seem to be steps backward from what was thought to be socialism. To some of the more nationalistic and ideological members of the party, it almost seems as if the revolution had never taken place.

Some traditionalists have even opposed an increase in foreign trade. After all, in the late 1960s, the official Chinese position was that the poorer countries of the world should be more self-reliant; that was the way to long-lasting and independent economic growth. In that era, few if any foreigners were allowed into China, and then seldom beyond the Canton trade fair. This was a complete reversal of the prerevolutionary open-treaty-port mentality. Today, however, foreign businessmen are swarming all over the country; and, just as in the bad old days, foreigners and the Chinese police themselves have begun to bar ordinary Chinese from some of the more elegant clubs and hotels. I remember seeing a policeman turn away the deputy mayor of Beijing from the Beijing Hotel until she could produce proper identity papers.

Such incidents have caused considerable resentment, but China's reformers continue to seek additional foreign investments and involvement. The state in July 1979 set up four special economic zones.[87] It selected the border areas of Shenzhen, Zhulai, Shantou, and Xiamen.[88] The bait to the foreign investment community to locate in these cities is that their businesses would be entitled to reduced customs duty, income taxes, rent, utility charges, and wage rates and to simplified border procedures.[89] The bait worked reasonably well. Even though the Chinese were disappointed that service-type activities, not manufacturing, accounted for a disproportionate share of the projects, the four zones had by late 1984 signed 4,700 contracts, involving an investment of $2 billion.[90]

While the Chinese are the major shareholders in most of the joint ventures, some foreign investors have been allowed to retain 100 percent control. One such corporation is the Minnesota Mining and Manufacturing Corporation. Located in Shanghai, it manufactures electronic resins, pressure-sensitive tape for electrical appliances, and other materials for the electronics industry.

Unfortunately, not all such initiatives involved high technology, and many turned out to be more promising than real. One consequence is that Chinese authorities have had to reinstitute some controls over foreign investment and procedures. These measures in turn provoked complaints from foreign investors. The foreigners are primarily interested in tapping the vast Chinese market and in taking their profits home in convertible currency, not in Chinese yuan. But the Chinese and, more recently, the Soviets have a very different agenda. They both see joint ventures as a way of obtaining high technology, increasing Chinese and Soviet exports, reducing or substituting imports, and learning Western managerial and production techniques. In addition, by financing these efforts with equity investment from the West, the Chinese and the Soviets are able to do all this without increasing their borrowing. That also explains why the Chinese and the Soviets are not eager to allow the joint ventures to take their profits out in convertible currency, unless the earnings are from convertible currency exports. This means that those who do not export will encounter difficulties in obtaining the convertible funds needed to import the components required to produce sophisticated products in China. (The Soviets are likely to behave in the same way.) In the case of a joint venture with American Motors, the American company ran out of convertible currency. It refused to put up more capital, since it had plenty of Chinese yuan. But the Chinese would not allow American Motors to change those yuan into convertible currency. As a result, the operations came to a halt, because American Motors could not import the necessary components.

Even those who do export are not necessarily immune to problems. They often have difficulty repatriating their profits to the home office. That, of course, assumes there are profits. Many foreign businessmen complain that it is not always as easy to make profits as they had been led to believe. The minute the Chinese sense that a firm is making profits, they raise the rent, which some say is higher in China than in Hong Kong, or they raise wages. Moreover, it is not easy to maintain quality control and fire workers in a system that is innately suspicious of foreign domination. Junior partners often end up being so junior that they cannot make the hard decisions that are necessary if the venture is to succeed. It seems improbable that the Soviets and their joint ventures will avoid running into exactly the same problems and frustrations. Just establishing a legal definition will take years, particularly given the Soviets' even greater concern about ideological purity.

The Chinese decision to resume economic relations with the West, especially the regulation to legalize special economic zones and joint ventures, was initially regarded by Soviet commentators as a serious heresy. Several Soviet writers insisted that the special economic zones and coastal foreign trade zones were not very different from the open-treaty-port concessions given to the imperialists in the nineteenth century.[91] The Soviets argued that the foreigners brought in little if any heavy industry —a complaint that again reflected Soviet priorities.[92] The Soviets stress that despite the concessions to foreigners the Chinese are being provided with little advanced technology and that when the foreigners do bring in technology, they often impose unreasonable regulations on its use.[93] Instead, as we saw, most of the foreign investments have been limited to service-type operations. This ensures the most rapid profit and also allows the investor to exploit the abundant and cheap Chinese labor —"a familiar imperialistic trick."[94]

One of the first signs that the Soviet attitude toward Chinese interaction with foreigners had changed was the appearance of an article by V. Portyakov and S. Stepanov.[95] The two authors presented a relatively straightforward description of Chinese special economic zones and the joint venture process. Although some of the articles that have appeared since were considerably more critical, it certainly appears to be more than mere coincidence that the Soviet authorities subsequently authorized the formation of joint ventures with foreign corporations.[96] Gorbachev may have had in mind something less than the creation of special economic zones, but he has gone so far as to suggest that Vladivostok be made an open city, so that it might become "a seat of trade and culture."[97] That suggestion may not encompass joint ventures, but since Vladivostok has traditionally been closed to foreigners, its opening would signify a marked change in policy, and there is good reason to assume that the change, if it comes, has been influenced by what has been happening in China.

The Chinese themselves are well aware that their opening up of their country has exposed them to some of the temptations that the Soviets criticize. Many Chinese view the special economic zones like Shenzhen as germs that may contaminate the rest of China with a bourgeois presence that could infect not only its ideology but also its social mores. That in part explains why these four cities are literally fenced off from the rest of China with barbed wire enclosures. An ordinary Chinese needs a special pass to visit Shenzhen. That is less difficult to obtain than a passport, but for most Chinese the one is just as unobtainable as the other.

Amid these criticisms, it was somewhat uncertain whether the effort should be abandoned. There was a rumor, for example, that Deng Xiaoping himself was so concerned that he decided to take several members of the Politburo to Shenzhen to judge the success or failure of the venture for themselves. The next morning Deng was said to have asked his colleagues for their impressions. "I cried," one general was reported to have replied. "Why?" asked Deng. "Because of what has happened to our revolution." An eyewitness report of Deng's visit indicates that this story is untrue.[98] However, it is true that some generals and some party officials oppose what is happening in Shenzhen. Nevertheless, Deng himself was bothered enough by the difference between promise and delivery, as well as by the lapse in moral standards, to declare that Shenzhen was still an experiment that "could fail."[99]

Despite his disappointment, Deng has decided that if China is to succeed, there must be more interaction with foreign corporations. For that reason, he has also designated fourteen coastal cities as special trade and manufacturing zones. The difference between the special economic zones and the fourteen ocean port cities is that the former have been transformed, as it were, into comprehensive economic regions, almost like customs free zones or open cities, while in the other cities just the factory sites, not the cities themselves, are special zones. All foreign operations in the special economic zones need pay only a 15 percent income tax (lower than the 18 percent collected in Hong Kong and the 30 to 55 percent paid in the rest of China), whereas in the fourteen cities only manufacturers are entitled to that rate.[100] By mid-1986, the overall effect of such change, at least on paper, was that China had attracted contracts for $18.1 billion in investment and 2,500 joint ventures, 127 of which are wholly owned foreign corporations.[101] Skeptics calculate, however, that only about $5 billion has actually been committed, if that much, and that most of the investment is by overseas Chinese in service activities or low- (not high-) technology industries, which are designed primarily to exploit China's cheap labor. The defenders of the concessions acknowledge the shortcomings but insist that one has to start somewhere, even if the benefits are meager. Technology transfer, as we also saw in the Soviet experience, is a slow and expensive process. Against that background, the Chinese results so far are not that disappointing.

VI

The attempt to attract foreign investment demonstrates as much as anything the costs that come with the benefits of these various reforms. Almost every move that makes the system more productive has not only economic but also political and social ramifications that some regard as a threat to the old order. A shift to more reliance on the market inevitably brings the dismantling of long-standing façades of order and economic stability that heretofore seemed to mask growing disproportions, blemishes, and stresses in the system. In effect, just as in Hungary, the lifting of the veil in China reveals the warts, such as suppressed inflation, unequal income distribution, class privileges and differences, unfavorable balances of trade, disguised unemployment, low productivity, frequent bankruptcies, technological backwardness, endemic corruption, and fallen moral standards, that were almost always there but that were usually powdered over.[102]

And, as might be expected, the popular reaction to the open acknowledgment of such shortcomings is usually negative and, on occasion, even politically dangerous. For example, despite an across-the-board salary supplement for every Beijing resident of 7.50 yuan in 1985, the complaints about inflation have been quite vocal. Reflecting that concern, the *Beijing Review* carried an article that explained what was being done to cope with inflation but noted that "despite assurances, some Beijing residents are worried." "Never have I seen such large-scale price raises since liberation [1949]. It's terrible," complained an elderly man who was standing in line waiting to purchase meat. "I don't think I can maintain or improve my standard of living as some officials have promised. This 7.50 yuan subsidy will not make up for my loss in the price rises." The article goes on to quote another woman as saying, "If reform means price rises, I prefer to maintain the status quo rather than reform. This bad news has confused people."[103]

Of course, similar phenomena, among them bankruptcy,

haunt the capitalist world and provoke similar complaints. The danger for any would-be reformer of the socialist system, including Gorbachev, is that the opponents of change will point to what appear to be these newly generated social evils and blame it not on a more realistic and open view of socialism but on the communicable diseases that seem to accompany any turn to a market, capitalism, or the West.

For many defenders of the status quo, the deficiencies they did not see, did not and do not bother them. Moreover, in many ways the moral and social climate did get better after the revolution. Drugs and prostitution disappeared, and public health, literacy, and food distribution improved considerably. To be sure, as we noted earlier, much of this came at the cost of draconic state and police control. Nonetheless, despite material improvements that the new system has brought and promises to bring, there remain many true believers who, given the option, would probably choose communist morality and hidden sins over the openness of improved economic efficiency and the excesses that reform entails.

The big unknown is what will happen when Deng dies. At the time of this writing, some uncertainty persists. Many Chinese specialists, both in and out of the country, feel that Deng has managed to put in power enough proponents of reform so that there will be no turning back. In addition, the striking improvement in agricultural and industrial production rates of growth has won over many skeptics. Even though the grain harvest fell in 1985 and again in 1986, it is still hard to ignore an average rate of growth in agricultural output of 11 percent from 1981 to 1984. In the same way, an increase in real GNP of 11 to 12 percent and a rise in industrial output of 18 percent in 1985 have been almost too impressive, since they tend to overheat the economy.[104] Even more important, all of this growth has generated an equally large increase in personal income and consumption, something that did not always happen earlier in China when its industrial and agricultural production increased.

But, as we saw, these gains came at a price, and there is no sign that the worrisome growth of economic problems and a decline of social morality will be resolved as long as the market system is allowed to flourish and individuals are encouraged to enrich themselves. There is wide agreement that in many ways these problems are exacerbated by the effort to couple a domineering government sector that is bureaucratic and jealous of its prerogatives to an expanding private sector that is pushing at the limits of what had, as recently as 1978, been sacred codes of behavior.

It could be argued, in fact, that the hardest and most dangerous part of the reform lies ahead, as party and state officials seek to accommodate and integrate the very different perceptions and concerns of the state and private sector. Take the question of bankruptcy. What should society do with an industry that produces goods inefficiently or produces items no one wants anymore? Ideally, the enterprise should be helped to increase its productivity or switch to new products. Yet, such readjustments do not always succeed. Indeed, many enterprises feel safe in being lax because of the assumption that the state will come to their rescue. As János Kornai has pointed out, most officials agree it is unfair to blame the managers for the poor performance of an enterprise when so much of what is wrong is usually a consequence "of central interventions, arbitrarily set prices and so on. Under such circumstances, the bureaucracy feels obliged to shelter the loss makers."[105] But should society then tax and divert resources from efficient enterprises in order to support the inefficient? Would it not be better to allow the efficient firms to keep their resources and become more efficient? Why penalize success and reward incompetence?

We saw a similar dilemma in Hungary, and if the Soviets decide to face up to it, their problem of how to handle the inefficient and obsolete will be equally difficult to solve. But the issue for China is even more important, because where one works also determines one's housing, pension, medical care, and almost everything else. For a Chinese worker, the unit, or *danwei,* is critical; without it, the worker has not only no source of income but also no one to look out for his general livelihood and well-being. The declaration of a factory's bankruptcy thus signals both a waste of material assets and a callousness to human needs.

Despite the risks, however, Chinese officials have apparently decided that the only way to ensure that Chinese managers do their best is to force enterprises that are consistently unprofitable to declare bankruptcy.[106] An instrument factory in Shenyang, in the north, was the first communist Chinese factory to be officially declared bankrupt. Similar moves in that direction are being made in Shenzhen and Beijing.[107]

The Chinese willingness to face up to the costs and benefits of bankruptcy is now also being discussed in the Soviet Union. Remember that Gorbachev and Ryzhkov themselves have called for the firing or, more properly, the reassignment of as many as ten million employees. The Soviets, however, have not yet begun to contemplate permitting bankrupcy in the Soviet Union. When discussing China, the Soviet commentators properly note that bankruptcy can be socially disruptive, particularly if there is no social security or no job location system for the unemployed.[108] Even with such support, one Soviet observer noted, the Shenyang bankruptcy case "aroused a strong response in the press, and since "about one out of every five Chinese enterprises operates at a loss," there may be "too many prospective bankruptcies."[109]

It may be unfair—to those who first took the leap into the unknown by introducing and authorizing the family responsibility system, small private enterprise, and foreign investment —to suggest that issues like bankruptcy, price flexibility, and unemployment may be even more dangerous to implement. Obviously, those initial steps were also audacious and risky. But something like bankruptcy highlights the more frequent and more intensive clashing that will take place as the market system, with its stress on efficiency and hard budgetary constraints, collides more and more with the centrally planned system, with its emphasis on stability and control. This is something that undoubtedly haunts Soviet reformers.

Deng's reforms are revolutionary in that they have moved

Chinese society farther out of the grasp of the Stalinist economic system than any other society has managed to move. Yet, the further Deng goes, the more expectations are heightened and present shortcomings exposed. It is a sort of twilight zone between limited and unimportant reforms and substantial, but disruptive, reforms. Those who have benefited from the reforms will probably continue to prosper and to support them, but the opponents may well come to feel more and more aggrieved and more and more determined to curb the excesses that offend them. In many ways, the traversing of this intermediate area is the most difficult and treacherous part of the whole reform process.

The opposition to the reforms will also grow as it becomes increasingly evident that not everyone has benefited equally. In both the rural and the urban areas of China, there are now some who have become very rich relative to their neighbors. Most of the new rich have made their money in the private or cooperative sector, but their wealth inevitably stirs resentment among the party cadres or bureaucrats, as well as among general employees of the state. Not surprisingly, this has given rise to strikes or slowdowns, as those who are left behind economically try to catch up.[110] Moreover, the average income earners in this still poor society are not reassured when they see these new rich spending their money in fancy, decadent discotheques, which the normal worker cannot afford even to enter. In addition, the corruption, bribery, and materialism—not to mention the prostitution and crime that have reemerged—have been deeply unsettling to many of the more traditional officials, such as Chen Yun, a member of the Standing Committee of the Politburo and an economic planner, who continues to long for a more egalitarian and virtuous society.[111] Leading the attack, Chen Yun has railed against the "evil winds" of corruption and the dangers that accompany the free market.[112] He has pointed specifically to cases like those of the local officials and entrepreneurs on Hainan Island, who by late 1984 had imported close to a billion dollars worth of Japanese cars and appliances for resale inside China, at double the normal price.[113] Chen

Yun's views are shared by other members of the Politburo, including Wang Zhen and Peng Zhen. They and a dozen or so leaders in their midfifties, such as Deputy Prime Minister Li Peng and Liu Hongru, who were educated in the Soviet Union in the 1950s seem to feel more comfortable with central planning and party control.[114] Their opposition to what they see as a weakening of central power is shared by some army generals who are also distressed by the shrinkage of their influence and privilege.[115] Such critics are cited frequently by Soviet skeptics who seem fearful that similar social dislocation will accompany any reform effort in the Soviet Union.[116]

The demonstration and calls for further economic and political reforms by the Chinese university students in December 1986 seemed to confirm the fears of China's political conservatives.[117] Sensing that the proponents of reform had gone too far, they apparently decided that the time for restraint had passed. Led by Chen Yun and Li Peng, the conservatives joined together to complain about what they deemed the excesses of the reform process. The conservatives were concerned that central planning and investment, as well as the party's role in economic activity, had been cut too much in favor of market influences. In addition, the fall in grain harvest for two years in a row indicated to them that the breakup of peasant land plots had gone to far. They were particularly distressed by what they saw as the diversion of resources from investment in land and as a curtailment of communal effort, such as irrigation and storage and other projects of benefit to the village as a whole, and by the dissipation of those funds instead on private pleasures like "weddings, funerals, and festival gifts."[118] The inroads made by foreign and capitalist influences through the foreign trade zones and joint ventures were especially worrisome.

In response to such complaints, Deng Xiaoping decided to fire Hu Yaobang as general secretary of the Communist party. Since Deng had handpicked Hu as his successor, this must have been a particularly painful decision. But Deng may have sacrificed Hu in order to fend off even more far-reaching reversals.

As it was, Deputy Prime Minister Li Peng and his allies began to insist on "a reemphasis on central planning, a slowdown of consumer spending and a return to the ethics of hard work and thrift."[119] If fully implemented, such proposals would represent a rejection of what had been unique and successful aspects of the Chinese reform effort.

Several Chinese officials insisted that the reform process would continue. The January reversals would be only temporary, just as "the Spiritual Pollution" campaign of 1982 had been temporary. But the concerns of some advocates of reform were reflected in the way one of the better-informed senior officials of the Chinese Academy of Social Sciences in Beijing responded to my question about whether the reforms would be reversed after Deng's death. Instead of giving the standard answer, "No, they wouldn't," he hesitated and then responded, "It all depends who dies first."

Because thus far the reforms have been successful and because they have built up a substantial body of support, it might seem that it will be politically impossible to undo what has been done. The complete revocation of the reforms would appear to be particularly difficult in the countryside, where peasants, who constitute such a large percentage of the population, seem strongly in favor of them. But, just as during the current Chinese reforms, economic growth during the Soviet NEP period increased in both aggregate and per capita terms in its early stages. Nonetheless, the Soviet peasants, who in the 1920s also made up a very large share of the Soviet population, were powerless to halt the collectivization of agriculture and the destruction of NEP. Admittedly, it took a Stalin to produce such a turnabout. The Soviet experience suggests that while the prospect seems dim now, given a strong enough leader, the possibility of a similar upheaval in China cannot be ruled out.

That this chapter on China is the longest in what purports to be a study of the Soviet economy is something more than false advertising. By undertaking such a reform, Deng Xiaoping and his associates have in effect provided Gorbachev and his associates with a laboratory experiment of what might happen if they should decide to undertake similar reforms. It is unlikely that Gorbachev will follow exactly in Deng's footsteps, but it is essential that we have some understanding of the type of difficulty Deng has had and will have to deal with, as we conclude this study with a chapter examining what lies ahead for Gorbachev.

8

The Choices and Obstacles That Lie Ahead

The task Gorbachev has set for himself is not an easy one. The time has come for us to examine what options are open to him. The main choices seem to be (1) a far-reaching reform that emphasizes a heavy reliance on the market, (2) an improved version of central planning and control, and (3) a hybrid system combining elements of each of the other systems. Other variations have been suggested, but these three options seem to be the main choices available to Gorbachev.[1]

A radical transformation of the economy, as Gorbachev called it initially, or even a radical reform, as he subsequently referred to it, is difficult under the best of circumstances. Those who have tried reform in other communist countries have had mixed results. Those who have attempted it in the Soviet Union have had uniformly poor results. The legacy of the Stalinist economic model is that it tends to perpetuate itself.[2] Huan Xiang, a senior official of the Chinese Academy of Sciences, put it precisely when, in describing the problem reformers in the communist world have to deal with, he noted that "the more centralized, the more rigid; the more rigid the economy, the lazier the people and the poorer they are; and the poorer the people are, the greater the need for centralization, forming a vicious circle" from which it is not easy to break out.[3]

The Stalinist model is more deeply embedded in the economic, social, and political fabric of the Soviet Union than in that of any other communist country, and any transition will therefore be more wrenching for the Soviets to make. We saw how difficult it has been for countries like China and Hungary to attempt the transition, and they were addicted for much briefer periods of time. If reforming the Chinese and Hungarian economies is comparable to turning around an oceangoing tanker, reforming the Soviet economy is analogous to turning around a dock that is firmly anchored to the shore.

But if anyone is to break the Soviet Union out of its trap, Gorbachev appears to be an excellent choice to do it. Before we consider his economic options in more detail, we will take a brief look at his political record. As we noted, he moved quickly to consolidate his power and to alter the makeup of the Politburo (see Table 10). Moreover, the sincerity of his desire to reform his country is beyond doubt. Within a year and a half of his accession to the post of general secretary of the Communist party, he had traveled through more of the Soviet Union than any previous Soviet leader, with the possible exception of Khrushchev, and Khrushchev had almost ten years to do his traveling. Wherever he has gone, Gorbachev has hammered in the need for economic revitalization, criticized inept bureaucrats and party leaders by name, and sought to rally the Soviet people to his cause. He has worked the crowds almost as if he were running for the presidency of the Soviet Union. Given his insight, enthusiasm, effort, and proselytizing style, he comes well equipped for the challenge.

Today, few Soviets doubt that Gorbachev means what he says. When Gorbachev in September 1985, visited Tyumen, in West Siberia, the main petroleum-producing region of the country, he brought with him a long list of organizations that had performed poorly.[4] Many of the criticized officials were subsequently fired. The lesson has not been lost on their successors, at least for the time being. In late 1983, before Gorbachev's accession to office, petroleum output began to decline; by 1985, it was 3 percent below what it had been a year earlier.

However, in response to Gorbachev's pressure, including his visit, petroleum production began to increase in early 1986. Production in 1986 was 3 percent higher than it had been in 1985. This was the result not so much of the discovery of new fields, although drilling has been increased, as of more careful work, better discipline, and a more sober work force.

However, impressive as Gorbachev's crackdown on discipline has been, unless there is a change in the underlying nature of the economic system, these production increases, which have also occurred in other segments of the economy, will again turn into declines. No matter how eager or resourceful a manager may be, he has to be able to depend on a smooth flow of materials and services from other sectors of the economy, and this will not come about through improved discipline and sobriety alone.

Nevertheless, even if such accomplishments are not a long-run solution, they are nonetheless something Gorbachev can take credit for. They enhance his record as a leader to be reckoned with and provide him with an important sense of momentum. The possibility that he will be in office for as much as twenty years means that those who might choose to oppose Gorbachev had better do so with discretion or, even better, with anonymity. At this stage of his tenure, the force for change would seem to be with him.

Gorbachev's record is not flawless. For instance, before he became general secretary of the party, his chief duty in the Central Committee was to deal with agricultural matters. He assumed responsibility in 1978, and by 1979 the Soviet Union had encountered a record series of bad harvests, which extended into 1986. A new agricultural program was unveiled in May 1982, but it contained little innovation. Like most new programs that have been unveiled since, it is at once more and less of what we saw in the past.

To some extent, Gorbachev's unimpressive record as an agricultural czar can be explained away by the fact that he was, after all, an underling in an administration run until November 1982 by Brezhnev and from February 1984 to March 1985 by

TABLE 10

CPSU Politburo and Secretariat (as of February 1, 1987)

Name (Date appointed)	Position	Birthdate
Politburo Full Members		
GORBACHEV, Mikhail Sergeyevich (10/80)	General Secretary, CC CPSU (1985)	03/02/31
ALIYEV, Geydar Aliyevich (11/82)	First Deputy Ch'man, USSR CM (1982)	05/10/23
CHEBRIKOV, Viktor Mikhaylovich (04/85)	Ch'man, KGB (1982)	04/27/23
GROMYKO, Andrei Andreyevich (04/73)	Ch'man, Presidium of USSR SS (1985)	07/18/09
*KUNAYEV, Dinmukhamed Akhmedovich (04/71)	First Sec'y, CC CP Kazhakhstan (1964)	01/12/12
LIGACHEV, Yegor Kuz'mich (04/85)	Sec'y, CC CPSU (1983)	11/29/20
RYZHKOV, Nikolai Ivanovich (04/85)	Ch'man, USSR CM (1985)	09/28/29
SHCHERBITSKY, Vladimir Vasilyevich (04/71)	First Sec'y, CC CP Ukraine (1972)	02/17/18
SHEVARDNADZE, Eduard Amvrosyevich (07/85)	Minister of Foreign Affairs (1985)	01/25/28
SOLOMENTSEV, Mikhail Sergeyevich (12/83)	Ch'man, Party Control Com'n, CC CPSU (1983)	11/07/13
VOROTNIKOV, Vitali Ivanovich (12/83)	Ch'man, RSFSR CM (1983)	01/20/26
ZAYKOV, Lev Nikolayevich (03/86)	Sec'y, CC CPSU (1985)	04/03/23
Candidate Members		
DEMICHEV, Petr Nilovich (11/64)	Minister of Culture (1974)	01/03/18
DOLGIKH, Vladimir Ivanovich (05/82)	Sec'y, CC CPSU (1972)	12/05/24

Candidate Members

SLYUN'KOV, Nikoly Nikitovich (03/86)	First Sec'y, CC CP Belorussia (1983)	04/26/29
SOKOLOV, Sergei Leonidovich (04/85)	Minister of Defense (1984)	07/01/11
SOLOV'YEV, Yuriy Filippovich (03/86)	First Sec'y, Leningrad Obkom (1985)	08/20/25
TALYZIN, Nikolay Vladimirovich (10/85)	First Dep. Ch'man, USSR CM (1985)	01/28/29
	Ch'man, Gosplan (1985)	
YAKOVLEV, Aleksandr Nikolayevich (01/87)		12/02/23
YEL'TSIN, Boris Nikolayevich (02/86)	First Sec'y, Moscow Gorkom (1985)	01/?/31

Secretariat

GORBACHEV, Mikhail Sergeyevich (1978)	General Secretary	03/02/31
BIRYUKOVA, Aleksandra Pavlovna (1986)		02/25/29
DOBRYNIN, Anatoliy Fedorovich (1986)		11/16/19
DOLGIKH, Vladimir Ivanovich (1972)	Head, Heavy Industry Dep't	12/05/24
LIGACHEV, Yegor Kuz'mich (1983)		11/29/20
LUKIANOV, Anatol Ivanovich (1987)		05/07/30
MEDVEDEV, Vadim Andreyevich (1986)	Head, Science and Educ. Dep't	03/29/29
NIKONOV, Viktor Petrovich (1985)		02/28/29
RAZUMOVSKIY, Georgiy Petrovich (1986)	Head, Organization Party Work Dep't	01/19/36
SLYUN'KOV, Nikoly Nikitovich (1987)		04/26/29
YAKOVLEV, Aleksandr Nikolayevich (1986)		12/02/23
ZAYKOV, Lev Nikolayevich (1985)	Head, Propaganda Dep't	04/03/23
ZIMYANIN, Mikhail Vasilyevich (1976)		11/21/14

*Removed from office December 1986.

Chernenko. That may also explain why, at a party session in October 1984 devoted to agriculture and where Gorbachev should have been a featured speaker, he uttered not a public word and was consigned to a back bench.

Gorbachev's shortcomings are not just the fault of others. The way he handled the explosion of the Chernobyl nuclear reactor, for example, was wanting. Admittedly, the Soviets have seldom done well with crisis management. As we saw, their relatively quick announcements about the sinking of the passenger ship *Admiral Nakhimov* and of their nuclear submarine in the fall of 1986, as well as the riots in Alma-Ata, suggest that, as part of the *glasnost* policy of openness and candor, they are trying to be more open and responsible. But because they have heretofore been more accustomed to suppressing their own news, this new policy is not always easy to carry out. There is also no denying that no one in any country has handled nuclear emergencies well. But Gorbachev's handling of the situation at Chernobyl was particularly inept.

The explosion took place at 1:23 A.M. on Saturday, April 26, 1986. Officials on the scene realized immediately how serious the explosion was when the roof over the reactor blew off and a fire generating heat of several thousand degrees centigrade ensued. Once that happened, they knew they had no choice but to call for outside help. American doctors have been told, for example, that Hospital No. 6 in Moscow was called within two hours of the explosion and ordered to send a medical team to Chernobyl and to ready itself to receive patients. The team left within six hours. Similarly, the Council of Ministers office in Moscow was called. It immediately created a special commission, whose members were quickly selected. As one of the scientists boasted, "Literally a few hours after it happened, the government decided to set up a commission. More than one half of the members of the commission were at the time in different parts of the Soviet Union, thousands of kilometers apart. And yet, we arrived there and got down to work on the same day."[5] Seldom has the Council of Ministers responded so quickly. It could have acted this way only with Gorbachev's involvement. This is further indicated by the acknowledgment of Valentin Falin, the chairman of the news agency Novosti, that Gorbachev was told about the explosion on that same Saturday.[6]

Even though senior Moscow officials, including Gorbachev, knew that there had been a serious accident at Chernobyl, they behaved as earlier Soviet leaders had—with lack of candor. Fearing panic among their own people and embarrassment in the outside world, they tried to hide what had happened as long as they could. There had been a somewhat similar accident in the Ural Mountains around 1957, in which twenty to thirty villages disappeared from the map, but no word of what had happened leaked out for about two decades.[7] Despite his insistence on *glasnost,* Gorbachev and the other Soviet leaders apparently thought they could handle Chernobyl in the same way. They did evacuate those caught at the plant site, but the residents of Pripyat, only four or five miles away, some of whom heard and saw the explosion, were left in their homes until Sunday at 2:00 P.M., a full thirty-six hours after the explosion and escape of radioactivity. Because of the failure of the leaders to respond, children were even permitted to play soccer in the town's streets.[8] The residents of the town of Chernobyl, ten miles away, were not moved until a full week after the blast, on Saturday, May 3, when a Politburo delegation—including Ligachev, Ryzhkov, and Shcherbitsky (but not Gorbachev)— paid a visit to the area and was horrified to see about 40,000 people still within a radius of eighteen miles of ground zero. Others remained in radioactive areas for as long as a month before they were finally evacuated.

As for Gorbachev, he waited until May 14, a full eighteen days after the event, before saying anything in public about what had happened. Then he insisted, "As soon as we received reliable initial information, it was made available to the Soviet people and sent through diplomatic channels to the governments of foreign countries."[9] This is not true. In addition to leaving the residents of Pripyat on their own for thirty-six hours with no advice about what to do Soviet authorities made no public announcement about what had happened until a three-sentence bulletin was finally read on Soviet television at 9:00 P.M., Moscow time, on Monday, April 28, 1986, almost three days after the event. That was the first the general Soviet public and the outside world knew for sure that there had been an explosion. Because they were receiving high readings of radio-activity, the Swedes, in particular, had on Sunday begun to call three Moscow ministries involved with nuclear energy to inquire if Soviet authorities could explain the source of the radio-activity. Even though each ministry had sent representatives to Chernobyl on Saturday morning as part of the special Council of Ministers commission, all three denied having any knowledge of any problem.

As the leader of the Soviet Union, Gorbachev must take responsibility for the delay in notifying his people and the world and for not removing nearby residents immediately. Since his May 14 speech some Americans have argued that instead of being criticized, Gorbachev should be praised for his openness. It is true that the Soviet Union did eventually become more open, but this view ignores the earlier mishandling of approximately 100,000 people in the immediate area, who were needlessly exposed to excessive amounts of radiation. Gorbachev in his speech tried to mask this misbehavior and his own very belated reaction (Stalin, despite his reported mental breakdown, waited only eleven days to address his people after the Nazi invasion of the Soviet Union in 1941), but more and more Soviet citizens, particularly the intellectuals, are coming to realize what happened. In the long run, this may seriously tarnish Gorbachev's image as an effective, responsive, and thoughtful leader. It may undermine his effort to induce the masses to follow his leadership into one of the most difficult tasks a society can undertake, the complete revamping of its deeply entrenched economic and political system. His overall record is still impressive, but if there is to be true *glasnost,* it must be acknowledged that he proved ineffective in dealing with an incident that demanded decisive action.

I

As powerful as he is, Gorbachev can only afford so many Chernobyls. The nuclear accident was particularly unfortunate because it seemed to confirm the rumors that had been circulating among some of the more superstitious Russians that catastrophes of this nature would plague Gorbachev. As bizarre as it might seem, because of the large birthmark on his forehead, it was whispered that Gorbachev had been cursed by the devil and branded with the mark of Cain. When Chernobyl was followed by a series of railroad accidents and coal mine disasters, as well as the ship and submarine sinkings, and even the unprecedented winter cold spell in 1986–87, this was taken by some as a sign that Russia would suffer as long as Gorbachev served as leader.

Part of the problem, of course, is that what appears to the old lady in the street to be an increase in catastrophes is due in part to Gorbachev's policy of *glasnost*. Previously the Soviet Union seldom acknowledged the existence of such tragedies. But there is little doubt that even if the Russian people were not so superstitious, once the policy of *glasnost* had been adopted, there would be a danger that the good news coming from the reforms would be swamped by the bad news. After all, as of March 1986, Gorbachev had been in office just two years. Nonetheless, Soviet workers had already begun to complain that the only change Gorbachev had brought them was an increase in the length of the vodka line, the institution of second and third work shifts, and more rigorous work requirements. For such reasons, it is important that Gorbachev have some success with his economic reforms, particularly if it appears the Chinese reforms are succeeding. For that matter, if China continues to make progress, the Soviets will find it increasingly difficult not to follow in China's footsteps and introduce similar reforms, something that will be painful for a country that sees itself, not China, as the leader of the communist world.

If he chooses, Gorbachev can cite a historical precedent for a move in what now appears to be the Chinese direction. That was Lenin's decision to adopt the New Economic Policy (NEP) in 1921. Some Soviet scholars have argued that Gorbachev should do just such a thing. Certainly, it would be ideologically safer for Gorbachev to seize the old NEP banner than to proclaim any move toward the market as his own conception. Whatever its source, "A Manifesto of the Movement for Socialist Renewal," which was released to the *Guardian* of England on July 22, 1986, also calls for a return to something like the NEP program. Its authors were reportedly a reform group originating in the Soviet leadership itself. While that seems doubtful, many elements of the economic program proposed by the movement have nonetheless been suggested by official spokesmen.

The NEP model would allow, at least initially, for state control of heavy industry and most means of production. It would, however, permit peasants and small private merchants to enrich themselves. As in the Asian and even the Bukharin models, this implies that the peasants could use their profits to satiate themselves until they had built up enough personal wealth and confidence in the system to reduce their hoards of goods. This also entails the decision to reverse priorities and allow light industry and private services to grow at the expense of heavy industry and the military-industrial complex.

Even if Gorbachev does not choose to call what he does a return to NEP, any move in the direction of the market can hardly avoid an evolution similar to that in China and Hungary. Neither the Chinese nor the Hungarians called what they were doing NEP (Hungary did refer to it as NEM), but it is fascinating to see how similar the pattern of reform has been in the two countries. In both cases, reforms followed in the wake of far-reaching political chaos and violence—the 1956 uprising in Hungary and the Cultural Revolution in China. That not only weakened the control of the Communist party but also forcibly awakened the people to the need for economic improvement. In both countries, this provoked the peasants, who out of desperation simply broke out of the collective and began to work the land for themselves. The initiative, in other words, came from the peasants, not from the center, which was distracted by questions of political survival.

If the Soviet Union were instead to opt for a more centralized reform, it would probably try to integrate enterprises into the central-planning and ministerial system largely the way the East Germans did. By bringing research, supply, and foreign trade activities under one roof, such as that of the *Kombinat*, the Soviet enterprise, like its East German counterpart, would presumably be able to upgrade its technology and involve itself directly in foreign trade. This would follow from the elimination of what has been viewed as a deadening and self-serving bureaucracy at the ministerial level, one that needlessly clutters decision making and stifles innovative and creative ideas. The *Kombinat* in East Germany is the ideal, but unrealistic, type. There would be no West German counterpart to underpin the Soviet effort.

The third option for the Soviet Union—rather than either pronounced decentralization or centralization—is to continue along much the same route it has been following since the beginning of the five-year plans. Various reformers will suggest cosmetic improvements in the way things are done. One will suggest greater central control; another will suggest more autonomy for the enterprise. There is no reason why two economists, or even the same person, might not suggest both courses at once. Politically, this would probably be the safest course to follow, and if Gorbachev can rouse himself to periodic bursts of bureaucratic reshuffling and anticorruption purges, the system should continue to grow. While Soviet technology may find itself falling farther and farther behind that of the rest of the world, living conditions would probably continue to improve, albeit in a slow, ponderous fashion, as they have in the past.

II

If Gorbachev were to seek outside advice, which of the three options might a Western economist, after years of studying the Soviet economy, recommend to him and the Politburo? I acknowledge in advance that the likelihood that the Soviets will follow such advice, particularly a radical move toward decentralization and the market, is very small or even nil. Were such prescriptions to be adopted, they might well cause the dismantling of the present communist system, as well as the secession of many of the Soviet republics. I nonetheless offer these recommendations as a way of indicating just how radical and controversial Gorbachev's transformation will have to be if he is serious about making the Soviet Union a world economic and technological leader.

Even though there is not as large a constituency for agricultural reform in the Soviet Union as in China, I would begin by allowing the peasants to increase the size of the private plots they already possess and to extend their private trading activities. I would start with the peasants, even though Gorbachev might prefer to help the urban workers first. The urban worker, like the peasant, will be reluctant to work harder and more carefully until he or she knows that there will be something worthwhile to purchase with the additional rubles that harder and more careful work will bring. That means, first of all, that more and better-quality food must become available. Thus, improved treatment of the peasants is a prerequisite for progress elsewhere in the economy.

The peasants as well as urban residents would also be allowed to engage in private handicraft and manufacturing. Wherever possible, Soviet entrepreneurs would be encouraged to join together voluntarily in cooperative groups. Gorbachev seems to be doing just that. Cooperatives are more acceptable from an ideological point of view, but for that very reason Soviet peasants and businessmen may be reluctant to join them. This reluctance stems from the fact that many things have been done in the Soviet Union in the name of the collective and cooperative, which have not given the members any input. Thus, when émigrés from the Soviet Union arrive in Israel, almost none will have anything to do with the Israeli kibbutz movement, because they assume, incorrectly, that the kibbutz members, like their counterparts in Soviet collectives, have no say in the management of the farm. There would be no restraint, however, on those who want to operate as private owners. Those operating service firms should be allowed to hire up to ten nonfamily members, and those in manufacturing should be permitted to hire up to twenty nonfamily employees—something, as we saw earlier, Gorbachev has so far refused to do.

This can be described as a return to the NEP. That would also mean that once the peasants and private proprietors, as well as *sovkhoz* and *kolkhoz* or service and manufacturing enterprises, both private and state, had paid a tax equal to 30 percent of their profits, they should be allowed to dispose of the remaining 70 percent of the profits as they choose. There would be no delivery quotas. Unlike the prototype contract responsibility system currently being used in the Soviet Union, this system would assign the limited tax not only to collective and state farms but also to individuals and families. Private producers and cooperatives would be allowed to compete if they could produce at the prices charged by state enterprises.

I would also recommend that Gorbachev follow many of the same reform principles in industry. While the state would continue to control large enterprises, procedures would have to be established for determining and controlling management. There is no reason why a high level of economic efficiency cannot be obtained with state ownership of some of the major means of production. That has occasionally happened in other countries. But state ownership is most effective when it is forced to compete, if necessary, with private or cooperative firms. Normally, the private sector will find itself unable to raise the capital needed to finance the heavy industrial projects of the sort created or operated by the state, but the possibility should not be precluded. For example, some relatively small entrepreneurs in the United States have discovered that mini steel mills can often produce steel more efficiently and thus more profitably than the larger integrated mills. The private and cooperative sector could challenge the state sector this way when the technology warranted.

Another approach to industrial reform that might be more acceptable than a return to private ownership would be to hand over ownership or control of state enterprises to the factories' employees. As in Hungary and some parts of China, the workers could form assemblies that have the power to select and fire a managerial board of directors—or the manager himself, in the smaller organizations. This would help ensure decentralization and a reduction in the state's control. Gorbachev in January 1987 suggested something like the election by workers of their managers, but there apparently was some resistance to the idea within the party. Worker control has sometimes resulted in excessive payment of bonuses, but an effort should be made to establish guidelines for the division of bonuses and for the reinvestment of profits.

Efforts would be made to ensure that the firms react to market-set prices. Prices for goods would be decontrolled as soon as possible. Prices for goods in short supply should be increased gradually, on a preannounced schedule, so that in something like three years all prices would operate freely. That might well bring severe inflation. Upper-income groups, especially those with savings, should be able to withstand the increase, at least until private and cooperative farms moved in to take advantage of those prices with increased production, which in turn should bring about lower prices. But lower-income groups would be given an immediate pay increase to help them cope with the higher prices. This would no doubt cause additional inflationary pressure, but it would be a necessary step for political as well as humanitarian reasons.

Some central planning in the production of major commodities might have to continue for two or three years, but the goal would be to abolish the direct administrative allocation of goods thereafter. Beginning immediately, however, plan quotas would be reduced to allow enterprises, even those producing priority goods, to sell an increasing proportion of their products on the market at market price and not through the plan.[10] Production for military needs would take place increasingly through the expenditure of tax proceeds and the open purchase of equipment.

New flexibility in the allocation of capital would be required to make it possible for private and state manufacturers to obtain the funds they need. Gosbank's monopoly would be broken and republics and large cities be able to establish their own banks. Enterprises and even individuals would also be allowed to join together to form lending institutions. Bond and stock markets would be established, too, to provide for even more capital mobility. Because central planning and administrative allocation of goods would be phased out over a period of time, access to rubles would take on meaning. For the first time, those with rubles would be able to purchase or rent equipment, materials, and buildings.

Initially, it might be difficult to generate a competitive mentality among the directors of existing state firms. Allowing private and cooperative firms to operate would help. It might be necessary, however, to reduce the long-standing emphasis on the amalgamation of enterprises and move to split them up instead. Enterprises, as well as individuals, would have to be allowed to expand imports over a three-year period if domestic producers found they could not compete in terms of price and quality. Both Hungary and China have had difficulty with producers who act as monopolists.

Another way to reduce the power of the monopolies would be to increase the economy's interaction with foreign producers. Even though the move would provoke serious shocks for many domestic producers, the ruble would be devalued in stages over a three-year period and export and import restrictions relaxed. The monopoly of the Ministry of Foreign Trade would be ended and foreign trade organizations dissolved. Joint ventures would also be encouraged, with the Soviet partner retaining 51 percent control. Provisions would be made for the progressively larger withdrawal of profits by the foreign partner.

To summarize, if a Western economist were to attempt to revitalize the Soviet economy, one of his first steps would be to seek a reduction in the role of the central planners and increase the authority of the enterprise managers. This means that while central planners would maintain control over the commanding heights of industry, those heights would be reduced gradually so that the price and market systems would come to play a growing role in the allocation of resources. The Soviets would be advised to legalize private property for the peasants and small businesses that engage in service or manufacturing operations. Cooperative service and manufacturing operations would also be legalized and encouraged. The state could continue to own and operate farms and factories, but they would have to learn to compete both among themselves and with the private and cooperative enterprises. The workers and managers would be rewarded with material incentives for their efforts, particularly for displays of extra creativity. That means that there would have to be an improvement not only in the way bonuses were calculated but also in what those bonuses could buy. There would have to be more emphasis on consumer and innovator sovereignty and less on the preferences of central planners. That is not to say that material interests would be ignored, only that those material interests would have to compete by means of rubles with other ruble holders.

Such measures would not be easy to implement. Indeed, some might argue that the combined effect of such actions would be to end the Soviet system. Yet, the Politburo has already agreed in principle to some of these changes, and other suggestions have been advocated separately, though not as a package, by reformers in the Soviet Union itself. The problem is that while such reforms, if undertaken earnestly, might bring the Soviet Union into the world economic system and enable it to share as never before in its successes, they might also cause the Soviet Union to share in its failures.

III

Once the reforms are decided upon, one still has to decide how to introduce them. Should one bring them in more or less all at once, as Ludwig Erhard did in Germany after World War II, or in piecemeal fashion as Deng and Kádár did? In all likelihood, it would be too much for the Soviet Union to switch all at once. In my scenario, I suggest a three-year break-in period because that would indicate a seriousness and immediacy of purpose and force Soviet managers to act now rather than procrastinate with the excuse that five years from now is a long way off. Most Soviet bureaucrats would no doubt delay as long as they could in hopes that some new proposal or ideological shift would spare them the hard choices they would otherwise have to make. That is why a short, meaningful limit for action is essential. Yet, given the deep roots of the Soviet system, it is necessary to recognize that it may be too traumatic to attempt such a transformation in a three-year period. So, as risky as it is, the reformers might opt instead for ten to fifteen years. West Germany, after all, before World War II had considerable experience with the market processes, and it was not necessary there to upend the whole political and economic system to bring the market back. Except in the Baltic republics, there are very few in the Soviet Union now who are old enough to have lived in a market-dominated environment. It would be irresponsible to expect that, without some time to prepare themselves, Soviet officials could administer a market system. Even if the state were to retain some of its administrative powers, the reform would presumably involve a gradual replacement of the basic role of central planning with new and increasing reliance on monetary and fiscal tools. Without time for preparation and reorientation, however, where would the Soviet Union find anyone with the requisite monetary and fiscal skills to implement such policies? Suddenly assigning a Soviet official from Gosbank or Gosplan to the task of fine-tuning the economy by using money supply variations and tax measures would be like assigning a railroad engineer who has never flown before to pilot a Boeing 747. Such a switch is not impossible, but it has its risks.

For that matter, Gorbachev will be lucky if he can move half as fast as leaders in Hungary or China did. Reform in both those countries was preceded by political and economic chaos. Nothing comparable has happened to the Soviet Union. In fact, to the extent that he is successful in increasing economic growth in the short run, Gorbachev actually lessens whatever urgency there might be for any extensive reforms. As we saw, this sense that the present situation is not serious enough to risk reform is typified by the reaction of Nikolai Baibakov, then the chairman of Gosplan, who was asked at a 1983 press conference about the likelihood of a radical reform away from central planning. Andropov had managed to rouse the economy to a considerably higher level of production than it had attained under Brezhnev. "Under the circumstances, why switch?" Baibakov asked. The economy, after all, was growing normally, so why should the Soviet Union abandon central planning and, by implication, switch to something as uncertain as the market and its inevitable inflation, bankruptcy, unemployment, and balance of trade problems? Since the rate of growth was then higher in the Soviet Union than in most Western countries, at least in the terms important to the Soviet Union, why should the Soviet Union give up a good thing?[11]

Gorbachev himself seems to recognize that this type of recovery does indeed complicate his task. During a visit to Vladivostok, he complained on national television, "It is naive and harmful to think that if economic indices have risen, then the restructuring of our work has been completely developed and is progressing everywhere at full speed. The situation is still far from that."[12]

It is not entirely facetious to suggest that Gorbachev's task might actually have been easier if Brezhnev had lived at least another four or five years and if Gorbachev had come to power immediately after Brezhnev's death. As it was, Brezhnev had brought the Soviet economy to a standstill, and the political and social system was stagnating. Economic malaise led to an increase in tensions, including outbreaks of strikes and clashes between groups of different nationalities. If this had continued for another four years or so, it might have brought the country to such a sorry state that, like China and Hungary, it might have been ripe for far-reaching and even radical change. But conditions in the Soviet Union were never desperate enough for radical reform. Now that the economy has once again begun to grow and corruption to diminish, there is still less incentive for systemic changes.

A meaningful move away from central planning, even under the worst circumstances, however, will be difficult to make, particularly if it implies greater recognition of the market. The Soviet Communist party, after all, regards itself as the keeper of the faith. Soviet leaders realize that any slackening of party discipline or dogma in the Soviet Union will almost inevitably be echoed elsewhere in the communist world—above all, in Eastern Europe. We saw how Liberman's suggestions about an increased role for profits and managerial autonomy were immediately picked up by almost all the countries in the bloc. This helps explain why the chief priests of ideology continue to speak out against what they see as an erosion of party doctrine. Therefore, ideological guardians like Yegor K. Ligachev must be extremely careful about what they propose and implement. Concern about ideological purity in large part explains the Soviet skepticism about China's encouragement of joint ventures and foreign investment, especially of those that are 100 percent owned by foreigners. Although a strong element of xenophobia is involved, party purists like Ligachev could scarcely feel comfortable with joint ventures on Soviet territory. Given Gorbachev's insistence, these joint ventures are all but certain to come, but it is safe to say that their arrival will evoke no enthusiasm from ideologists of Ligachev's stamp.

Concern about a watering down of communist authority also helps explain Ligachev's attack on Gorbachev's call for more openness. Some in the Politburo seem deeply concerned that too much openness will encourage too much criticism of party functionaries, and thus a loss of respect for the party as a whole. For example, in what is at least an implicit attack on Gorbachev, Gromyko warned, "On the pretext of encouraging healthy and necessary criticism, no one must be allowed to resort to the fantasy of cracks in our party and Soviet society. Criticism and vilification of honest communists are not the same thing; they are not the same thing at all."[13]

Agreeing with Gromyko, Ligachev acknowledged that there has been good criticism of "everything improper," but he cautioned, "Unfortunately some newspapers have permitted lapses and *Pravda's* editorial office has not escaped this."[14] His fear of what reform might mean for party doctrine and what signals it might send to communist parties in other countries also helps explain why Ligachev found it necessary to deny that the Soviet economic reform would lead to an increase in the role of the market and private enterprise.[15] As the chief defender of the faith, Ligachev, in particular, must worry about where such alien notions as open criticism, private enterprise, and free markets might lead and what he must do to frustrate such initiatives. This probably also explains the July 1, 1986, decree, mentioned earlier, that imposes strict curbs on what the Soviets describe as unearned income. The decree bans the private use of hired labor and the selling of products or crops that the seller did not produce himself. Reportedly, the July 1, 1986, crackdown was supposed to have been introduced simultaneously with the November 1986 decision authorizing individual and family private businesses as of May 1, 1987. However, party ideologists apparently insisted that the crackdown should precede any liberalization.[16] Such hard-line opposition probably also explains why, unlike those in China and Hungary, private businessmen in the Soviet Union are prohibited from hiring and, thereby, exploiting anyone else outside the family. Moreover, as we saw with the crackdown, the law was written with such a broad sweep that it has had the effect of discouraging permissible as well as illegal activities. This incident highlights how reluctant party ideologists seem to be to accept some of these more radical proposals.

IV

Even if the party faithful could be convinced of the need for a significant reduction in the role of central planning, the central planners or industrial ministers would be unlikely to share that conviction. On the surface, their lack of enthusiasm may not look all that important. Khrushchev simply dispensed with them when he dissolved most economic ministries in 1957 and created the regionally based *sovnarkhozy* in their place. But, as Khrushchev quickly discovered, a Soviet leader cannot act unilaterally when it comes to reorganizing the bureaucracy. This is nothing new; the czars had the same problem. John Stuart Mill noted back in 1859, "The Czar himself is powerless against the bureaucratic body; he can send any one of them to Siberia, but he cannot govern without them, or against their will. On every decree of his they have a tacit veto, by merely refraining from carrying it into effect."[17] In just this way, Soviet bureaucrats blocked Khrushchev, and before long he had to back off and return more and more of the decision-making power and organization to Moscow.[18] The first thing his successors, Brezhnev and Kosygin, did was to abolish the *sovnarkhozy,* a mere seven years after they had been created, and reinstitute the ministerial system.

Like Khrushchev's establishment of *sovnarkhozy* in 1957, Gorbachev's abolishing or limiting of central control and planning would amount to a fundamental alteration of the Soviet system. There is good reason to worry that, without the control of the central planners, the various republics would begin to siphon off more resources for themselves. The experience with the *sovnarkhozy* proved that.

At the same time, an increase in the autonomy of the enterprise and a move toward decentralization would tempt the managers and regional officials throughout the country to put more of their output aside for current consumption and other worldly pleasures. Were this to happen, the military-industrial complex would not have access to the resources for the heavy

industry and military expenses that it has come to expect. So-
viet generals would most likely come to fear that the Soviet
Union would lose its status as the military equal of the United
States. This is certainly something they worry about.[19]

Rumors have already cropped up that Gorbachev has asked
the military to tighten its belt, although he has publicly said he
would not do such a thing.[20] Gorbachev reportedly gave a
speech in May 1985 to the general staff in Minsk in which he
complained that the Soviet military-industrial complex had had
too many cost overruns and had asked for too many new weapons systems. That he treats the military with less respect and
may supply it with less funds than his predecessors did is implied by his decision not to make Marshal Sergei L. Sokolov,
the minister of defense, a full member of the Politburo, as was
Dmitri Ustinov, Sokolov's predecessor. The contrast is all the
greater because Sokolov is only a candidate member of the

ILLUSTRATION 4

Party and government officials at funeral of Leonid Brezhnev. *Chernenko*

Politburo, while Viktor Chebrikov, the head of the KGB, has been made a full member. Gorbachev's downgrading of the military is also suggested by a comparison of the newspaper photographs that appeared after the funeral for Brezhnev with that of Chernenko's funeral, which Gorbachev ran (see Illustrations 4 and 5). Whereas the minister of defense in the earlier funeral is pictured next to the new general secretary (Andropov, at Brezhnev's funeral) and four generals are at the far left, in the pictures of Chernenko's funeral no one in uniform is next to Gorbachev and the generals have been cropped.

Conceivably, the generals can be mollified as some of their counterparts in China seem to have been, with the argument that a reallocation of resources now will make it possible to devote more resources to improve technology, which in turn will make possible a more sophisticated technology. Only in this way will Soviet military strength actually be increased.

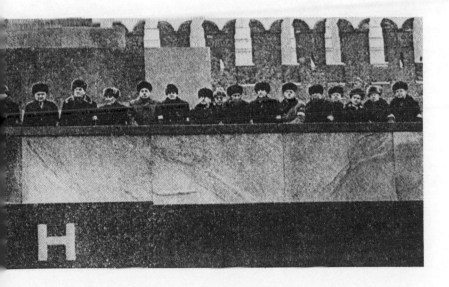

Whether such a rationalization will go over with Soviet generals remains to be seen. In all likelihood, something considerably more than a short-run diversion of resources will be required if the Soviets are to enhance their technology. However, if Gorbachev is to reduce his military expenditures, he will need some relaxation of tension, which in turn means a downplaying of the threat from the United States. Such a downplaying could have important repercussions inside the Soviet Union. Some Soviets have argued that the main justification for strict political control and large military expenditures in the Soviet Union is that the country is in danger of imminent attack from the United States. Consequently, if tensions seem to have been relaxed too much and if no threat is apparent, there is no longer

ILLUSTRATION 5

Party and government officials at funeral of Konstantin Chernenko.

any need for tight internal security and the restrictions on political freedom. In other words, this change could undermine the very nature of the Soviet political system.[21]

Soviet leaders are probably well aware that what begins as a call for economic reform is very likely to end up as a call for political reform. They saw this in Czechoslovakia, and if they look, they will find the same process unfolding in China, where, as we noted earlier, intellectuals, economists, and university students, began to call for reforms in the political structure and for academic and press freedoms.[22] For that matter, some in the Soviet Union have already called for similar changes there. The manifesto leaked to the *Guardian* in July 1986 contained an appeal for just such rights. Even though the manifesto may not

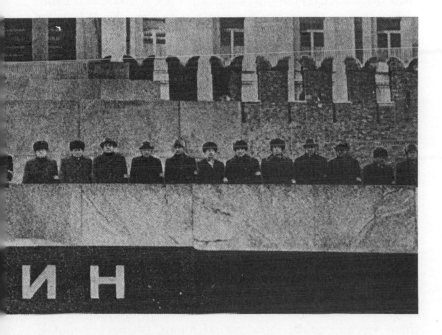

be authentic, its message was obviously important enough to provoke Gorbachev to reject it indirectly in a radio speech he made to the Soviet public during his trip to Khabarovsk, in late July 1986.[23] Despite this rejection, Gorbachev himself subsequently proposed some of the same ideas. In his January 27, 1987, speech to the Communist party's Central Committee, he called for secrets elections and the nomination of more than one candidate for party and state offices as high as the republic level. The Central Committee agreed only in part. Such elections would be permitted only at lower party levels.

The rejection of Gorbachev's original, more far-reaching proposal reflects the fear of the conservatives that relaxation in one area in a one-party state inevitably gives rise to calls for relaxation in other areas. That is not to deny that the Soviets can reverse course and squelch any political initiatives that may appear. Yet, any challenge to the system is bound to make Soviet bureaucrats nervous. It is not surprising, therefore, that their instinctive reaction to complaints about abuse and inefficiency in the system has been to punish the whistle-blowers rather than the abusers of the system.[24] It mattered not that these critics act in response to Gorbachev's call for more openness and candor in dealing with malfunctions in the system. They are challenging the system, and the safest strategy, when in doubt, is to draw up the black limousines and rally around the bureaucrats.

V

The reaction of the senior ministry officials as well as of the middle-and lower-level functionaries when reform threatens their prerogatives, and even their jobs, is not unique to the Soviet Union; it resembles that of petty bureaucrats anywhere in the world. However, Soviet petty bureaucrats feel a special urgency because Gorbachev has made a point of stressing that his reforms, even in their more modest version, will entail a major shrinkage in the number of state functionaries.[25] In case there was any doubt about his intentions, Gorbachev moved boldly in late 1985 to amalgamate the five ministries dealing with agriculture into one, and in the process he dismissed over 3,000 one-time functionaries in the various ministries. They were urged to look for jobs in the provinces, which, after all, is where the peasants are but which, unfortunately for the bureaucrats, is not where Moscow and its high life are.

Gorbachev's call for continued consolidation of this sort should serve as a clear warning to other bureaucrats that the same thing may happen to them. To demonstrate their indispensability, some Soviet bureaucrats have begun to intensify what can be called the "red tape shuffle"—the attempt to create as much red tape as possible, so that nothing can be done without their involvement. One Soviet critic has even created a fictional "Mr. X" (literally, Iks Igrekovich Zetov) who, to justify his own existence, will do everything he can to make sure that the 208 indicators he supervises are not done away with.[26] Assuming that index checkers like Mr. Iks are spread through the system and that their jobs and privileges depend on the protection, if not the expansion, of that red tape, anyone seeking reform must be prepared to do battle with them. Since the bureaucrats have so much to lose, they will not give up easily. Abel Aganbegian has observed, "Since the reform's fundamental aim is the real expansion of factories' autonomy, this means that many officials and ministries, state bodies and banks will have to transfer some of their powers to managers of factories or groups of factories. Since the bureaucratic apparatus is accustomed to giving orders, we expect passive resistance to the innovations."[27] The writer Vasil Bykov anticipates that the typical reaction of those affected will be to issue "a sea of words absolutely correct in form, but just as inert in essence. They will talk but they won't lift a finger to get things moving. More likely, they will move in the other way."[28] (See Illustration 6).

VI

As if it were not enough to have to do battle with senior party officials and intermediate bureaucrats, Gorbachev has also

ILLUSTRATION 6

Administrative Reform

"We have reorganized! We now work in the new fashion."

IVANOV	PETROV	SIDOROV
PETROV	SIDOROV	IVANOV

From *Ekonomicheskaia gazeta,* December 1986, no. 50, p. 24.

found that most factory managers do not seem very eager for any far-reaching change. To the extent that a manager has been successful under the old system, he is likely to be reluctant to switch to a new way of doing things, particularly if what he did well under the old system turns out to be of little or negative value under the new system. Undoubtedly, a really good and daring manager will welcome a new, even diametrically opposite, kind of challenge. But Gorbachev will be lucky if even a small percentage of his manager will welcome rather than sabotage new ways of doing things. For example, in explaining why the Proletarian Hammer Plant continued to produce the Vega 2E refrigerator, despite the widespread recognition that it was poorly made, I. I. Pudkov, then head of the Ministry of Machinery for Light Industry, Food Industry and Household Appliances, explained that the plant's closing would leave the workers with nothing to do.[29] Such resistance is recognized by Professor Aganbegian; in his list of those who can be expected to oppose the reform, he includes not only the bureaucrats but also "the managers unable and unwilling to adopt the new kind of management."[30] Aganbegian adds another category, "those excessively lazy and insufficiently energetic managers who prefer decisions to come from above and who consider the expansion of their sphere of authority and responsibility a nuisance. Many people will not like taking risks." Leonid Abalkin, a corresponding member of the Academy of Sciences, has warned about the same problem: "Many managers are none too eager to enjoy their freedom, like birds unwilling to quit an open cage."[31]

VII

The reluctance to try something new extends to the workers and the general population as well. *Pravda* has noted the lack of enthusiasm for reform among the general population.[32] Everyone seems to complain that nothing is being done and yet does nothing about it. Gorbachev himself has remarked that many people applaud his ideas but that "locally everything is going as it did in the old days."[33] Even Gorbachev's enthusiasm has begun to wane. His frustration occasionally breaks through, as it did during a visit to Khabarovsk on July 31, 1986: "It needs to be said beforehand, comrades, that if there is no organizational work to fulfill the decision, its fate will be the same as that of the previous ones, which, incidentally were passed by your very requests. The unsatisfactory state of affairs at many sections is connected precisely with the bad implementation of the measures mapped out and with the unsatisfactory utilization of reserves and existing possibilities."[34] Undoubtedly, it is an overstatement, but after such high hopes and so much frustration it is understandable why Gorbachev has apparently come to feel that in order to achieve his reforms he may have to begin "by reorganizing man himself."[35]

VIII

To the outside observer, Gorbachev's continued emphasis on human failings and narrow parochialism makes one wonder whether Gorbachev understands that the difficulty in reforming the Soviet economy is not just a consequence of human frailty. That certainly is a problem, but a bigger dilemma, one that tends to bring out what seems to be so much Soviet resistance is that the system itself is at fault. In other words, it is not enough to select the best managers and engineers, train them in the most advanced technique, and instill in them a passion for service to the state. This will have little long-range effect if, once the experts start to work, they find that the machinery they have to work with is ill designed and obsolete, that the incentive system leads the work force to shoddy production, and that their suppliers are more highly rewarded when they supply poor quality, ill-suited goods than when they deliver high-quality, appropriate products. The first secretary of the Sverdlovsk oblast party committee, Yurii Petrov, put it more succinctly when he complained, "Political and administrative methods do not suffice, particularly when the economic incentives are working in the opposite direction . . . instead we have an economic paradox. What is good for the consumer and consequently the state, is bad for the producer."[36] To illustrate his point, he gave an example of what happened when the pipe producers in Sverdlovsk tried to improve the quality of their pipe. Like other officials cited earlier, he complained, "We find that right now, without remodeling or any other change, the factory can produce pipe that is equal to the best in the world. But if it did so, its volume indicators (which determine the size of the bonuses) and, consequently, its incentive funds would decrease."

On occasion, some highly motivated manager does break through the bounds and turn out high-quality and innovative products. When this happens, however, the innovator may end up causing more problems than he solves. For instance, a farm manager in Belorussia decided he could significantly increase the production of vegetables if he built an extensive network of hothouses.[37] He built so many and they were so successful that the peasants began to spend more time in the hothouses than on the regular fields of the farm. This annoyed local officials, who in anger tore down the hothouses, explaining that despite their successes they were taking up more space than had been authorized. In a speech to the Central Committee, Gorbachev himself referred to a comparable incident.[38] An engineer, A. I. Chabanov, had developed a new, advanced machine tool in a research institute, but no factory would manufacture these tools. Temporarily, Chabanov found himself as acting manager of a factory, and he immediately started producing those machines. But four bureaucrats complained that Chabanov had "breached regulations and padded his reports." As a consequence, the ministry and regional party officials joined together to fire him from his job, expel him from the party, and charge him with a crime. To top it off, when Chabanov wrote to Moscow seeking an appeal, the local party officials intercepted his letter and destroyed it.

The hothouse and machine tool incidents illustrate how difficult it is to be creative in a system that is centrally controlled and where creativity has traditionally been frowned upon. It sometimes appears that in order to generate the decentralization of decision making he wants, Gorbachev will have to issue centralized orders from Moscow on how to act independently of Moscow.

Because of the absence of independent power centers, there tends to be little room for nonconformity and spontaneity, even if nonconformity and spontaneity mean a more efficient operation. When a plant director does manage to make an organizational breakthrough, he may still be frustrated because the minute he finds he must turn elsewhere in the economic system for supplies and support, the disruption and obstruction begin again.

This need to interact with the rest of the economy will limit, if not defeat, any effort to rationalize the economy, at least as long as the experiments are made piecemeal. Take the 1986 experiment at the VAZ Zhiguli factory in Togliatti and its counterpart in Sumy. As we noted, over 200 major enterprises were converted to the same type of system in early 1987, and ultimately all Soviet factories will be operating the same way.[39] It turns out, however, that this may not be any cure-all. Thus, the Togliatti experiment itself has been frustrated by the failure of suppliers elsewhere in the economy to respond properly. Because the auto parts suppliers have not provided quality parts in a timely manner, output at Togliatti has also fallen victim to delays and poor quality. This interdependence has been belatedly acknowledged by senior officials, from Gorbachev down to the Togliatti plant manager himself.[40] A. P. Alexandrov, the then president of the Soviet Academy of Sciences, noted similarly that the same problem of poor interaction among ministries and unreliable supply delivery thwarts the development of the high-technology sector.[41]

High-technology innovation in the Soviet Union is not only a matter of better coordination among ministries. The major challenge is to unleash the innovative talents of Soviet engineers, inventors, and managers and to link up that creativity with the equally imaginative efforts of those who control the capital resources. If the argument in the preceding pages is correct, this will involve an approach very different from the one Gorbachev seems to be taking. The age of high technology does not lend itself to centralized decision making and to a squeezing of the managers and workers. But an attempt to win the creative enthusiasm of managers and workers will have to be accompanied by a reversal of priorities. There will be no expansion of creativity until the standard of living improves, and there will be no increase in the quality and quantity of consumer goods without some feeling by all Soviets, including the peasants, that their efforts will be properly appreciated. This is why an agricultural reform is so intimately linked to and in many ways the key to technological innovation.[42] The road to structural transformation is a long one, and much has to accompany such reform, including the decentralization of decision making and the allocation of capital. Moreover, if it is to be successful, a meaningful reform requires a very different set of economic priorities.

His actions so far suggest that Gorbachev believes that all these forces can be mobilized within a system that continues to be centrally supervised by the state. Even though he acknowledges that the Soviet Union has become too large for everything to be manipulated from the center, he has done very little to decontrol investment and finance, a critical step he must take if he is to prevent Soviet technology from falling into the "systems trap" described in Chapter 4—a fall that might cause the Soviet Union to lag behind the rest of the developed world for years to come.[43]

To be fair, we must acknowledge that in no society do all the institutions interact harmoniously. Every society, ours included, is afflicted by clashes between groups working at cross-purposes. This even happens occasionally in Japan, one of the most harmonious societies in today's industrial world. But the lack of coordination seems greater in the Soviet Union than in most other economies, and meshing the parts more efficiently is probably one of Gorbachev's greatest challenges. The reforms he ultimately designs must have more coordination and commonality of purpose than the present Soviet system has. Managers and workers must believe that their individual well-being will be enhanced to the extent that they also help others improve their well-being. As Gorbachev himself has put it, "A house can be put in order only by a person who feels that he owns the house."[44]

IX

So what are the prospects for reform? Under Gorbachev, they are probably better than they have been for a long time, but even so the odds are that Gorbachev will have to settle for less than he seems to aspire to. While he may come to feel increasingly impressed by developments in China, it will be difficult to follow the Chinese very closely. The Soviet system is more deeply entrenched. Moreover, if the reform is to begin in agriculture, as it did in China and Hungary, it will not have the far-reaching impact it has had in those countries, because the smaller Soviet agricultural population means there will be fewer people in the Soviet Union who will be its immediate beneficiaries. This smaller base of support for the reforms makes it hard to see how Gorbachev can duplicate the immediate improvement that took place in China. Immediate improvement in economic well-being and increased economic growth are essential, however, in order to offset the warts of inflation, unemployment, bankruptcy, and bad balance of trade that accompany such reforms. Some officials have already begun to warn that a free price system during the NEP period gave rise to serious inflation.[45]

All this is not to argue that there will be no reform. Some improvements will occur, probably in foreign trade, joint ventures, agriculture, and the service sector, although the decree of July 1, 1986, which attempts to curb income not earned in state enterprises, suggests that reform of the service sector will come slowly. It is also likely that enterprise managers will end up with more power and more financial autonomy, but not as much as they need to free themselves from the petty tutelage of central officials. In other words, there will be improvements and improved productivity, but not the breakthrough Gorbachev seems eager to achieve.

The likelihood is that in its effort to seek improved economic efficiency, the Soviet leadership will continue to experiment. Many of these initiatives will in fact be remodeled versions of earlier efforts, and many of their experiments will still move in a direction opposite to that of other, sometimes simultaneous reforms. Yet, it must not be forgotten that the Chinese reforms also began with experiments that eventually grew and became the norm. Admittedly, China has not eliminated all contradictions in its system or all opposition to change. Moreover, many onerous regulations and much interference remain. Yet, despite periodic backsliding, Chinese managers and peasants do seem to have more freedom to maneuver than they had a decade ago. It is conceivable that the Soviets will adopt the Chinese approach, but it does not seem likely. Instead, the Soviet Union will probably continue to look to East Germany as a model of reform, making a marginal and even radical change here and there, and to operate much as it did in past periods of reform. There will probably be some improved efficiency and maybe more borrowing from the West, but it is hard to see how even Gorbachev can bring about the far-reaching reforms he seeks. Nonetheless, because the Soviet Union is so rich in resources, it can go on using its raw materials to finance its other shortcomings. It may never become the dominant economic power in the world—but it never has been. That need not mean an end to the Soviet Union's political or military prominence. However, without the ability to stay abreast of high technology produced elsewhere, the Soviet Union may find that the maintenance of its world position will be increasingly difficult, but not impossible.

Gorbachev confronts an unpleasant dilemma. Without a radical economic and political upheaval, the Soviet Union will probably be unable to sustain its economic power and compete in the ever-faster-moving arena of high technology. Essential to such an upheaval, however, is a decision to slash Soviet military expenditures and divert more resources to decentralized consumption and innovation, but this in turn will force, at the very least, a temporary reduction of its military might and prestige. In other words, it is hard to see how he can achieve the economic modernization and power he wants without sacrificing some current political and military power.

American policymakers have not always understood Gorbachev's situation. It is not that Gorbachev needs a renewed period of détente to prevent the collapse of his system, as some in the White House have argued. The Soviet system is not in danger of collapse. Instead, Gorbachev needs a relaxation of

East-West tensions so that he can divert resources from heavy industry to implement the far-reaching economic reforms he feels he must have to prepare the Soviet Union for economic and technological competition in the twenty-first century.

But Gorbachev has another choice. He can settle for somewhat more modest economic reforms that will bring marginal improvements and that will not impinge very much on the country's military prerogatives and expenditures. As long as technology does not move too fast beyond its reach, the Soviet Union can probably maintain its military and political role even though its civilian economy is likely to slip farther and farther behind that of a growing number of other countries.

Either choice involves some risk. If he decides on a radical reform and a reduced military posture, Gorbachev has no guarantee that he will be able to withstand either the opposition from the ideologues and the military-industrial complex or the political and economic chaos that may well ensue. Moreover, there is always the chance that, in the process of doing all this, Gorbachev will fail in bringing about economic reform but succeed in relegating the Soviet Union to a lesser military and political position. Yet, if he chooses the somewhat safer second alternative, he must give up his plan for a major economic improvement in his country. He will also have to take a risk that military technology will not move too far beyond the Soviet Union's reach. Neither choice is very attractive, especially given Gorbachev's initial hopes and expectations, but the odds are that, given the resistance his reforms will face, and the risks a really radical reform entails, he will opt for the more conservative route.

Short of some unexpected catastrophe, the Soviet economy is unlikely to come close to collapse, but without some equally unexpected transformation neither is it likely to improve its standing among the world's economic leaders. In the end, Gorbachev, like his predecessors, will probably have to settle for an economy that has to rely more on its natural riches than on its creative potential.

New Initiatives in the U.S.S.R.

3/11	Gorbachev becomes General Secretary of the Communist Party.
5/85	Factory experiment at two factories—Togliatti and Sumy—which allow firms to keep 70 percent of profits to finance themselves.
10/85	Eleven machine tool ministries put under the jurisdiction of the Bureau for machine building.
11/85	Six agriculture ministries combined into Gosagroprom.
11/85	Summit meeting between Gorbachev and Reagan in Geneva.
2/86	27th Congress of the Communist Party.
2/86	Anatoly Shcharansky freed from prison and allowed to emigrate.
3/86	Collective farms allowed to sell up to 30 percent of their output in cooperative stores in urban areas at high prices.
3/86	Bureau for Fuel Energy Complex established to coordinate energy ministries.
4/86	Explosion at Chernobyl nuclear energy plant.

7/86	Crackdown on private trade activities.
8/86	American journalist Nicholas Daniloff arrested.
8/86	Soviet Union seeks admittance to GATT as an observer.
8/86	Politburo authorizes creation of joint ventures with Socialist and capitalist partners.
9/86	Monopoly of Ministry of Foreign Trade is broken and selected enterprises and ministries can now arrange their own export and import.
10/86	Iceland summit meeting between Gorbachev and Reagan.
11/86	Authorization provided for formation of new semi-private cooperatives.
12/86	Release of Andrei Sakharov from exile in Gorky.
12/86	Two-day riots in Kazakhstan.
1/87	1500 factories must now have their production certified as to quality before workers are paid.
1/87	Seven ministries and 36 enterprises are converted to new self-financing experiment introduced in 5/85 at Togliatti and Sumy.
1/87	New emigration law goes into effect which restricts emigration to invitations from immediate family members.
1/87	Release of more than 150 political prisoners.
1/87	Plenum of Communist Party convened. Gorbachev calls for election of party, government and industry officials and managers. Final resolution authorizes many fewer elections than Gorbachev requested.
2/87	New law spelling out regulations for operating state enterprises—to be patterned on Togliatti and Sumy experiment—in all enterprises as of 1990.
5/87	Individual- and family-run businesses authorized to open.

Notes

ABBREVIATIONS

CDSP	*Current Digest of the Soviet Press*
CIA	Central Intelligence Agency
Ekon. gaz.	Ekonomicheskaia gazeta
FBIS	Foreign Broadcast Information Service Daily Report: Soviet Union
FBIS, China	Foreign Broadcast Information Service Daily Report: People's Republic of China
JEC, *China*, 1982	Joint Economic Committee of the Congress of the United States, *China under the Four Modernizations: Selected Papers,* vol. 1 (Washington, D.C.: GPO, 1982)
JEC, *China*, 1986	Joint Economic Committee of the Congress of the United States, *China's Economy Looks toward the Year 2000,* vol. 1 (Washington, D.C.: GPO, 1986)
JEC, *Eastern Europe*	Joint Economic Committee of the Congress of the United States, *East European Economies: Slow Growth in the 1980's,* vol. 1 (Washington, D.C.: GPO, 1985); vols. 2–3 (ibid., 1986)
Lit. Gaz.	*Literaturnaia gazeta*
Nar. khoz.	Tsentral'noe statisticheskoe upravlenie, *Narodnoe khoziaistvo SSSR v 1961 gody* (Moscow: Gosstatizdat, 1962) (cited with the appropriate statistical year)
NYT	*New York Times*
RFE/RL	Radio Free Europe/Radio Liberty
Sots. ind.	*Sotsialisticheskaia industriia*

CHAPTER ONE

1. *NYT,* June 17, 1983, p. A7.
2. *CDSP,* May 28, 1986, p. 8.
3. *Pravda,* June 10, 1986, p. 3; *CDSP,* July 9, 1986, p. 21.
4. *Pravda,* July 20, 1986, p. 2.
5. *FBIS,* April 9, 1986, p. R3.
6. *Pravda,* April 24, 1986, p. 1.
7. *CIA, Statistical Abstract, 1985* (Washington, D.C.: n.p., 1985), p. 25.
8. *Izvestiia,* November 19, 1983, p. 3; January 29, 1985, p. 3; *Sots. ind.,* September 29, 1982, p. 3; November 14, 1984, p. 2; *Nedelia,* June 21–26, 1982, p. 6; *Lit. gaz.,* December 8, 1982, p. 12; Seweryn Bialer, *The Soviet Paradox: External Expansion, Internal Decline* (New York: Alfred A. Knopf, 1986), p. 61.
9. *Moskovskaia pravda,* January 5, 1986, p. 1; July 20, 1986, p. 3.
10. RFE/RL 117/86, March 11, 1986, p. 1; *Pravda,* March 2, 1986, p. 3.
11. *Pravda,* August 19, 1985, p. 3; June 19, 1986, p. 1; *FBIS,* June 20, 1986, p. R11.
12. *Pravda,* April 9, 1986, p. 2; *FBIS,* April 11, 1986, p. R6.
13. Henry Rosovsky, in *NYT,* September 6, 1985, p. 23; *Fortune,* September 16, 1985, p. 33, October 13, 1986, p. 26.
14. Abel Aganbegian, in *Problems of Economics,* April 1985, pp. 9–11.
15. *Pravda,* August 3, 1986, p. 1.
16. U.S. Arms Control and Disarmament Agency, *World Military Expenditures and Arms Transfers* (Washington D.C.: n.p., 1985), p. 81.

CHAPTER TWO

1. Alexander Baykov, *The Development of the Soviet Economic System* (New York: Macmillan, 1948), p. 279; Alexander Gerschenkron, *Economic Backwardness in Historical Perspective* (Cambridge: Harvard University Press, 1962), p. 255.
2. Abram Bergson, "National Income," in Abram Bergson and Simon Kuznets, eds., *Economic Trends in the Soviet Union* (Cambridge: Harvard University Press, 1963), p. 6.
3. *Nar. khoz.,* 1962, p. 196.

4. *Ibid.*, 1961, p. 357.
5. Janet G. Chapman, "Consumption," in Bergson and Kuznets, eds., *Economic Trends*, p. 235.
6. Anthony Sutton, *Western Technology and Soviet Economic Development, 1917–1965* (Stanford: Hoover Institution, 1973), vol. 3, p. 1.
7. Robert Campbell, *Soviet Economic Power* (Boston: Houghton Mifflin, 1960), p. 195.
8. U.S. Senate, Sub-Committee to Investigate the Administration of the Internal Security Act and Other Internal Security Laws of the Committee on the Judiciary, *Exports of Strategic Materials to the USSR and Other Soviet Bloc Countries: Hearings*, 87th Cong., 2d sess. (Washington, D.C.: GPO, 1963), pt. 3, p. 382.
9. CIA, *Handbook of Economic Statistics, 1985*, p. 132.
10. Seymour Melman, "Promotion of and Exchange of Information on Research in Industrial Economies" (European Productivity Agency, Organization for European Economic Cooperation, Paris, June 30, 1959, Mimeographed), pp. 5, 10.
11. Raymond Vernon, "Apparatchiks and Entrepreneurs: U.S.-Soviet Economic Relations," *Foreign Affairs*, January 1974, p. 260.
12. Alexander Erlich, *The Soviet Industrialization Debate, 1924–1928* (Cambridge: Harvard University Press, 1960), pp. 10, 16, 82.
13. *FBIS*, August 20, 1986, p. S2.
14. Ibid.
15. Joseph S. Berliner, "Planning and Management," in Abram Bergson and Herbert S. Levine, eds., *The Soviet Economy: Towards the Year 2000* (Boston: Allen and Unwin, 1983), p. 353.
16. *Pravda*, August 31, 1985, p. 1.
17. *Ibid.*, December 12, 1984, p. 3; August 22, 1985, p. 1; *Ekon. gaz.*, September 1985, no. 39, p. 3.
18. Evsei Liberman, in *Pravda*, November 20, 1967, p. 5; Abel Aganbegian, in *Trud*, November 17, 1981, p. 2; Tatiana Zaslavskaia, "The Novosibirsk Report," *Survey*, Spring 1984, p. 88.
20. Fyodor I. Kushnirsky, *Soviet Economic Planning, 1965–80* (Boulder, Colo.: Westview Press, 1982), p. 20.
21. *CDSP*, December 28, 1983, p. 3.
22. *NYT*, October 14, 1985, p. D8.
23. United Nations Association, New York City, *Discussions with the Soviet Economic Panel, Moscow, January 1983*, (New York: UNA, 1983), p.30; idem, *Moscow Economic Dialog, UNA Exchange*, (New York: UNA, 1985), p. 3.
24. *Pravda*, September 6, 1985, p. 2.
25. *Trud*, August 28, 1984, p. 2.
26. Ibid.
27. *Pravda*, January 26, 1985, p. 1.
28. *Sots. ind.*, January 24, 1985, p. 2.
29. *FBIS*, July 28, 1986, p. R6.
30. *Trud*, August 28, 1984, p. 2.
31. N. Baryshnikov and G. Galakhov, "Kapital'noe stroitel'stvo reshaiushchii uchastok sotsialisticheskogo vosproizvodstva, *Planovoe khoziaistvo*, March 1982, pp. 25–30.
32. *FBIS*, July 31, 1986, p. R3.
33. Ibid., p. R2.
34. *Pravda*, August 15, 1985, p. 2.
35. *CDSP*, December 28, 1983, p. 4.
36. S. P. Zverev, "Trudovaia distsiplina vo mnogom zavisit to mestnoi initsiativi," *Ekonomika i organizatsiia promyshlennogo proizvodstva*, no. 5, 1984, p. 45.

37. *CDSP,* July 6, 1983, p.3.
38. For other instances of such behavior, see *CDSP,* April 17, 1985, p. 8; August 21, 1985, p. 17; *Sots. ind.,* October 14, 1982, p. 2.
39. Douglas Diamond, "Soviet Agricultural Plans for 1981–85," in Seweryn Bialer and Thane Gustafson, ed., *Russia at the Crossroads: The Twenty-sixth Congress of the Communist Party of the Soviet Union* (London: Allen & Unwin, 1982), p. 117; D. Gale Johnson and Karen McConnell Brooks, *Prospects for Soviet Agriculture in the 1980s* (Bloomington: Indiana University Press, 1983), p. 6.
40. *CDSP,* September 1, 1982, pp. 4, 6.
41. *Sots. ind.,* January 24, 1985, p. 2.
42. See RFE/RL 321/85, September 25, 1985, p. 1.
43. *FBIS,* August 4, 1986, p. R11.
44. David Sedik, "The Growth of Savings Deposits in the USSR: Two Views among Soviet Economists," *Radio Liberty Research,* RFE/RL 321/85, September 25, 1985, p. 2.
45. Radio Liberty, August 4, 1986, *Annotation* from *Ekonomika sel'skogo khoziaistva,* March 1986, pp. 59–64; *Ekon. gaz.,* October 1984, no. 43, p. 15; Les Voskresensky, *The Food Program: Its Aims* (Moscow: Novosti Press Agency, 1982), p. 41; *CDSP,* June 29, 1983, p. 22; December 19, 1984, p. 21.
46. *Pravda,* December 7, 1982, p. 3.
47. *CDSP,* January 5, 1983, pp. 25–26.
48. Ibid., November 7, 1982, p. 21.
49. Ibid., January 5, 1983, pp. 25–26.
50. *Pravda,* May 28, 1986, p. 2.
51. *Kazakhstanskaia pravda,* December 3, 1982; *CDSP,* February 9, 1983, p. 18.
52. *Pravda vostoka,* June 26, 1984 (from RFE/RL, August 30, 1984, p. 4; *Pravda,* February 18, 1985, p. 18; *CDSP,* October 6, 1982, p. 21; July 24, 1984, p. 4.
53. *CDSP,* September 1, 1982, p. 23; November 23, 1983, p. 10; October 23, 1985, p. 3.
54. *Sots. ind.,* April 9, 1982, p. 3; September 29, 1982, p. 3; *Ekon. gaz.,* June 1986, no. 26, p. 6.
55. *Lit. gaz.,* September 16, 1981, p. 10.
56. *NYT,* June 21, 1982, p. D8.
57. *CDSP,* September 7, 1983, p. 10.
58. *Pravda,* August 6, 1982, p. 3; *Izvestiia,* October 8, 1983, p. 2.
59. *Izvestiia,* October 8, 1983, p. 2. In the R.S.F.S.R., farms are only about sixty miles from meatpacking facilities.
60. *Izvestiia,* February 4, 1982, p. 2.
61. *Pravda,* June 8, 1981, p. 3; Johnson and Brooks, *Prospects,* p. 9.
62. *CDSP,* November 7, 1982, p. 2.
63. *Nar. khoz.,* 1983, p. 362.
64. *Pravda,* May 28, 1986, p. 2; *FBIS,* August 22, 1986, p. T1.
65. *CDSP,* September 28, 1982, pp. 1–5; *Izvestiia,* June 26, 1982, p. 3; June 28, 1982, p. 2.
66. Lazar Volin, *A Century of Russian Agriculture: From Alexander II to Khrushchev* (Cambridge: Harvard University Press, 1970), p. 314.
67. *Molodoi kommunist,* January 1985, p. 51.
68. Ibid.
69. Lester Brown, *The United States and Soviet Agriculture: The Shifting Balance of Power* (Washington, D.C.: World Watch, October 1982), p. 14.
70. Johnson and Brooks, *Prospects,* p. 154.
71. Ibid., p. 52.

72. *CDSP,* November 3, 1982, p. 4.
73. Johnson and Brooks, *Prospects,* p. 31; *NYT,* June 21, 1982, p. D8.

CHAPTER THREE

1. *Pravda,* September 20, 1985, p. 1.
2. *FBIS,* August 6, 1986, p. R9.
3. Ibid., August 4, 1986, pp. R5, R8.
4. *Ekon. gaz.,* September 1985, no. 37, p. 3.
5. János Kornai, "The Hungarian Reform Process: Visions, Hopes and Reality," *Journal of Economic Literature,* December 1986, p. 1693.
6. *FBIS,* July 28, 1986, p. R7.
7. Baykov, *Development,* p. 297; Harry Schwartz, *Russia's Soviet Economy* (New York: Prentice-Hall, 1950), pp. 174, 177, 190, 271.
8. *Nar. khoz.,* 1958, p. 494.
9. *FBIS,* August 6, 1986, p. R17.
10. Michael Voslensky, *Nomenklatura* (Garden City, N.Y.: Doubleday, 1984), p. 243.
11. E. Liberman, "O planirovanii promyshlennogo proizvodstva i material'nykh stimulakh ego razvitiia," *Kommunist,* no. 10, July 1956, p. 75.
12. Gertrude E. Schroeder, "The Soviet Economy on the Treadmill of 'Reforms,' " in *Joint Economic Committee of Congress of the United States, Soviet Economy in a Time of Change* (Washington, D.C.: GPO, October 10, 1979), p. 313.
13. *Pravda,* September 6, 1985, p. 2; *CDSP,* October 9, 1985, p. 6.
14. *Ekon. gaz.,* February 1981, no. 9, p. 23.
15. Schroeder, "Soviet Economy," p. 329.
16. Ibid., p. 335.
17. Ibid.; *CDSP,* October 23, 1985, p. 3.
18. *Soviet News,* October 21, 1969, p 28.
19. Schroeder, "Soviet Economy," p. 316.
20. Ibid., p. 336.
21. *Izvestiia,* November 3, 1985, p. 2; *CDSP,* November 30, 1983, p. 28.
22. Karl-Eugen Wadekin, "The Private Agricultural Sector in the 1980s," RFE/RL 251/85, August 2, 1985, p 4; *CDSP,* October 16, 1985, p. 19.
23. *Ekon. gaz.,* February 1985, no. 8, pp. 1, 11.
24. *Izvestiia,* June 1, 1985, p. 3.
25. Wadekin, "Private Agricultural Sector," p. 6.
26. *Izvestiia,* June 1, 1985, p. 3.
27. Ibid.; G. I. Shmelev, "Sotsial'no-ekonomicheskii potentsial semeinogo podriada," *Sotsiologicheskie issledovaniia,* April 1985, p. 14.
28. *CDSP,* June 15, 1984, p. 14.
29. Ibid.
30. *FBIS,* August 8, 1986, p. R11.
31. Wadekin, "Private Agricultural Sector," p. 1; *Sel'skaia zhizn',* January 18, 1981, p. 1.
32. *Nedelia,* September 16–22, 1985, p. 2.
33. *CDSP,* February 20, 1985; *Komsomol'skaia pravda,* February 6, 1985, p. 2.
34. *Pravda,* March 11, 1981, p. 1; see Karl-Eugen Wadekin, "Raion Agricultural Associations and Brezhnev's Food Program," RFE/RL 125/82, March 17, 1982, p. 1.
35. *FBIS,* April 29, 1986, p. S1; *Pravda,* January 18, 1986, p. 2.
36. Karl-Eugen Wadekin, "The Major Restructuring of Soviet Farming?" RFE/RL 56/85, February 20, 1985, p. 2.
37. *Pravda,* March 21, 1986, p. 1; *Lit. gaz.,* April 16, 1986, p. 2.

38. *FBIS,* July 31, 1986, p. R4.
39. RFE/RL 322/86, August 26, 1986, pp. 2, 4.
40. *Pravda,* November 22, 1985, p. 1.
41. *Ibid.,* October 18, 1985, p. 1.
42. *FBIS,* January 28, 1987, p. R4.
43. *Zaria vostoka,* November 26, 1981, p. 1; *Izvestiia,* September 29, 1981, p. 1; *Lit. gaz.,* September 16, 1981, p. 10; "Soviet Area Audience and Opinion Poll," RFE/RL, April 1982, p. 5.
44. *Trud,* October 17, 1981, p. 2.
45. *FBIS,* August 6, 1986, pp. R16, R17; August 4, 1986, p. R13.
46. *Pravda vostoka,* September 26, 1985, p. 2; November 22, 1985, p. 2; January 23, 1986, pp. 1–2.
47. *NYT,* February 8, 1985, p. 1; *CDSP,* September 8, 1982, p. 3; April 27, 1983, p. 13; November 30, 1983, pp. 21, 28; December 28, 1983, pp. 22, 25; August 15, 1984, p. 21; Timothy J. Colton, *The Dilemma of Reform in the Soviet Union* (New York: Council on Foreign Relations, 1986), pp. 26–27.
48. *Washington Post,* August 3, 1983, p. 1; *Survey,* Spring 1984, p. 83.
49. *Pravda,* August 18, 1983, p. 4; *NYT,* August 18, 1983, p. 1.
50. *NYT,* August 18, 1983, p. A13.
51. *Pravda,* December 11, 1984, p. 2.
52. Ibid., June 12, 1985, p. 1.
53. Ibid., November 9, 1985, p. 2.
54. Ibid., June 19, 1986, p. 2; RFE/RL 250/86, July 2, 1986, p. 1.
55. *Izvestiia,* August 19, 1985, p. 3.
56. Ibid., January 23, 1985, p. 2; *Ekon. gaz.,* October 1986, no. 43, pp. 15–16.
57. *Izvestiia,* October 27, 1985, p. 2; May 28, 1986, p. 2; *Pravda,* July 14, 1986, p. 3.
58. *Ekon. gaz.,* August 1985, no. 33, p. 1. Subsequently, the Elektrovypriamitel' was apparently dropped from the scheme.
59. *Izvestiia,* July 29, 1985, p. 2.
60. Ibid., July 28, 1985, p. 2. A report in *Pravda* subsequently indicated that the associations could keep only 25 percent of their hard-currency receipts. *Pravda,* March 10, 1986, p. 2.
61. *FBIS,* June 19, 1986, p. R12, from *Pravda,* June 17, 1986, p. 3.
62. *CDSP,* January 1, 1986, p. 23.
63. *Izvestiia,* July 28, 1985, p. 2.
64. Alice C. Gorlin, "The Power of Soviet Industrial Ministries in the 1980s," *Soviet Studies,* July 1985, p. 366.
65. *FBIS,* November 25, 1986, p. R4; *Izvestiia,* November 23, 1986, p. 2.
66. Gorlin, "Power," p. 364.
67. Stephen S. Rosenfeld, in *Washington Post,* August 5, 1983, p. A19.
68. Philip Hanson, in RFE/RL 291/85, September 4, 1985, p. 3; RFE/RL 200/85, July 17, 1985, p. 1.
69. Philip Hanson, "All Quiet on the Reform Front?" RFE/FL 328/86, August 29, 1986, p. 3.
70. *Izvestiia,* August 19, 1986, p. 2.
71. *NYT,* October 7, 1986, p. A21.
72. *Izvestiia,* June 7, 1986, p. 2.
73. *FBIS,* August 7, 1986, p. S4.
74. *Pravda,* August 29, 1986, p. 1; *FBIS,* September 12, 1986, p. S1.
75. *FBIS,* July 28, 1986, p. R7.
76. *Izvestiia,* June 11, 1986, p. 6.
77. *Ekon. gaz.,* March 1986, no. 10, p. 8.

78. Evgenii Ambartsumov, "Analiz V. I. Leninym prichin krizka 1921 g. i putei vykhodka iz nego," *Voprosy istorii*, no. 4, April 1984, p. 15.
79. E. Bugaev, "Strannaia pozitsiia," *Kommunist*, no. 14, September 1984, p. 119.
80. *Ekon. gaz.*, October, 1986, no. 43, p. 15.
81. *Izvestiia*, November 20 1986, p. 5; *FBIS*, November 26, 1986, p. S1.
82. *NYT*, September 25, 1986, p. D1; *Sots. ind.*, September 23, 1986, p. 1; *Journal of the US-USSR Trade and Economic Council*, vol. 2, no. 4, 1986, pp. 13–17.
83. *FBIS*, July 26, 1986, p. R15; *Pravda*, August 15, 1986, p. 1.
84. *FBIS*, August 4, 1986, p. R3.

CHAPTER FOUR

1. *Economist*, August 23, 1986, p. 8; U.S. Department of Commerce, *An Assessment of U.S. Competitiveness in High Technology Industries* (Washington, D.C.: GPO, 1983), p. 41. This study sets a higher percentage of scientists and a higher ratio of research and development to sales than does the *Economist*.
2. Ibid.
3. *Wall Street Journal*, March 13, 1985, p. 1.
4. *NYT*, February 16, 1986, p. 58.
5. Morton I. Kamien and Nancy L. Schwartz, *Market Structure and Innovation* (Cambridge: Cambridge University Press, 1982), p. 6; *The State of Small Business, A Report of the President*, Transmitted to the Congress, May 1985 (Washington, D.C.: GPO, 1985), p. 129; *Harvard University Gazette*, May 6, 1983, p. 1.
6. Oliver Williamson, "The Modern Corporation: Origins, Evolution, Attributes," *Journal of Economic Literature*, December 1981, pp. 15, 37.
7. *Wall Street Journal*, September 3, 1985, p. 1.
8. *NYT*, September 8, 1985, Financial section, p. 1.
9. *Fortune*, October 13, 1986, p. 35.
10. Joseph S. Berliner, *The Innovation Decision in Soviet Industry* (Cambridge: MIT Press, 1976), pp. 348–50; *CDSP*, January 11, 1986, p. 23.
11. *CDSP*, January 11, 1986, p. 23.
12. *FBIS*, July 28, 1986, p. R7.
13. *Pravda*, January 7, 1986, p. 2.
14. *FBIS*, August 19, 1986, p. S2.
15. *Sovetskaia Rossiia*, January 12, 1986, p. 3; Viktor G. Afanasyev on Soviet television, August 16, 1986, as reported in *FBIS*, August 19, 1986, p. S2.
16. *Izvestiia*, October 11, 1983, p. 6; *Pravda*, January 3, 1985, p. 2; January 9, 1985, p. 2; *Sots. ind.*, April 2, 1985, p. 2; *Wall Street Journal*, April 24, 1985, p. 1; *Fortune*, October 13, 1986, p. 36.
17. Ia. Orlov, "Spros naselenie i zadachi proizvodstva i torgovli," *Voprosy ekonomiki*, September 1983, p. 104; *Izvestiia*, March 22, 1984, p. 2; *Sovetskaia Rossiia*, January 12, 1986, p. 3; *Znanie*, Economics ser., no. 4, 1984, p. 44.
18. Manfred Kharder, "O nekotorykh pokazateliakh otsenki deiatel'nosti kombinatov i predpriiatii GDR," *Problemy teorii i praktika upravleniia*, April 1984, p. 38.
19. S. E. Goodman, "Technology Transfer and the Development of the Soviet Computer Industry," in Bruce Parrott, ed., *Trade, Technology and Soviet-American Relations* (Bloomington: Indiana University Press, 1985), p. 131.
20. Loren Graham, "The Soviet Union Is Missing Out on the Computer Revolution," *Washington Post*, March 11, 1984, p. C1.
21. RFE/RL 323/86, August 18, 1986, p. 1; *Komsomol'skaia pravda*, January 11, 1987, p. 4.
22. Goodman, "Technology Transfer," p. 135.
23. *Pravda*, September 26, 1985, p. 1.

24. U.S. Department of Defense and CIA, *The Soviet Acquisition of Militarily Significant Western Technology: An Update* (Washington, D.C.: n.p., September 1985).
25. Philip Hanson, "New Light on Soviet Industrial Espionage," RFE/RL 36/86, January 20, 1986.
26. U.S. Department of Defense and CIA, *Soviet Acquisition,* pp. 8–9.
27. Anatol Fedoseyev, "Design in Soviet Military Research and Development: The Case of Radar Research in Vacuum Electronics" (Paper no. 8 in the Soviet Science and Technology Eyewitness Account Seminar, Russian Research Center, Harvard University, May 1983). These statements were made in discussion following the lecture.
28. John W. Kiser III, "Tapping Eastern Bloc Technology," *Harvard Business Review,* March–April 1982, p. 85; "Soviet Technology: The Perception Gap," *Mechanical Engineering,* April 1979, p. 22.
29. Dr. Mark Goldberg, "Experience of a Mathematician at Kharkov Institute of Low Temperature Physics" (Paper no. 7 in the Soviet Science and Technology Eyewitness Account Seminar, Russian Research Center, Harvard University, April 1983), pp. 9, 17, 21; *Fortune,* October 13, 1986, p. 35.
30. Gerschenkron, *Economic Backwardness,* pp. 362–63.
31. U.S. Department of Defense and the CIA, *Soviet Acquisition,* p. 12; see also Goodman, "Technology Transfer," p. 126.
32. Zaslavskaia, "Novosibirsk Report," pp. 91, 95.
33. *Krasnaia zvezda,* May 9, 1984, pp. 2–3.

CHAPTER FIVE

1. U.S. Department of Defense and the CIA, *Soviet Acquisition.*
2. *Izvestiia,* June 10, 1985, p. 2; *Pravda,* February 27, 1986, p. 5.
3. *Trud,* April 17, 1981, p. 2.
4. *Pravda,* August 20, 1981, p. 3; March 10, 1982, p. 3; December 21, 1983, p. 2; July 17, 1984, p. 2; June 11, 1985, p. 2; *Sots. ind.,* June 7, 1979, p. 2; October 4, 1981, p. 2; October 12, 1984, p. 2; August 1, 1985, p. 2; *Trud,* April 17, 1981, p. 2; July 24, 1981, p. 2; *Izvestiia,* October 8, 1983, p. 2; October 5, 1984, p. 2.
5. *Sots. ind.,* June 18, 1985, p. 2.
6. *Pravda,* February 24, 1981, p. 2.
7. *Ibid.,* April 6, 1966, p. 7.
8. *Nedelia,* November 25–December 1, 1985, p. 12; *FBIS,* January 28, 1987, p. R9.
9. Philip Hanson, *Trade and Technology in Soviet-Western Relations* (New York: Columbia University Press, 1981), chaps. 9–11.
10. *Pravda,* July 13, 1985, p. 2.
11. *Izvestiia,* June 10, 1985, p. 2.
12. *Pravda,* December 21, 1983, p. 2; July 30, 1985, p. 2.
13. *Ibid.,* July 30, 1985, p. 2; Philip Hanson, "Soviet Assimilation of Western Technology," in Parrot, ed., *Trade,* p. 67.
14. *Izvestiia,* May 21, 1984, p. 2.
15. *Vestnik, AN SSSR,* no. 6, 1982, p. 10; Gordon B. Smith, ed., *The Politics of East-West Trade* (Boulder, Colo.; Westview Press, 1984), p. 6.
16. *Sots. ind.,* July 6, 1979, p. 2; *Pravda,* June 14, 1980, p. 3; June 29, 1981, p. 2.
17. Parrot, ed., *Trade,* pp. 24, 71.
18. *Izvestiia,* May 21, 1984, p. 2.
19. *CDSP,* April 17, 1985, p. 8; July 6, 1983, p. 3; *Sots. ind.,* October 14, 1982, p. 2; Josef C. Brada, "Soviet-Western Trade and Technology Transfer: An Economic Overview," in Parrot, ed., *Trade,* pp. 16–17.
20. Brada, "Soviet-Western Trade," p. 16.

21. Ibid.
22. Address to the Khabarovsk Party Collective, July 31, 1986, in *FBIS,* August 4, 1986, p. R5; *FBIS,* August 26, 1986, p. S4.
23. *Boston Globe,* September 22, 1985, p. 3.
24. *NYT,* September 7, 1985, p. 8.
25. Louis Lavoie, "The Limits of Soviet Technology," *Technology Review,* November–December 1985, p. 72.
26. Padma Desai, "The Productivity of Foreign Resource Inflow to the Soviet Economy," *American Economic Review,* May 1979, pp. 70–75; Judith Thornton, "Differential Capital Charges and Resource Allocation in Soviet Industry," *Journal of Political Economy,* May/June 1971, pp. 545–61; Padma Desai and Ricardo Martin, "Efficiency Loss from Resource Misallocation in Soviet Industry," *Quarterly Journal of Economics,* August 1983, pp. 442–56; Donald W. Green and Herbert S. Levine, "Implications of Technology Transfers for the USSR," in NATO, *East-West Technological Cooperation* (Brussels: NATO Economic Directorate, 1976); Donald W. Green and Herbert S. Levine, "Soviet Machinery Imports," *Survey,* Spring 1978, pp. 112–26; Martin L. Weitzman, "Technology Transfer to the USSR: An Econometric Analysis," *Journal of Comparative Economics,* June 1979, pp. 167–77; Yasushi Toda, "Technology Transfer to the USSR: The Marginal-Productivity Differential and the Elasticity of Intra-Capital Substitution in Soviet Industry," ibid., pp. 181–94.
27. *FBIS,* July 29, 1986, p. R15.
28. *Pravda,* August 16, 1986, p. 1.
29. *Pravda,* September 24, 1986, p. 1.
30. *Ekon. gaz.* February 1987, no. 6, p. 4.

CHAPTER SIX

1. *Boston Globe,* July 27, 1986, p. 6.
2. Much of what follows is based on Paul Marer, "Economic Reform in Hungary: From Central Planning to Regulated Market," in JEC, *Eastern Europe,* 1986, p. 237, and on János Kornai, "The Hungarian Reform Process: Visions, Hopes, and Reality," *Journal of Economic Literature,* December 1986, p. 1687.
3. Evsei Liberman, "O planirovanii promyshlennogo proizvostva i material'nykh stimulakh ego razvitiia," *Kommunist,* no. 10, July 1956, p. 75; Kornai, "Hungarian Reform Process," pp. 1689, 1724.
4. Marer, "Economic Reform," p. 237.
5. Ibid., p. 229.
6. M. Czizmadia, "New Features of the Enterprise Structure in the Hungarian Agriculture and Food Industry," *Acta Oeconomica,* vol. 31, nos. 3–4, p. 229.
7. Ibid., pp. 226–27.
8. Ibid., p. 232; E. Czizmadia, "Lasting Elements and Changing Circumstances in the Hungarian Agrarian Development," *Acta Oeconomica,* vol. 32, nos. 3–4, p. 354.
9. Thomas A. Vankai, "Hungarian Agricultural Performance and Prospects during the 80's," in JEC, *Eastern Europe,* 1986, p. 341.
10. Ibid., p. 350.
11. Ibid., p. 357.
12. Ibid., pp. 356–57.
13. Michael Marrese, "Hungarian Agriculture: Moving in the Right Direction," JEC, *Eastern Europe,* 1986, p. 328.
14. L. Szamuely, "The Second Wave of the Economic Mechanism Debate in the 1968 Reform in Hungary," *Acta Oeconomica,* vol. 33, nos. 1–2, p. 49.
15. Marer, "Economic Reform," p. 239.

16. Paul Hare, Hugo Radice, and Nigel Swain, eds., *Hungary: A Decade of Economic Reform* (London: Allen & Unwin, 1981), p. 15; Marer, "Economic Reforms," pp. 234, 247; Adam Zwass, *The Economies of Eastern Europe in a Time of Change* (Armonk, N.Y.: M. E. Sharpe, 1984), p. 7.
17. Zwass, *Economies,* p. 7.
18. Ibid.
19. Ibid., Marer, "Economic Reform," p. 247.
20. Rudolf L. Tokes, "Hungarian Reform Imperatives," *Problems of Communism,* September–October 1984, p. 1.
21. Kornai, "Hungarian Reform Process," p. 1726.
22. János Kornai, *Contradictions and Dilemmas* (Cambridge: MIT Press, 1986), p. 33.
23. Zwass, *Economics,* p. 8.
24. Tokes, "Hungarian Reform Imperatives," p. 2; Marer, "Economic Reform," p. 247; Paul Hare, "Hungary: Internal Economic Developments" (Paper prepared for the NATO conference on Economies of Eastern Europe and Their Foreign Economic Relations, Brussels, April 1986, Mimeographed), p. 10; Zwass, *Economics,* p. 14; Marton Tardos, "How to Create Efficient Markets in Socialism" (Institute of Economics, Hungarian Academy of Sciences, Budapest, September 1984, Mimeographed), p. 34.
25. Hare, "Hungary"; Marer, "Economic Reform," p. 247.
26. Marer, "Economic Reform," p. 253.
27. Ibid., p. 254.
28. Ibid., p. 258.
29. Ibid., p. 249.
30. Tokes, p. 17.
31. Zoltán Sabov, "Enterprise Reform in Hungary; A Gradual Privatization" (n.d., Mimeographed), p. 5.
32. Hare, "Hungary," p. 14.
33. Marer, "Economic Reform," p. 251; Sabov, "Enterprise Reform," p. 5.
34. Marer, "Economic Reform," p. 270.
35. Ibid., p. 253; Kornai, "Hungarian Reform Process," p. 1703.
36. Tardos, "Efficient Markets," p. 48, table 4.
37. Marer, "Economic Reform," p. 254.
38. Hare, "Hungary," p. 15.
39. Marer, "Economic Reform," p. 255.
40. Tardos, "Efficient Markets," p. 35; Marer, "Economic Reform," p. 256; Hare, "Hungary," p. 15.
41. *NYT,* January 14, 1985, p. D4; *Soviet Business and Trade,* April 9, 1986, p. 1.
42. *NYT,* July 8, 1986, p. A2.
43. *Wall Street Journal,* November 20, 1985, p. 11.
44. *Sots. ind.,* June 8, 1986, p. 3.
45. *Soviet–East European Report,* RFE/RL, vol. 1, no. 25, September 20, 1984, p. 1.
46. Tardos, "Efficient Markets," p. 32 n. 20 and p. 5.
47. *Financial Times,* September 2, 1986, p. 2.
48. *Soviet–East European Report,* RFE/RL, vol. 1, no. 25, September 20, 1984, p. 1.
49. Kornai, *Contradictions,* p. 33.
50. Marer, "Economic Reform," p. 253.
51. Ibid., p. 254; Hare, "Hungary," p. 17.
52. *Buda Press,* October 1, 1984, II-27A, p. 3.
53. Hare, "Hungary," p. 16.
54. Ibid., p. 17.
55. Ibid.
56. Marer, "Economic Reform," p. 254.

57. Hare, "Hungary," p. 17.
58. Ibid., p. 18.
59. *Soviet–East European Report,* RFE/RL, vol. 3, no. 15, March 1, 1986, p. 1.
60. Tokes, "Hungarian Reform Imperatives," p. 10.
61. *NYT,* March 31, 1985, p. 17.
62. *Wall Street Journal,* April 1, 1985, p. 27.
63. *NYT,* March 31, 1985, p. 17.
64. *Wall Street Journal,* August 28, 1985, p. 15; *Soviet–East European Report,* RFE/RL, vol. 3, no. 23, May 20, 1986, p. 1.
65. *Boston Globe,* August 17, 1986, p. A8.
66. *Pravda,* March 19, 1983, p. 2; *Lit. gaz.,* January 22, 1986, p. 2; *Sots. ind.,* June 8, 1986, p. 3.
67. *Radio Liberty* 227/86, June 10, 1986, p. 2.
68. Ibid.
69. Seweryn Bialer and Joan Afferica, "The Gensis of Gorbachev's World," *Foreign Affairs,* America and the World, no. 3, 1986, p. 612.
70. Thad P. Alton, "East European GNP's: Origins of Product, Final Uses, Rates of Growth, and International Comparisons," in JEC, *Eastern Europe,* 1985, p. 120.
71. CIA, *Handbook of Economic Statistics, 1985,* p. 39.
72. Doris Cornelsen, "Economic Development in the German Democratic Republic" (Paper prepared for the NATO conference on the Economies in Eastern Europe and Their Foreign Economic Relations, Brussels, April 1986, Mimeographed), p. 2.
73. Manfried Melzer and Arthur A. Stahnke, "The GDR Faces the Economic Dilemmas of the 1980's: Caught between the Need for New Methods and Restricted Options," in JEC, *Eastern Europe,* 1986, pp. 139, 166.
74. Zwass, *Economies,* pp. 30–31.
75. Karl C. Thalheim, "The Balance Sheet," in Hans-Hermann Hohmann, Michael Kaser, and Karl C. Thalheim, eds., *The New Economic Systems of Eastern Europe* (Berkeley: University of California Press, 1975), p. 532.
76. John Garland, "FRG-GDR Economic Relations," in JEC, *Eastern Europe,* 1986, p. 180; Cornelsen, "Economic Development," p. 1; Maria Haendske-Hoppe, "German Democratic Republic: Foreign Economic Relations" (Paper prepared for the NATO conference on the Economies of Eastern Europe and Their Foreign Economic Relations, Brussels, April 1986, Mimeographed), p. 2.
77. Cornelsen, "Economic Development," p. 2.
78. Ibid., p. 3.
79. Melzer and Stahnke, "Economic Dilemmas," p. 140.
80. Ibid., p. 144.
81. Cornelson, "Economic Development," p. 5.
82. Ibid., p. 8.
83. *Financial Times,* October 23, 1985, p. 3.
84. Ibid., August 22, 1985, p. 3.
85. Garland, "FRG-GDR Economic Relations," p. 169.
86. Ibid.
87. Ibid., p. 170.
88. *Polityka,* June 7, 1986, p. 4., reprinted in *FBIS,* June 26, 1986, p. BB6.

CHAPTER SEVEN

1. Robert F. Dernberger, "The Chinese Search for the Path of Self-Sustained Growth in the 1980's: An Assessment," in JEC, *China,* 1982, p. 21; Jan S. Prybyla, "From Mao to Market," *Problems of Communism,* January–February 1986, p. 21.

2. Dernberger, "Chinese Search," p. 21.
3. Ibid., p. 24. *Jingji Guanli,* December 5, 1984, pp. 7–11, reprinted in *FBIS, China,* February 20, 1985, p. K14, reports that wages were frozen for twenty years. For a dissenting view, see Dwight Perkins, "The Prospects for China's Economic Reforms," in A. Doak Barnett and Ralph N. Clough, eds., *Modernizing China: Post Mao Reform and Development* (Denver: Westview Press, 1986), p. 39.
4. Nicholas Lardy, "Agricultural Reform," *Journal of International Affairs,* Winter 1986, p. 91.
5. Ibid.
6. Perkins, p. 39; *Jingji Yanjiu,* January 1984, p. 23, in *FBIS, China,* March 7, 1984, p. K2.
7. Based on an interview in Beijing with officials of the Institute of Development under the State Council on Rural Development (hereafter cited as the Institute for Rural Development).
8. David Zweig, "Opposition to Change in Rural China: The System of Responsibility and People's Communes," *Asian Survey,* 7 July 1983, p. 880.
9. Interview with officials in the Institute of Rural Development, June 25, 1986, Beijing. Officials in the Institute of Economics of the Chinese Academy of Social Sciences report the same findings. Interview, Beijing, June 24, 1986.
10. David Zweig, "Context and Content in Policy Implementation: Household Contracts and Decollectivization 1977–1983" (Paper in David M. Lampton, ed., "Policy Implementation in the Post-Mao Era," Mimeographed), p. 6.
11. Institute of Economics interview, June 24, 1986, Beijing.
12. Ibid.
13. Zweig, "Opposition," pp. 880, 884–85.
14. Zweig, "Policy Implementation," p. 7.
15. Ibid., p. 21.
16. Ibid., p. 5.
17. Zweig, "Opposition," pp. 882–83.
18. Zweig, "Policy Implementation," p. 8.
19. Lardy, "Agricultural Reform," p. 95.
20. Perkins, "Prospects," p. 49.
21. Frederic W. Crook, "The Reform of the Commune System and the Rise of the Township-Collective Household System," in JEC, *China,* 1986, p. 362.
22. Zweig, "Opposition," p. 885.
23. *Beijing Review,* June 30, 1986, p. 14.
24. Institute of Rural Development interview, June 25, 1986, Beijing.
25. Frederic M. Surls, "China's Agriculture in the 80's," JEC, *China,* 1986, pp. 338–39.
26. Ferdinand Kuba, "China's Agricultural Revolution," *Current World Leaders,* Biography and News/Speeches and Report Issue, May 1986, p. 318.
27. CIA, "China: Economic Performance in 1985" (Report presented to the Subcommittee on Economic Resources, Competitiveness and Security Economics of the Joint Economic Committee, Washington, D.C., March 17, 1986, Mimeographed), p . 2.
28. Lardy, "Agricultural Reform," p. 93.
29. Surls, "China's Agriculture," p. 339.
30. CIA, "China," p. 2.
31. G. I. Shmelev, "Sotsial'no ekonomicheskii potentsial semeinogo podiada," *Sotsiologicheskie issledovaniia,* April 1985, p. 16.
32. Ibid., p. 19.
33. Ibid., p. 20.
34. Zweig, "Policy Implementation," pp. 28a–29; David Zweig, "Up from the Village

into the City: Reforming Urban-Rural Relations in China" (Paper presented at the Thirty-second North American Meeting of the Regional Science Association, Philadelphia, November 15–17, 1985, Mimeographed), p. 27.
35. *FBIS*, September 18, 1986, p. R8 (emphasis added).
36. *Pravda*, January 26, 1986, p. 2.
37. Zweig, "Policy Implementation," p. 28a.
38. Dernberger, "Chinese Search," pp. 32, 56–57.
39. Report of the Delegation of American University Presidents, "Teng Hsiao-ping's interview with the Delegation of American University Presidents, November 14, 1974," (Mimeographed), p. 7.
40. *Beijing Review*, July 28, 1986, p. 1.
41. U.S. Arms Control and Disarmament Agency, *World Military Expenditures and Arms Transfers* (Washington, D.C.: GPO, 1985), p. 58; *Beijing Review*, July 28, 1986, pp. 4, 77.
42. U.S. Arms Control and Disarmament Agency, *World Military Expenditures*, p. 81.
43. Ibid., p. 85.
44. Shmelev, "Sotsial'no," p. 19.
45. Institute of Rural Development interview, June 25, 1986, Beijing; *Boston Globe*, January 25, 1987, p. 101.
46. JEC, *China*, 1986, pp. 340, 457.
47. *Ekon. gaz.*, June 1986, no. 26, p. 6.
48. Marshall I. Goldman, *The U.S.S.R. in Crisis: The Failure of an Economic System* (New York: W. W. Norton, 1983), p. 81.
49. Lardy, "Agricultural Reform," p. 94.
50. Vladimir Kurbatov, "Problems of Agriculture," *Asia and Africa Today*, no. 3, 1985, p. 29.; V. Fetov and V. Matveyev, "China's Economic Growth," *Far Eastern Affairs*, no. 3, 1984, p. 125.
51. Fetov and Matveyev, "China's Economic Growth," p. 125.
52. *Pravda*, March 17, 1986, p. 4; August 8, 1986, p. 5.
53. *Izvestiia*, November 15, 1983, p. 5.
54. Ibid.; Z. Muromtseva, "The Modernization of Agriculture in the PRC: The Question of Capital Investment," *Far Eastern Affairs*, no. 2, 1985, pp. 95–100.
55. *Izvestiia*, June 1, 1985, p. 3; *Pravda*, October 25, 1984, p. 5.
56. *Lit. gaz.*, June 11, 1986, p. 14
57. Christine Wong, "The Second Phase of Economic Reform in China," *Current History*, September 1985, p. 260.
58. John Maynard Keynes, *The General Theory of Employment, Interest and Money* (New York: Harcourt, Brace and World, 1964), p. 383.
59. Institute of Economics interview, June 24, 1986, Beijing.
60. Evsei Liberman, "O planirovanii promyshlennogo proizvodstva i material'nykh stimulkh ego razvitiia," *Kommunist*, no. 10, July 1956, p. 75.
61. Evsei Liberman, in *Pravda*, September 9, 1962, p. 3; November 3, 1962, p. 13; "Planirovanie proizvodstva i normativy dlitel'nogo deistviia," *Voprosy ekonomiki*, August 1962, p. 104; *Ekon. gaz.*, November 10, 1962, p. 11.
62. Nina Halpern, "Making Economic Policy: The Influence of Economists," in JEC, *China*, 1986, p. 136.
63. Institute of Economics interview, June 24, 1986, Beijing.
64. Wong, "Second Phase," p. 261.
65. Ibid.
66. Ibid., p. 260; Dorothy J. Solinger, "Industrial Reform," *Journal of International Affairs*, Winter 1986, p. 109.
67. Solinger, "Industrial Reform," p. 109.
68. *Beijing Review*, August 11, 1986, p. 4.

69. Robert F. Dernberger, "Economic Policy and Performance," in JEC, *China*, 1986, p. 30; *Wall Street Journal*, June 6, 1986, p. 28.
70. P. Kaprolov, "Inflationary Processes in China," *Far Eastern Affairs*, no. 3, 1982, p. 99; A. Kruglov, "Small-Scale Industry in China," ibid., no. 1, 1985, p. 77.
71. Kruglov, "Small-Scale Industry," p. 79.
72. Ibid., p. 77; S. Manezhev, "Foreign Entrepreneurial Capital in the PRC's Economy," *Far Eastern Affairs*, no. 1, p. 44; *FBIS*, March 29, 1985, p. 4.
73. *FBIS*, March 29, 1984, p. 4; RFE/RL 48/85, February 13, 1985, p. 2.
74. *Izvestiia*, August 8, 1985, p. 5.
75. Kruglov, "Small-Scale Industry," p. 78.
76. *Pravda*, August 5, 1984, p. 5.
77. Solinger, "Industrial Reform," p. 109.
78. Institute of Economics interview, June 24, 1986, Beijing.
79. *Wall Street Journal*, August 29, 1986, p. 21.
80. *Beijing Review*, July 14, 1986, p. 5; *NYT*, February 11, 1985, p. D4.
81. *NYT*, February 11, 1985, p. D4.
82. *Boston Globe*, August 6, 1986, p. 67; *NYT*, September 28, 1986, p. 17; December 25, 1986, p. 34.
83. Interview in Beijing, June 1986. *Izvestiia*, January 20, 1987, p. 5, reports the figure as 17 million.
84. *Lit. gaz.*, July 31, 1985, p. 14; *NYT*, August 4, 1985, p. 16; July 31, 1985, p. D14; *Nanfang Ribao*, July 26, 1985, pp. 1–2, in *FBIS, China*, August 2, 1985, pp. 5, 9.
85. *Asian Wall Street Journal*, June 27–28, 1986, p. 1.
86. *Beijing Review*, June 23, 1986, p. 4; *Far Eastern Economic Review*, July 18, 1985, p. 93.
87. Guochang Huan, "China's Open Door Policy, 1978–1984," *Journal of International Affairs*, Winter 1986, pp. 6–7.
88. *FBIS, China*, August 2, 1985, p. K8; Perkins, "Prospects," p. 47.
89. Interview with city officials of Shenzhen, July 2, 1986; Guochang Huan, "China's Open Door Policy," pp. 6–7.
90. *FBIS, China*, August 2, 1985, p. K9.
91. *Pravda*, July 20, 1984; E. Paschenko, "Some Legal Aspects of Chinese 'Open Door Policy,'" *Far Eastern Affairs*, no. 2, 1985, p. 74; *Pravda*, October 25, 1984, p. 5.
92. S. Manezhev, "Foreign Capital," p. 44.
93. Ibid., p. 43.
94. Ibid.; *Pravda*, August 5, 1984, p. 5; *Izvestiia*, January 20, 1987, p. 5.
95. V. Portyakov and S. Stepanov, "China's Special Economic Zones," *Far Eastern Affairs*, no. 2, 1986, p. 36.
96. *Izvestiia*, August 13, 1986, p. 5; *Trud*, July 18, 1986, p. 3; *Kommunist Tadzhikistana*, July 10, 1986, p. 3; *Izvestiia*, January 20, 1987, p. 5.
97. *FBIS*, July 29, 1986, p. R18.
98. Interview in Shenzhen, July 2, 1986.
99. *Beijing Review*, July 15, 1985, p. 6; *NYT*, September 23, 1985, p. D10.
100. See *China Business and Trade*, September 23, 1984, pp. 2–3.
101. *Wall Street Journal*, July 17, 1986, p. 12.
102. *Beijing Review*, July 15, 1985, pp. 7–8.
103. Ibid.
104. CIA, "China," pp. 2–3.
105. Kornai, "The Hungarian Reform Process," p. 1697.
106. *Beijing Review*, March 3, 1986, p. 6; *Boston Globe*, July 17, 1986, p. 3.
107. Interview in Shenzhen, July 2, 1986.

108. *Izvestiia*, August 28, 1986, p. 5.
109. Ibid; *Izvestiia*, January 17, 1987, p. 6.
110. *NYT*, April 24, 1986, p. 2.
111. *FBIS, China*, August 7, 1985, p. K6; *Hongqi*, July 1, 1985, pp. 7–10; *Financial Times*, May 21, 1986, p. 13; *FBIS, China*, p. P5, from the *Nanfang Ribao*, July 26, 1985, pp. 1–2.
112. *FBIS, China*, August 7, 1985, p. K4, from *Jingji Ribao*, August 2, 1985, p. 1.
113. *Boston Globe*, June 23, 1985, p. 81.
114. *NYT*, February 13, 1987, p. A8.
115. *FBIS, China*, December 10, 1984, p. W7, from Ming Pao, December 5, 1984, p. 4.
116. *Ekon. gaz.*, August 1986, no. 33, p. 20.
117. *NYT*, Febraury 1, 1987, p. E3; *Christian Science Monitor*, February 5, 1987, p. 1.
118. *Boston Globe*, January 25, 1987, p. 101.
119. *NYT*, February 1, 1987, p. E3.

CHAPTER EIGHT

1. Berliner, "Planning and Management," p. 350.
2. Egon Neuberger, *Central Planning and Its Legacies* (Santa Monica: Rand Corporation, December 1966), p. 6.
3. *Beijing Review*, May 20, 1958, p. 15.
4. *Ekon. gaz.*, September 1985, no. 37, p. 3.
5. Soviet radio, May 6, 1986, reported in *FBIS*, May 7, 1986, p. L6.
6. From an AFP dispatch, as reported in *FBIS*, May 12, 1986, p. L1.
7. A. Zhores Medvedev, *Nuclear Disaster in the Urals* (New York: W. W. Norton, 1979), p. 10.
8. *Boston Globe*, November 16, 1986, p. 31.
9. *Pravda*, May 13, 1986, p. 1.
10. Dwight Perkins has spelled out the importance of such steps in more detail. Perkins, "Prospects," p. 39.
11. *Pravda*, August 18, 1983, p. 4; *NYT*, August 18, 1983, p. 1.
12. *FBIS*, July 29, 1986, p. R1.
13. *Pravda*, February 27, 1986, p. 6.
14. Ibid., February 28, 1986, p. 4.
15. Philip Hanson, in RFE/RL 291/85, September 4, 1985, p. 1, quotes from the Tanjug news agency; *NYT*, December 1, 1985, p. F3.
16. *Pravda*, May 28, 1986, p. 2; *Boston Globe*, November 28, 1986, p. 13.
17. John Stuart Mill, *On Liberty* (Baltimore: Penguin Classics, 1974), p. 183.
18. According to an unauthorized report, Gorbachev gave a speech to Soviet writers on June 19, 1986, in which he compared the apparat's opposition to his reforms to the earlier opposition to Khrushchev's reforms and noted how the apparat had managed to break Khrushchev's neck and would, if it could, do the same to him. For a somewhat similar version, see *FBIS*, October 9, 1986, p. R1, and *NYT*, December 22, 1986, p. 10.
19. *NYT*, August 26, 1986, p. A4; *FBIS*, July 29, 1986, p. R27.
20. *Boston Globe*, July 28, 1986, p. 5.
21. Alexander Gerschenkron, *Continuity in History and Other Essays* (Cambridge: Harvard University Press, 1968), p. 284.
22. *FBIS, China*, July 16, 1986, p. K9; *NYT*, January 18, 1987, p. 1.
23. *FBIS*, August 4, 1986, p. R2.
24. Ibid., p. R13.

25.*Pravda*, June 17, 1986, p. 2; *FBIS*, June 18, 1986, p. R4.
26. *Sots. ind.*, July 19, 1985, p. 2; *Pravda*, July 4, 1986, p. 1.
27. *FBIS*, July 25, 1986, p. S2, taken from *L'espresso*, July 6, 1986, pp. 44–47.
28. *CDSP*, July 23, 1986, p. 10.
29. *Izvestiia*, October 9, 1983, p. 1; *CDSP*, November 9, 1983, p. 7.
30. *FBIS*, July 25, 1986, p. S2, from *L'espresso*, July 6, 1986, pp. 44–47.
31. Letter to the editor, *Financial Times*, July 12, 1986, p. 7.
32. *Pravda*, May 12, 1986, p. 1.
33. *FBIS*, April 8, 1986, p. R6.
34. *FBIS*, August 4, 1986, pp. R6–R8.
35. *FBIS*, April 9, 1986, p. R5.
36. *Pravda*, March 2, 1986, p. 6.
37. *Lit. gaz.*, August 6, 1986, p. 10. I am indebted to Erich Goldhagen for drawing my attention to this article.
38. *Pravda*, June 17, 1986, p. 4.
39. *FBIS*, June 18, 1986, p. R12.
40. *Sots. ind.*, July 24, 1986, p. 1; *Pravda*, March 1, 1986, p. 4; *FBIS*, August 26, 1986, p. S4.
41. *Pravda*, February 27, 1986, p. 5. The same problem exists in the video industry. See *Pravda*, June 8, 1986, p. 2.
42. Some economic historians are now beginning to argue that the First Industrial Revolution was in fact preceded by just such an economic takeoff in the English countryside. For more on this issue, see Jeffrey G. Williamson, "Debating the British Industrial Revolution," a paper prepared for *Explorations in Economic History*. See especially N. Crafts, "British Economic Growth, 1700–1850; Some Differences in Interpretation," 1986. Tim Sullivan drew this debate to my attention.
43. *FBIS*, June 18, 1986, p. R4.
44. *Ekon. gaz.*, February 1987, no. 6, p. 6.
45. *Pravda*, September 7, 1985, p. 2.

Index